"This book, which throws new and much-needed light on
one of the least understood groups of children—the gifted
learning-disabled—will be a real eye-opener to the many
who are confused by their problems. It provides the best
and most useful advice I know of for parents and teachers
of these very special boys and girls. Its many case histories
make fascinating reading. A much-needed book."

> —Louise Bates Ames, Associate Director,
> Gesell Institute of Human Development

"Priscilla Vail reveals that students' minds are as varied as
their bodies or their personalities. Her cogent and
important book is filled with sensible suggestions about
how these different minds can best be cultivated."

> —Dr. Howard Gardner, Professor,
> Boston University School of Medicine,
> author of *Frames of Mind:
> The Theory of Multiple Intelligences*

PRISCILLA L. VAIL is the Learning Specialist at the
Pippowam-Cisqua School in Bedford, New York, and a
member of the Advisory Board of the Fisher-Landau
Foundation. Her previous books included *The World of the
Gifted Child, Clear and Lively Writing,* and *Gifted,
Precocious or Just Plain Smart*.

PRISCILLA L. VAIL

Smart Kids with School Problems

Things to Know and Ways to Help

A PLUME BOOK

PLUME
Published by the Penguin Group
Penguin Books USA Inc., 375 Hudson Street, New York, New York 10014, U.S.A.
Penguin Books Ltd, 27 Wrights Lane, London W8 5TZ, England
Penguin Books Australia Ltd, Ringwood, Victoria, Australia
Penguin Books Canada Ltd, 10 Alcorn Avenue, Toronto, Ontario, Canada M4V 3B2
Penguin Books (N.Z.) Ltd, 182–190 Wairau Road, Auckland 10, New Zealand

Penguin Books Ltd, Registered Offices: Harmondsworth, Middlesex, England

Published by Plume, an imprint of Dutton Signet, a division of Penguin Books USA
Inc. This is an authorized reprint of a hardcover edition published by E.P. Dutton
and published simultaneously in Canada by Fitzhenry and Whiteside Limited,
Toronto.

First Plume Printing, August, 1989

20 22 24 26 28 30 29 27 25 23 21

Grateful acknowledgment is made for permission to reprint excerpts from the
following works:

"Coaching for the SATs: What the Colleges Think," by William C. Hiss.
Reprinted by permission from *Independent School* (October 1984), copyright ©
1984 by the National Association of Independent Schools.

Book review of *Frames of Mind: The Theory of Multiple Intelligences* by
Howard Gardner, and Priscilla L. Vail. Reprinted by permission from
Independent School (February 1984), copyright © 1984 by the National
Association of Independent Schools.

"Richard's Story," by Richard C. Strauss. From *Bulletin of The Orton Society* 28
(1978). Reprinted by permission of the author.

"SAT Preparation and Independent Schools," by Dorothy H. Dillon. Reprinted
by permission from *Independent School* (October 1984), copyright © 1984 by
the National Association of Independent Schools.

REGISTERED TRADEMARK—MARCA REGISTRADA

Original hardcover design by Earl Tidwell

LIBRARY OF CONGRESS CATALOGING-IN-PUBLICATION DATA
Vail, Priscilla L.
Smart kids with school problems.

1. Gifted children—Education—United States. 2. Learning disabilities—
United States. I. Title.
LC3993.9.V35   1988   371.95   88-9863

PRINTED IN THE UNITED STATES OF AMERICA

BOOKS ARE AVAILABLE AT QUANTITY DISCOUNTS WHEN USED TO PROMOTE PRODUCTS
OR SERVICES. FOR INFORMATION PLEASE WRITE TO PREMIUM MARKETING DIVISION,
PENGUIN BOOKS USA INC., 375 HUDSON STREET, NEW YORK, NEW YORK 10014.

TO
DONALD VAIL,
WHO GIVES ME
CARE, CRITICISM, AND COURAGE

CONTENTS

Contents

ACKNOWLEDGMENTS

To my lodestars, mentors, and companions, thank you.

Jean Anderson Luke, her colleagues Margaret Lawrence and Helen Ross, Katrina de Hirsch, Rita Rudel, Louise Bates Ames, and Leah Levinger opened windows on human development.

My colleagues in The Orton Dyslexia Society and the National Association of Independent Schools, particularly on the Academic Committee, have taught me a great deal. Through their national and regional conferences these organizations make research and practical educational techniques available to teachers and parents. But speakers finish speaking, and seminar planners fold up their easels; the printed word remains. To Blair McElroy, champion of wombats and editor of *Independent School*, and to Rosemary Bowler, meticulous, droll editor of *Annals of Dyslexia*, thanks on behalf of the millions of smart kids with school problems who benefit from the knowledge you make available.

The Fisher-Landau Foundation focuses on gifted children with learning disabilities. To Emily Fisher Landau, thanks for your great generosity, and for beaming in on this population. I appreciate the

Acknowledgments

privilege of sitting on the Advisory Board and working alongside such distinguished colleagues.

Thanks to the Rippowam-Cisqua students, and others I have worked with, for sparking ideas, being willing to take risks, hanging in when the going was rough, and chanting that beautiful phrase "Oh, now I get it!"

To my colleagues in our profession, which, though beleaguered, is surely the most exciting in the world, thank you for all you give, daily, to students, parents, and one another. To parents of conundrum kids, thank you for trusting educators with your children. We shall try to be deserving.

Unending thanks to those companions who have test-driven this manuscript; left me alone when I needed to work, and been there when I emerged; offered suggestions, made me laugh, and kept me going. Particular thanks to Waldo, Margaret and Bill, Anne and Johnny, Gordon, Buzz, Soulsister Jane, and Betty.

To my family: Donald, Melissa, Norman, Luke, Thomas, Lucia, Jesse, Polly, Mark, and Angus, thanks for moral support, for enduring burned or tepid dinners, and understanding "sure, after the book is done." To those yet unborn, warm welcome when you arrive. To those no longer here, thank you for knowledge I sometimes fought against receiving.

To Ida Genovesi in Bedford and Gail Woodrow in Stonington, thank you for the comfort of your patient practical help.

Paula Diamond, new but valued friend; Margot Marek, teacher and author; Dick Marek, editor and publisher: what a wonderful team you are. I am proud to work with you.

Thanks.

PRISCILLA L. VAIL

Bedford, New York

PREFACE

Anger, fear, self-doubt, frustration, and pressure are typical of the reactions that intensify when an intelligent student has a school problem. Negative responses contaminate the classroom, invade the home, and squeeze the spirit and intelligence of smart kids. In their confusion, parents, teachers, and students themselves may be quick to lay blame. This book offers ways to find the roots of academic problems and suggests specific ways to circumvent or surmount them.

Smart kids with school problems often shine in the arts, athletics, or interpersonal skills or show great promise in mathematics, engineering, or science. But many are turning away from education because their school problems are misunderstood.

What are these kids like? They may be young people who welcome challenge outside school, but avoid it in the classroom. They may be students who relish thinking and problem solving but have poor organizational skills. Some are imaginative, verbal students whose written work is poor. Others remember their experiences, people, and emotions but can't seem to memorize schoolwork.

Some have trouble listening and following directions. Others don't seem to harness their intelligence. Often, for reasons we shall explore, they do not get high scores on standardized tests. This increases their vulnerability to pressure because many current cries for educational reform are really calls for higher test scores. These students need recognition, understanding, and help from concerned adults because their bright promise is at risk, and because there are many of them.

How many? Probably between 20 and 30 percent of any school population. Among the obvious learning disabled there are those with high though hidden intellectual potential. Among the gifted there are those with subtle learning disabilities. Among the "average" students are those in whom giftedness and disability mask one another, pulling academic performance into the middle range. Thus these students may be found in the top, middle, or low groups of any grade.

How should we describe them? We might call them gifted and learning disabled, learning disabled and gifted, academic ugly ducklings, street smart and school dumb, atypical learners, or smart kids with school problems. Because each one is a glorious though challenging puzzle, I name them after a type of puzzle: I call them *conundrum kids*.

The long-term implications of being a conundrum kid are exhilarating whenever talent and self-respect are kept alive. The student who is understood and helped faces short-term periods of discomfort and hard work as well as times of great satisfaction. But the student who is not diagnosed and helped faces short-term academic discomfort snowballing into long-term self-doubt, a poor education, diminished professional opportunities, and, often, an unfulfilled life.

In spite of the difficulties, the message of this book is optimistic. As a learning specialist, diagnostician, teacher of children, leader of teacher training workshops, and parent, I have puzzled over—and taught—smart kids with school problems. By following the research, trying different methods and materials, watching master teachers, and noticing what strategies work in which circumstances, I have learned some things to know and ways to help.

This book is laid out in ten chapters.

Preface

Chapter 1 describes traits and emotional needs frequently found in bright or gifted students, discusses different learning styles, and cites school problems conundrum kids may meet at particular grade levels.

Chapter 2 discusses the young child's developmental readiness for schoolwork and offers guidelines for grade placement in the early years.

Each of the next five chapters explores one learning system. Just as the health of a human body depends on separate but inter-related systems, active learning relies on its own discrete but interdependent systems. Healthy people and successful students needn't bother teasing them apart, but in times of trouble it is important to see which systems are functioning smoothly and which are causing trouble. We shall look at strengths and weaknesses in visual learning, motor function, auditory learning, language and learning, and psychological availabililty for schoolwork.

Chapter 8, "Testing Demystified," explores testing and interpretation of test scores in general and gives examples of constructive ways to use test results to help conundrum kids.

Chapter 9 looks at maturation and higher education for smart kids with school problems.

Chapter 10 tells the stories of three gifted people who survived schooling and have realized their true potential.

P.L.V.

1

RECOGNIZING, UNDERSTANDING, AND HELPING CONUNDRUM KIDS

The jagged learning profile of a conundrum kid looks like a cross section of the Alps. One student may have high conceptual power and low ability to read, write, and spell. Another may be strong with words and weak with numbers. Another may have great artistic talent but flounder in formal academics. The discrepancy between the highs and the lows is uncomfortable, even painful, for the student. The greater the discrepancy the more intense the discomfort: unexercised talents itch, unsupported weaknesses ache.

Because failure is easy to see, unenlightened adults may ignore the student's talent, fostering a negative self-concept by focusing on what he can*not* do. (To avoid the cumbersome use of double pronouns, I have arbitrarily settled on the general use of *he* for students and *she* for teachers.) Many kids with high potential face discouragement every time they walk in the school door. Smart kids with school problems need the advocacy of informed adults to help them acquire necessary skills and, equally important, to protect the talent, originality, and power they offer.

For example, Charlie, an eighth grader, built a tree house with a cantilevered deck and sold five of his paintings at the community art show. He made the drawings for the poster but couldn't do the lettering because each time he tried to copy the words *Community Historical Association* he made a different mistake. Although he understands advanced mathematical concepts and has a natural interest in science, he scores poorly on standardized tests, his written work is weak, and he is failing history

Looking at Charlie's test scores, his spelling, and his history exam, it would be easy to think him stupid. In his case, as is true with many other students we shall meet throughout the book, specific talents are often the flip side of specific disabilities.

Although talent and trouble are intertwined in every conundrum kid, by looking at giftedness and other atypical learning styles separately, we have a better chance of understanding the child who carries both. Let's look first at giftedness.

GIFTEDNESS

The criteria for giftedness are numerous, often nit-picking, and they differ widely from place to place or from test to test. They often identify good test takers or high scorers who may or may not be original thinkers, and they frequently eliminate gifted kids who do not excel in traditional ways. Therefore, in this book I use *gifted* to describe those who happen to meet the criteria and also those who are highly intelligent, talented, or just plain smart. Trying to distinguish among these categories takes time that could be better used by meeting the students' needs.

Gifted people frequently have clusters of the following ten traits: rapid grasp of concepts, awareness of patterns, energy, curiosity, concentration, exceptional memory, empathy, vulnerability, heightened perceptions, and divergent thinking. While these traits invigorate learning, they may also create friction in the classroom or in the home. In fairness to the students we are trying to understand, we need to acknowledge that singly, or in combination, they can be both blessings and burdens.

RAPID GRASP OF CONCEPTS

Gifted people grasp concepts so quickly it seems as if the knowledge has been inside them all along, waiting to be awakened simply by being mentioned. While such *instant learning* can be stimulating, it can also be unsettling to classmates, teachers, and the student himself.

Classmates may resent a peer who learns without apparent effort, and teachers may resent students who learn without explanations. Students themselves are often perplexed by their instant learning, enjoying the excitement but wondering whether it is dishonest—a sort of intellectual shoplifting—and worrying whether knowledge that arrives without effort might vanish without warning. Some gifted students who learn quickly think easy learning doesn't count, and they develop a cynical attitude toward schooling in general.

AWARENESS OF PATTERNS

Gifted people are unusually alert to patterns. They recognize symmetry in nature, in seashells or leaves, and in such man-made creations as architecture and art. They notice patterns of interval and repetition in mathematics and music, frequently relating the one to the other. They understand the abstract conceptual patterns that may connect such seemingly different disciplines as science and art, and, through language, they recognize the psychological patterns in literature that parallel those in daily living. Thinking in patterns is a way of thinking by analogy, the foundation of much higher level academic work. But it is not always easy for others to understand the patterns the gifted student sees. Adults or peers may think he is being purposely obscure, just as he may become annoyed by their apparent slow-wittedness.

ENERGY

Intellectual and psychological energy levels may exceed a gifted person's level of physical energy. Although physical energy is more evident to the casual observer than the other two, these energies of the mind are the fuel for abstract exploration and discovery. Unfortunately, an uncertain or weary adult may misinterpret a student's high intellectual energy as personal challenge instead of recognizing it as the urge to pursue a problem longer and more deeply than other people. The student who persists with "but have you stopped to think about . . ." or "I know something else about that that no one else thought of" is sometimes an unwelcome challenge.

CURIOSITY

Curiosity spurs vigorous investigation of physical, intellectual, or psychological realms. It is as natural a force to gifted thinkers as physiological hunger and thirst. Questions like Why? How come . . . ? Where did . . . ? When was the first . . . ? What is . . . made of? have led to great discoveries, but such questions are not always welcome in school. They may take time from the matter at hand, and they are seen as diversions. Sadly, too, teachers who are uncomfortable not knowing an answer resent students with wide, deep curiosity. When a student of any age finds his curiosity unwelcome in school, he often saves it for extracurricular endeavors.

CONCENTRATION

Many gifted people can focus their intellectual energies for long periods of time. While the ability to concentrate is admirable and deserves exercise, it is often at odds with academic schedules and family living. Big ideas need generous pieces of time if they are not to be lost, but school schedules are built of forty- or fifty-minute class periods, and the clock governs such family activities as car pools, soccer practices, music lessons, and dentist appointments, not to mention mealtimes. The gifted need large unstructured pieces of time.

EXCEPTIONAL MEMORY

The gifted person may have an encyclopedic memory for people, events, and emotions, both in his experience and from his reading. He may have a vivid recollection of the blue front door to his grandmother's house, which he hasn't seen since the age of four. Paradoxically, this same student may forget last week's spelling rule, the multiplication tables, or the capital of North Dakota. This discrepancy between a powerful experiential memory and a weak memory for specific factual information may create an incorrect impression of a kid who "doesn't care," "hasn't studied," or "only learns what he feels like learning."

EMPATHY

The gifted person is often highly sensitive to the feelings of others. If he feels welcome in school, he will use his empathetic skills positively, enhancing the quality of everyone's life in the classroom, on the athletic field, in the lunchroom and halls, or wherever he happens to be. But the unwelcome gifted thinker whose traits create friction in conventional academic settings may choose to use his empathy negatively, knowing just how to gain attention or make trouble.

VULNERABILITY

While a young poet creating new patterns or metaphor may trust his own sense of innovation and be invulnerable to the criticisms of an unimaginative teacher, this same individual is often socially and emotionally more vulnerable than his peers, particularly to loneliness and the kind of self-doubt that comes from perceptive self-scrutiny and the knowledge of being different. A look at real children shows that intellectual strength confers no immunity to emotional pain.

HEIGHTENED PERCEPTIONS

Like the other traits, heightened perceptions complicate life for gifted people. They focus on beauty and also on ugliness, on joy and also on pain, on the attainable and on the unattainable. These perceptions cast a mercilessly bright light on the discrepancies between reality and the ideal, sometimes throwing the perceiver off balance. For example, young children with heightened perceptions often become intellectually aware of the idea of death before know-ing how to make emotional peace with its inevitability. The knowl-edge arrives spontaneously, pushing the child into a period of distress aroused by his heightened perceptions but not alleviated by them.

DIVERGENT THINKING

Divergent thinkers who enjoy open-ended questions see prob-lems and situations from unusual angles, and can tolerate the am-biguity of seeing things from several different points of view. They are willing to wrestle with "What if . . ." and are happiest exploring questions that have no verifiable answers in the back of the book. Their ability to recognize patterns, combined with their heightened perceptions, often lead them to insights that are bewildering to the rest of us, or seem "off the track" or "beside the point." This kind of originality can create friction between a gifted student and a teacher who wants everyone in the class to use identical procedures.

Students with clusters of these traits have high intellectual potential, but keeping this promise alive is no easy task. Although these characteristics are precursors of discovery and innovation, many of them are inconvenient or disruptive in routine academic settings.

It is important to remember that high grades are not always evidence of gifted thinking: precocity may accompany giftedness but does not certify it, and the ability to memorize does not guarantee the ability to think. Many intellectually powerful students do poorly on rote exercises, and are uninterested in filling in workbook blanks or selecting answers from multiple-choice options. For reasons we shall explore in detail in Chapter 8, "Testing Demystified," test scores alone are unreliable indicators of the presence or absence of gifted thinking.

LEARNING STYLES

An individual's learning style is his intellectual fingerprint, unique and permanent. The term *learning style* refers to the way a student learns: aptitudes, compensations, and weaknesses. The math student who learns easily with *manipulatives* (blocks, chips, or rods) may struggle with worksheets. The failing reader may be unable to remember sight words but catch on quickly with phonics. One student may learn as quickly from a demonstration as another may from a verbal explanation. Current neurological research indicates that learning styles reflect individual brain development and architecture.[1]

According to Geschwind, Galaburda, Masland, and Behan, to name but four outstanding contributors to this field, the mother's level of testosterone (the male sex hormone) influences the migration of cells to certain parts of the fetal heart and brain between the sixteenth and twentieth weeks of gestation. Stimuli that cross the placenta prompt a response in the brain that, in turn, accounts for reorganization of brain architecture. This reorganization may predispose a person both to particular types of talents and aptitudes and to "a climate inhospitable to language," which could account for many school problems in highly intelligent kids.

These patterns of brain architecture underlie such seemingly unrelated conditions as left-handedness, learning disorders, autoimmune disease, allergies, migraine, some types of ulcerative colitis, and specific types of epilepsy. Left-handedness does not cause a learning disorder any more than allergies cause epilepsy; they are manifestations of a common set of circumstances.

Of note is the frequent coincidence of people with remarkable talent in three-dimensional work—architects, mathematicians, engineers, scientists, and surgeons—who are also left-handed or ambidextrous, who are vulnerable to the previously cited conditions, and who have or had school problems.

These patterns of brain architecture occur in a 4 to 1 male/female ratio. Trying to explain why, scientific researchers now hypothesize that female fetuses affected by the agent causing brain reorganization do not survive gestation as often as males. This hypothesis reverses previously held ideas that the male is more vulnerable to learning disorders and also provides a neuroanatomical explanation for male aptitude for such disciplines as math, reducing the impact of cultural influences.

Teachers and parents need to understand that there are neuroanatomical reasons for learning styles; that a student who learns one way but not another isn't being purposely uncooperative. In teaching we also need to remember that, while individual preferences remain, students who are skillfully taught can develop alternative or compensatory ways of learning.

Often a smart kid's school problem arises from a mismatch between his learning style and the methods and materials used in the curriculum. When this happens, it is the student who is diagnosed as learning disabled, instead of the material's being labeled inappropriate.

Learning disabilities can be created as well as inherited. Some should properly be called *pedagenic*: they spring from inappropriate schooling. They may be *chronogenic*, caused by a poor match between the age of the child and the concepts being introduced, or they may be *sociogenic*, springing from an inhospitable or even hostile setting. Others, to be sure, are truly *genetic*, springing from being "just like Uncle Charlie."

The term *learning disability* may be appropriate or it may have lost its precision through overuse. *Learning disability*, translated literally, means being not able to learn, but although learning disabled (LD) kids have trouble learning in some situations, many learn rapidly in others.

The term *learning disability* has an air of finality that promotes pessimistic thinking at home and at school: "He has a learning disability so there's nothing I can do. He needs a specialist." An alternative term, *learning difference*, has the optimistic ring conundrum kids deserve. They can learn, and often, with some adjustments in materials and methods of presentation, they can learn in the regular classroom.

Learning differences can account for the discrepancies between one learning system and another and also for highs and lows within a single learning system. Here are some examples:

In the visual learning system, a student who is highly talented in the visual arts may have trouble learning to recognize letters or sight words.

In the motor system, the highly skilled athlete with exquisite coordination may have barely legible handwriting.

In the auditory learning system, the student with perfectly good hearing may not remember oral instructions.

In the language system, the talkative student may have trouble understanding what he reads or organizing his written work.

In psychological availablity for schoolwork, the imaginative thinker may have trouble focusing his attention.

As we investigate these learning systems in the ensuing chapters we shall see some reasons for such discrepancies and examples of ways smart kids can be helped.

Learning differences are lifelong, and although they may create embarrassment or failure during school years, later on they may be part of personal charm.

For example, I have a friend, an extremely successful administrator, who can't sing on key or cut tidily with scissors. She was embarrassed by these "disabilities" in her elementary school years but they don't matter now. In fact they are considered humorous idiosyncrasies. One of my favorite authors was considered a weak student because she was a slow reader. Now that she is a successful author, her enjoyment of individual words invigorates her writing and is no longer a weakness. A distinguished lawyer whose agile mind can go directly to the center of a complicated issue sometimes has trouble with rote memory. Telephone numbers don't stick in his head, and when he is tired or under stress he spells incorrectly. As a student he disguised his spelling with sloppy handwriting. As a professional adult, he dictates to a secretary in the office, uses a word processor with an automatic spelling corrector at home, or ducks the whole question by making a telephone call instead of writing a letter. School problems may cease to matter after graduation. They are what they are called: school problems.

PERSONAL NEEDS

To help smart kids overcome their school problems concerned adults must recognize their personal as well as curricular needs. The combination of intellectual power and school problems intensifies these students' needs for belonging, care giving, output as well as intake, three-way development, adult leadership, and humor.

THE NEED TO BELONG

Conundrum kids are particularly vulnerable to loneliness and isolation, and often seek what Frankie, in Carson McCullers's *The Member of the Wedding*, called "the we of me." Ninth grader Julie, a talented young dancer who is failing algebra and Latin, said, "I guess I'm a different species. I mean, giraffes can find other giraffes, porcupines have other porcupines, adults have adults, even kids have other kids . . . and then there's me."

Common-interest groups, being read to, and appropriate grade placement all foster a sense of belonging. Weekend or vacation groups that offer activities in the student's area of strength can help him find others with similar interests. In addition to traditional opportunities for athletes to join local teams, many associations for the gifted and talented sponsor Saturday Clubs with topics ranging from electronics to chess to magic. Increasing numbers of colleges cooperate with parent groups and local schools in programs for the gifted in story writing, computers, drama, drawing, and sculpture. Science museums, art museums, and libraries often provide exciting opportunities for hands-on learning. The number of mentors, adults with an interest or skill they are willing to share with young people, is growing, particularly in large cities where people are actively seeking ways to meet others with similar interests. Although some programs for the gifted require the student to submit an IQ score, many will waive that requirement if the student is genuinely interested in the topic.

Another way to reinforce a sense of belonging is for adults to read aloud *to* kids in school and at home. Students who feel different are profoundly reassured to find that other people enjoy the same stories they do, catching their breath, laughing, crying, and shuddering at the same episodes. The selections need not be lengthy; it is hearing a story as part of a group that builds a sense of community. Because of their universal themes, myths, folk tales, and fairy tales are particularly well suited to these students' needs.

Like myths and folk tales, fairy tales deal in a permissible way with the emotional forces our students feel but often fear. The triumph of the seemingly weak over the seemingly strong is a welcome theme to the smart kid with school problems, as are the explorations of jealousy, revenge, and power these tales offer.

Discovering that people in other times and cultures have puzzled over the questions about creation that appear in mythology and folk tales is heartwarming to the student who enjoys open-ended exploration and has clusters of the traits mentioned earlier.

Appropriate grade placement is another way to help a student belong. Putting a child with others who are at a different developmental level isolates him immediately. Some parents hesitate to place an intellectually advanced child with his chronological, social-emotional peers, fearing their child will be bored. They need to meet Michael, whose story I heard from Leah Levinger, child psychologist and professor at Bank Street College of Education in New York.

Michael was a four-year-old who understood the concept of time. Not only could he call out the hour and minute on demand, but he really understood what the numbers meant. He had a solid grasp of present, future, and past tenses and could even anticipate elapsing time. For example, if his mother said, "We'll be going in half an hour," he would appear at her side twenty-nine minutes later, without looking at his watch or being reminded.

To celebrate his ability to tell time, his parents gave him a watch. Although its round face was bigger than the width of his four-year-old wrist, he strapped on his timepiece proudly and wore it everywhere. His classmates would ask him what time it was and he would call out joyfully "10:22" or "9:55." They didn't know whether that was correct, nor did they really care; it was just a companionable litany they called back and forth.

One day when it was time for the group to go to Rhythms class, Michael seemed nervous about his beloved watch and asked his teacher to hold it for him. In passing it from his hand to hers, he dropped it on the cement floor. Seeing it was broken, he sobbed while she tried in vain to console him: "It was an accident." His tears continued to flow. "No one will be angry with you . . . it was an accident." His shoulders were shaking with his crying. "Your parents will get you a new watch." By now he was trembling all over. "I'll get you a new watch." Nothing soothed his distress until the teacher's aide came from the other side of the room. "Here, Michael, do you want to borrow my watch?" Instantly the crying stopped. He fastened the replacement, snuffed up the last of his tears, and, holding his hand tightly over the watch face, said with relief, "Good. Now my mother will know when it's the right time to pick me up."

Michael's powerful intellect had absorbed the invisible concept of time, but emotionally he was a four-year-old magical thinker who equated the loss of his timepiece with the risk of abandonment. His feelings told him that if time weren't firmly anchored to his body, he might not get his mother there to collect him. His watch was more than a recorder—it was the creator of time. Michael didn't need to learn letters and numerals ahead of schedule. He would get those in due course and make good use of them. He needed to be four with other fours and be cared for by those who understood the needs of a four-year-old's heart as well as mind.

THE NEED TO GIVE CARE

Many of the traits of gifted thinkers make it difficult for them to make friends, and many students with learning differences feel both unloved and unlovable. The conundrum kid who carries both burdens may need extra help with relationships. In being responsible for another living creature, the growing child finds the confirmation of being needed, which shows him he can give as well as receive.

An eighteen-year-old girl won a prestigious literary award for her poem about grief and mourning. When asked how she knew about such things, she gave the credit to her hamster. She said that as a child she had been sharp-tongued and lonely. Because she was a voracious reader who enjoyed doing her homework, she was usually quick to answer the teacher's questions. With her ready tongue and book learning, she squelched the other kids in class, and they avenged themselves on the playground.

She was unhappy in school, but at home she had a hamster who seemed to love her as much as she loved him. She played with him, confided in him, made him Valentines, and even gave him a birthday party. Her affection poured out. One day the hamster discovered how to open his cage, and began a series of daily escapes, finding his way to the closet, into the hall, and finally to the bathroom, where he learned how to scale the towel rack and go from there to the toilet seat, which he ran like a racecourse. One Friday, he fell into the toilet and drowned. Margaret found him when she got home from school. She said, "I sobbed and grieved for the whole weekend and my mother didn't interfere. She didn't try to tell me everything would be all right, and she didn't buy me another hamster. I touched the bottom of sadness. Then we had a funeral, and I could deal with life again, but I never forgot."

THE NEED FOR OUTPUT AS WELL AS INTAKE

The ten traits of giftedness mentioned earlier act as wide-diameter pipes for the intake of information, ideas, and experiences. Students with vast capacity for intake need equally generous outlets to regulate the flow. But a word of caution: Because we know gifted thinkers are capable of high achievement, we sometimes overlook their need to be allowed the error half of trial and error, forgetting that a project-gone-wrong can be the seedbed of discovery. If we encourage output while insisting on perfection, we jeopardize students' willingness to take risks. By thwarting exploration, we condemn gifted thinkers to living in other men's discoveries.

Output needn't always be academic. Something as simple as making up a batch of cookies is the type of output that allows a conundrum kid to extend a friendly hand to a world that often misinterprets his actions. Making cookies with another child may be a way of making a friend, and offering to share them may show a generosity other people don't recognize.

THE NEED FOR THREE-WAY DEVELOPMENT

True education encourages the development of the student's aesthetic and moral values as well as academic progress.[2] But a culture that rewards high test scores and verifiable answers frequently shortchanges exploration of ambiguities and time-consuming enigmas. The student whose education emphasizes rational-scientific factual work at the expense of aesthetic and moral development is being prepared to function as a machine rather than a human being.

Aesthetic nourishment is essential for students with heightened perceptions, awareness of patterns, and delight in divergent thinking. In addition to traditional art, music, or dance classes, interdisciplinary projects that encourage students to join poetry with paintings, to illustrate stories, to combine words and art with music, or to find patterns in their surroundings are exercises in aesthetic development that enrich the entire educational atmosphere. Most smart kids with school problems excel at this kind of endeavor, but, ironically, such opportunities are often considered "enrichment," reserved for high-scoring students, and offered in the same time block as the remedial training conundrum kids need.

Students need opportunities to probe moral and ethical questions, to learn what Abraham Tannenbaum of Columbia University calls "the moral consequences of having a very good idea." A glance at history provides examples of brilliant ideas that caused deep human suffering: the scholarly writings of Karl Marx, the invention of DDT, or the splitting of the atom. Today's students are going into uncharted moral, ethical worlds in which even death and life are being redefined. With their capacity for original insight, intellectual power, and barrier-breaking work, our students need to develop their ethical and moral codes before being asked to rely on them.

THE NEED FOR ADULT LEADERSHIP

Gifted students need adult leaders to help them make choices, take chances, and accept themselves when they fall short of perfection. Adult leaders can help young people avoid unnecessary disappointment by helping them choose potential projects according to degree of difficulty and likelihood of success.

Some high-scoring students need adult leadership to liberate them from the prison of their own accomplishments. Early and continual academic success can make a student so dependent on perfect papers and correct answers that he relinquishes an original idea because it might earn a *C* instead of an *A*. Conundrum kids under pressure to improve their grades may also limit their work to what they think will please the teacher. When parents or teachers praise high grades extravagantly, they impoverish both the weak and the strong students' innovative capacities.

Effective adult leadership can promote creativity and liberate a student who is imprisoned in a grid of grades by offering projects and exercises that honor originality over conformity.

Gifted thinkers resent failure and blame themselves when they cannot meet their own expectations. The gifted thinker with a learning difference hates failure as much as his unencumbered peers but meets it twice as often. Warm adult leadership can remove some obstacles, help him over others, and reassure him he is understood.

THE NEED FOR HUMOR

Sometimes adults take school and school problems so seriously that they overlook the nature of children and the importance of laughter. Humor is a dowser's wand to the pools of affect and energy that characterize real learning. If we can locate these pools through humor and tap them through the academic exercises we offer in school, we encourage the student to join his natural energy to academic requirements.

Cartoons, skits, articles or stories in the student newspaper, satire, dramatic productions, and verse are but a few of the many appropriate vehicles for student humor that encourage the abstract thinking underlying funny things.

As part of a schoolwide cleanup and antilitter campaign, students in kindergarten through grade twelve read (or heard) Shel Silverstein's poem about the girl who refused to do her household chore: "Sarah Cynthia Sylvia Stout Would Not Take the Garbage Out."[3] Each verse gives vivid descriptions of rotting refuse. As their literary contribution to the campaign my fourth-grade language arts class made a poster of a garbage can labeled "Great Garbage," to which they attached their own garbage poems, and invited other classes to contribute. Here are three gourmet selections.

Eyeballs bulging out of frogs
Coffee cans and catalogues
Bread crusts soaked in soup from tortoise
Two dead mice with rigor mortis.

Crushed-up mushed-up lollipops
Rusty broken bottle tops
Purple spotted old band-aids
Ripped-up dirty window shades
Mystery mushrooms, sour cider
Kitty litter, squished-up spider.

Dribbling, drooling purple eggnog
Slimy leg and skin of frog
Snouty mouty old fish heads
Cookie crumbs from unmade beds.

The authors of these verses were conundrum kids, two years ahead
of their classmates in math and two years behind them in reading
and spelling.

We can encourage humor in school in the tasks we give students
to do, the selections we give them to read, and, above all, in the
example we set through our perceptions of ourselves.

PRINCIPLES OF GOOD PRACTICE

The smart kid with school problems needs coordination of support,
evaluation of strengths and weaknesses, anticipation of curriculum
demands, and accommodation of learning style.

COORDINATION OF SUPPORT

Conundrum kids need coordinated support from the professionals and nonprofessionals in their lives. From the educational
field they need sympathetic administrators who understand their
needs and are willing to bend some of the institutional machinery.
They need classroom teachers who accept atypical learning styles

and are willing to use a variety of materials and teaching techniques. Although they need specialists to help lay out the particulars of their programs, they do not always need to be taught by specialists. They need one person to plan and oversee their total educational program, a person I call the *overseer*.

This overseer must be available for consultation with the student's teachers, for conferences with the student's family, and for planning with the student himself. Whether this overseer is a learning specialist, an administrator, a counselor, a school psychologist, a guidance counselor, or a seasoned senior teacher acting as an academic adviser doesn't matter. But the student needs a continuing advocate whose job it is to offer encouragement and smooth the way, to make educational recommendations on the basis of diagnosis and clinical observations, and to interpret test results to the family and the school. The overseer should be able to deflect, yet understand, parental anxiety or rage at slow progress and be tactful enough to make suggestions to teachers without putting them on the defensive. The job requires a combination of gentleness and strength.

In coordinating their support and working with the overseer, teachers and parents need to recognize one another's vulnerabilities.

Teachers need to understand that parents suffer vicarious pain when their children struggle. Pain brings fear and often fatigue. Confused and apprehensive parents may blame themselves, find fault with the school, or lose faith in the student. Teachers who make themselves available for conferences, and who sympathize with a student's dilemma, can help parents grow as they increase their understanding of academic problems.

Parents need to understand that teachers want their students to succeed and suffer self-doubt when they don't. When personal uncertainty turns inward, it causes discouragement; turned outward, it causes defensiveness. Parental support of teacher efforts can bring out the best in the situation; blame worsens it.

True coordination requires the educators and parents to compare notes. The high-achieving student who takes three hours an evening on homework other students complete in an hour is sending an important signal. His parents need to know how long the assignments are meant to take; the teacher needs to know how much effort is going into the task. The student who seems pulled together in school but is temperamental at home may be functioning under too much pressure. Parents and teachers need to be aware of both kinds of behavior. The student who is passive in school but active outside it is leading the kind of double life that drains psychological energy. Bed-wetting, nail-biting, stomachaches, and headaches are the kinds of symptoms teachers and parents need to share.

Other nonprofessional adults in the student's life, be they grandparents, coaches, aunts, uncles, family friends, or mentors, have important support to give. In order to believe in himself, the struggling student needs acceptance, love, and optimism to counteract the message of inadequacy school problems convey.

EVALUATION OF STRENGTHS AND WEAKNESSES

A master file is vital to the evaluation and education of a conundrum kid. Ideally the parents and overseer maintain the file together. If this is not possible, the parents should assume the primary responsibility, either on their own initiative or at the suggestion of the educators. Evaluation should begin the minute a teacher or parent thinks, "There's something different about this kid."

The master file should begin with the first dated notes listing concerns, questions, traits, indications of learning differences, and the student's personal needs. (The earlier part of this chapter provides a useful framework.) The more specific the notes the better. "Tom has trouble concentrating when people are moving around, but noise doesn't seem to bother him" tells more than "Sometimes Tom gets distracted." The format can be informal, but good evaluation is a cumulative process, which depends on a flow of written records.

The master file should contain test scores and report cards as well as a few samples of the student's work demonstrating both strengths and weaknesses.

Each year's work samples, report cards, and any anecdotal materials should be clipped together, and at least twice a year the adults in charge of the student's schooling should use the master file for review and planning. They need to return to the original dated paper to note consistency or change in patterns, to judge the efficacy of remedial measures, and to be sure talent is being kept alive. Once again, they should write down their comments. Written notes from these twice-yearly sessions should be clipped to the other papers from that year.

Understanding the root of the problem is the basis for on-target remediation. Putting a runner with a sprained ankle in a sling or offering crutches as a headache remedy doesn't help any more than giving academic support that doesn't match the need. But it is a sorry truth that many conundrum kids are getting general tutoring— a diffuse combination of pep talks and homework help—rather than the specific training they need. Chapters 2 through 8 are designed to help educators and parents focus their efforts precisely.

An individual psychoeducational evaluation makes an important contribution and belongs in the master file. We shall explore the when, why, and how in detail in Chapter 8, "Testing Demystified."

A careful review of the student's learning history and samples of work can distinguish the true conundrum kid from the student who is simply the victim of unrealistically high parental expectations. Sometimes a parent will label an average learner LD because he is not at the top of the class. It is easier for some parents to say "My kid is LD" than it is to say "My kid is average." The contents of the master file may give the overseer material to help the family set realistic expectations.

The master file should be shared by teachers, parents, the overseer, and the student himself as soon as the adults agree he is mature enough to understand its contents.

ANTICIPATION OF CURRICULUM DEMANDS

Educators and parents who understand a conundrum kid's learning style can often prevent trouble by anticipating the demands of the curriculum and giving early help.

Here is a general sequence of curriculum showing different types of thinking required at successive grade levels, and tied to Piaget's learning stages: *preoperational*, approximately ages two to seven or eight; *concrete operations*, approximately ages seven to eight to eleven to twelve; and *formal operations*, eleven to twelve continuing through life. Teachers accustomed to working with one particular age group or subject matter may find this overview helpful. So may parents who remember their own schooling but haven't studied learning.

Kindergarten and first-grade students are in the *preoperational stage* in which behavior and thinking are still egocentric. The student grows ready for mental symbols and symbolic play and learns through simple trial and error rather than logic.

In kindergarten the conundrum kid who is very quick at some tasks and slow or disabled in others has trouble fitting in with a standardized curriculum. Because early school experiences color the student's view of himself as a learner, it is easy for the smart kid to decide he is either omnipotent or inadequate.

In first grade most children learn to read, write, spell, and do paper-and-pencil arithmetic, and the child who is unready or unable to learn these skills usually feels different and scared. The next chapter, "The Young Child: Developmental Levels and Academic Requirements," explores some specifics of kindergarten and first-grade readiness.

Students from roughly the second through sixth grades are in Piaget's stage of *concrete operations*. The student learns to make groupings of classes and relations and begins to develop logic, which is initially bound to the manipulation of objects. The student develops the concept of *conservation*, understanding that four ounces of water is four ounces of water even though one four-ounce pouring barely covers the bottom of a big pot and another fills a juice glass.

In second grade, students consolidate their basic language arts and math skills. The conundrum kid who missed them is likely to be overwhwelmed by the double burden of trying to grasp and consolidate simultaneously. The student who has not developed the concept of conservation doesn't really know the "fourness" of four and will have trouble understanding math.

In third grade, those reading, writing, spelling, and math skills, which had previously been goals in themselves, now become the foundations of reading comprehension, creative writing, and the solving of practical problems in arithmetic. The student with inadequate reading, writing, language, or math skills is in the precarious position of trying to build a structure with a half-full tool box. Chapters 3, 5, and 6, "Visual Learning," "Auditory Learning," and "Language and Learning," demonstrate the connections be-tween these systems and the three *R*s.

In fourth grade, students are expected to increase the fluency of their written expression. Because writing competence tradition-ally lags behind reading facility, the shaky reader will have trouble meeting this requirement, as will the poor speller or student with handwriting difficulties. We shall explore the far-reaching effects of early handwriting problems in Chapter 4, "Motor Function and School Achievement."

Fifth and sixth graders are expected to acquire information and organize their thoughts. The student with a weak language base will have trouble with both. Former problems with reading may seem to bloom anew as the volume and complexity of assignments in-crease. Handwriting problems will undercut conceptually good work.

Around seventh grade, the student enters the age of *formal operations,* which brings the ability to think abstractly without work-ing with physical objects, the ability to coordinate several variables in thought or action, and a refinement of the ability to hypothesize, predict consequences, and consider implications in new situations.

In seventh and eighth grades, the intelligent student is ex-pected to integrate the skills from the earlier years, using them to absorb and express concepts, orally and in written work, on in-creasingly abstract levels with reliable mechanical skills. The co-nundrum kid who is still collecting those skills falls further and further behind.

In high school the successful student relies on a good memory, organization, well-developed concepts, reasonable psychological stability, and solid mechanical skills. Students with ragged devel-opment may have trouble with the transitions these years encom-pass: from childhood to adulthood, from one subject matter to another, and from enjoyment of the activities they're good at to struggles with subjects that are difficult. Intelligent or brilliant young people who feel unsuccessful in school during this period may reject the idea of any further education. They may drop out, turn against society, or harm themselves.

College is a time for exploring new disciplines, or old disciplines at new levels. The atypical student may need help assembling his credentials for admission, and must anticipate his needs for special support once he starts college. Otherwise, he risks being turned down or flunking out. There are specific suggestions for help in Chapter 9, "Maturation and Higher Education."

If there are so many hurdles and perils, what makes the process worthwhile? Theodore Sizer, former dean of the Harvard Graduate School of Education and author of *Horace's Compromise, The Dilemma of the American High School* (see Annotated Bibliography), says that a true education confers these three: *power, agency,* and *joy.*

Smart kids with school problems need the *power* of basic skills to support their ideas. And they need psychological power to keep their dreams alive during the years when school problems bring discouragement.

Agency refers to the opportunity to exercise and display that power. Good students have easy access to agency; they can write for the school newspaper, be on the debating team, or enter Olympics of the Mind contests. Conundrum kids often have trouble finding appropriate places or ways of displaying their power in school and need adult help in finding a showcase.

Joy, the outgrowth of power and agency, is what makes learning worthwhile. The smart kid with school problems has as great a capacity for joy as his unencumbered classmates but needs help to keep it alive.

Anticipation of curriculum demands and perils particular to conundrum kids at successive grade levels can help head off difficulty. Prevention can build power, provide for agency, and protect joy.

ACCOMMODATION OF LEARNING STYLE

To accommodate the atypical learner's needs, adults in charge of his program need to budget time for the nurture of talent, for remedial help, and for steady progress with regular schoolwork.

Talent withers without nurture. Because it is talent that will bring joy long after the legal requirement for schooling is satisfied, ample time must be allocated for the student's particular interest.

Remedial help may come from several sources. In some instances, classroom teachers can provide it themselves without relying on specialists. In more serious situations, a specialist may need to prescribe the materials or provide remedial training. It is fortunate when sufficient help is available through the school system. When it is not, the parents must pick up the slack, either hiring a tutor or trying to provide the help themselves, using materials suggested by the overseer or teacher. Although trying to combine the roles of parent and teacher is difficult, and can have negative results, sometimes it is the only available option.

Remedial help can be given as prevention as well as cure. This is the best type of accommodation. Unfortunately, some smart kids don't get the help they need until they are failing.

A thoughtful, worried parent called me last fall. She and her husband had just moved to our area with their sixth grader son. When the boy was in first and second grades, he had needed extra help with reading and writing, which the school had provided. They predicted he might need help again later on, but all went well in third and fourth grades, where his interest in science really bloomed. His reading problem began to surface again in fifth grade when the pace picked up: he had a different teacher for each subject, and more work was required. Because this boy had good early training, he is not in real trouble; his A in science pulls his overall average up, but nevertheless he is discouraged and scared. He wants to get to the top but realizes he is only just getting by. He is caught in a school policy that says a student must be two years below grade level in reading before receiving extra help. "Where can we turn?" his mother asked. "He's too strong to qualify for help and too weak to manage without it."

Accommodation sometimes means lifting a requirement. A sophomore at a competitive New England college was failing French. When she received a letter from the academic dean, she was certain it was a notice of academic probation and was astonished at the message: "In view of your persistent difficulty with languages, evident in your high school transcript and college record, we suspect you may have the kind of learning disability which will exempt you from the foreign language requirement. Please make an appointment through this office to have the appropriate testing." She passed the test by failing it, the foreign language requirement was lifted, and she traded French for a course in engineering.

Learning styles must be accommodated in the regular classroom as well as in special situations. The classroom teacher can help the atypical learner do regular schoolwork through careful grouping. Conundrum kids need to work alone, as well as in small groups, and with the whole class.

Because they need to work at their own level and pace (which may be faster or slower than their peers', depending on the subject), they need opportunities for independent study.

They also need to work in small groups where talents can combine; the artist who spells poorly, working with an accomplished writer, can create a work more powerful than either could achieve alone.

Most regular schoolwork is done with the whole class, and the conundrum kid can often hold his own if given appropriate remedial support and such alternative teaching strategies as we shall explore in the ensuing chapters.

To accommodate divergent thinking, heightened perceptions, awareness of patterns, and other traits of giftedness, the wise adult, either teacher or parent, will offer exercises that honor originality over conformity. Children of all ages can create folk tales describing the origins of such natural phenomena as fire or thunder. They can write about and illustrate their own imaginary creatures. They can listen to three-fourths of a story and then try to write an ending different from the one they think the author has used. Just as there is no such thing as a wrong poem, there is no wrong fable, wrong imaginary animal, or wrong origin of the first rainbow. Gifted students are often interested in future studies. They can design means of transportation, new foods, or games for the future.

Mathematics offers brainteasers and mind-benders with infinite numbers of different, yet correct answers. I watched a group of seven-year-olds deciding "How many ways can you add and subtract to get seven?" In a very short time, the group had brainstormed over forty! Moving quickly beyond $3 + 4 = 7$, and its companion $4 + 3 = 7$, they went on to such elaborations as $2 + 1 + 1 + 1 + 2 = 7$ and $9 - 6 + 4 = 7$ and $100 - 90 - 3 = 7$.

Later in the day I watched some ninth graders use the "four

fours" trying to build every number from zero to fifty. The rules require the use of all four fours, along with any mathematical sign or process, to reach a specific number. For example, twenty could be $4/4 + 4 \times 4 = 20$. Sixteen might be $4 + 4 - 4 \times 4 = 16$, or, equally correctly, it could be: $4 \times 4 \div 4/4 = 16$. The combinations are endlessly fascinating to those who enjoy playing with numbers, and there is a wide variety of equally correct answers.

Even though it takes time and care to accommodate conundrum kids' learning styles, teachers become better teachers by increasing their repertoires of styles and materials, schools are richer for the contributions these kids make to the fabric of school life, and our society needs their power, agency, and joy. Many great intellectual, artistic, and scientific contributions have come from those who had severe academic problems, or would have, had they been required to attend school. From Leonardo da Vinci to Albert Einstein the list is long and the intellectual power great. It includes the geniuses, the highly accomplished, and the just plain competent.

A CASE HISTORY: BART

Angry, curious, and *gentle* were the three words Bart's mother chose to describe her eighth grader son. His father said, "He's all contradictions. He's smart in thinking but dumb in school; he remembers the hard things and forgets the simple ones. He's always gotten along with us and our friends but can't get along with his teachers." Bart said of himself "I always mess up," "Max is the smart one in our family," and "I used to be smart when I was little."

Bart was an early stairclimber, walker, tricycle rider, and block builder, but a late talker. Although he understood everything, he said little, and his speech was difficult to understand. His father was proud of Bart's physical prowess and overlooked his verbal difficulties, but Max mimicked him and often reduced him to tears. His mother arranged for a course of speech therapy when Bart was three, which proved successful. Although some minor misarticulations linger (he says *vis* for *this* and *Mattasusetts* for *Massachusetts*), these, like his unusual combination of blue eyes and dark hair, simply contribute to his individuality.

When he started first grade, his speech sounds were clear but his conversation came in pauses and spurts. He had trouble associating letters with sounds, didn't learn his sight words, and frequently tangled letter sequence in spelling. Max would never let him forget the time he signed his paper "B-r-a-t."

Although Bart could create intricate structures with blocks, sugar cubes, tongue depressors, or whatever was at hand, his pencil control was poor. By the end of second grade, his letters and numerals were still large and awkwardly formed. He struggled with reading and the pencil-paper aspects of school but enjoyed classroom discussion and taking care of the guinea pig.

Using phonics in third, fourth, and fifth grades, he consolidated his reading skills, but his spelling contained such errors as: *pepul, wus, thay, sed,* and *on perpis,* and his handwriting problems persisted.

By sixth grade Bart's silent reading and comprehension were strong, but his oral reading was jerky and rushed. His written work was untidy, disorganized, and littered with incorrect spelling. As his ideas increased in pace and complexity, his hand lagged further and further behind. His speech rhythms of pause and spurt continued, and he didn't use punctuation for either phrasing or logic. In one exercise, omitting a vital comma and question mark, he wrote "when are we going to eat Max."

He had a different teacher for each subject, and his performance varied widely. On the athletic field, in the science lab, in the art room, on the stage, or in independent reading, Bart was competent and confident. In math class he understood the concepts but his papers were sloppy. He frequently "forgot" his homework, and he did poorly on tests because, in his haste to write the problems and the answers, his columns would drift or he would transpose the numbers, writing 17 for 71, or 256 for 265. Although he handled lab materials skillfully, he was so ashamed of his science notebook, and so afraid his mother (or Max) would see it, that he threw it away, pretending he had lost it on the bus.

In social studies he enjoyed immersing himself in other cultures, but his written work was helter-skelter. He would jump from one topic to another, and couldn't seem to use a topic sentence and a paragraph to organize his thoughts.

The comment on his sixth-grade report card was "Bart nearly failed language arts. He will be taken out of art and physical education if he doesn't improve next term."

He entered seventh grade angry with himself and the system. His teachers considered him a troublemaker. His father thought Bart wasn't trying, Max thought Bart was dumb, and his mother hoped he was simply going through a bad time.

This tall, strong, angry boy who enjoyed problem solving in math, art, and the out-of-doors had very poor rote memory, handwriting, and spelling. He was misunderstood while being exhorted to try harder and do better.

When Bart was in eighth grade, his parents decided to take him to a psychologist for testing. Combining Bart's parents' descriptions, quoted earlier, with a review of his school history and the results of the testing, the psychologist found recurrent patterns of wide discrepancies in Bart's learning style. This jagged profile accounted for many of his academic highs and lows.

The psychologist felt Bart's anger came from the frustration of feeling smart and dumb simultaneously, and offered several suggestions. The first was to share the test results with Bart himself. Seeing his high scores should boost the boy's self-confidence, and identifying the weak areas would help him see them as specific difficulties instead of symptoms of overall stupidity.

The next suggestion was to find a tutor to work with Bart five times a week in hourly sessions for the remainder of the academic year and over the summer. The goals would be to improve his handwriting, work on his spelling, combine the spelling and handwriting training with one another, and develop organizational skills for written work. In addition, the psychologist suggested that Bart's parents buy a computer with a word processor and have him learn both touch-typing and the use of the word-processing program as soon as school let out in June. With such training under his belt, Bart could return to school in September with brighter prospects for success.

At first, Bart did not want to talk to the psychologist or review his test results, but when he agreed to go he was enormously relieved by what he heard. Although he is not delighted to sacrifice his summer freedom to remedial work, he has agreed and is particularly looking forward to having a computer. His parents feel able to plan intelligently now that they understand the specifics of Bart's difficulties. They will stay in touch with the psychologist, who will act as an overseer in coordinating Bart's education. They have begun a master file. Because Bart is understood, he and his family have traded fear and frustration for "things to know and ways to help."

2

THE YOUNG CHILD

DEVELOPMENTAL LEVELS
AND
ACADEMIC REQUIREMENTS

A good fit between the student's developmental levels and the academic requirements of the school promotes joyful, solid learning. Mismatches can create learning disabilities, distort personal relationships, cap creativity, and impoverish the overall quality of a human life. Talented, intelligent children are not simply a national resource, they are a universal treasure. To dull the glow of their promise through inappropriate placement is a form of child abuse.

This chapter is designed to help educators and parents ward off unnecessary school problems by exploring developmental readiness for kindergarten and first grade, and appropriate grade placement in the early years of schooling. It is so much easier to start out at the right level than to try to undo the harm of a poor placement decision by later retention or acceleration. Since the child's view of himself as a learner—as a worthwhile human being—is heavily influenced by his first experiences in school, the initial placement decision has lifelong impact.

FACTORS IN A STUDENT'S DEVELOPMENTAL LEVEL

A student's developmental level is a combination of his age, social-emotional maturity, and intellectual development. Let's explore them one by one.

AGE

Turning five doesn't automatically make a child ready for school. Chronological level may be the least important of the three developmental components, yet it is often the major determinant of school placement.

Birth date frequently controls the decision about who should enter school and in which grade. For example, in six public school districts in or adjoining the town of Bedford, New York, policies variously state that a child who is going to turn five during the school year by either December 1, December 15, or December 31 should enter kindergarten in September of that school year. When the child's birthday is near the cutoff date, or in cases of unusual psychological, intellectual, or developmental function, the school may recommend, or parents may request, a departure from standard procedure. Although the parent has the option to request accelerated or delayed entry, the school retains the authority to make the final decision, and, increasingly, in public, parochial, and independent schools (which some people call private), schools recommend waiting. This is particularly true as more and more kindergartens step up the curriculum with formal academic training.

Instead of, or in addition to, using birth dates, some schools encourage a "three before first" policy. They want their students to have three years of preschool, including kindergarten, before first grade. These can be two of nursery school and one of kindergarten; one of nursery school, one of kindergarten, and one in a transitional kindergarten–first grade program; or one of nursery school and two of kindergarten.

Traditionally, independent schools throughout the country have used earlier birth-date requirements, selecting September or June as the cutoff date rather than December. In addition, many are pleased with the results of using different cutoff dates for boys and girls: to be eligible for kindergarten in the fall, a girl must turn five by September 1, and a boy must have turned five by the previous June 1. This policy is born of many years of observing the relative readiness of male and female children.

"Three before first" and birth-date cutoff policies can be shifted if necessary, but they may buy the child the extra time he needs for developmental growth, at the same time helping anxious parents save face. It's easy to say, "He missed the kindergarten deadline, so he'll go a year later."

Research, such as that done by Jeannette J. Jansky at Columbia University, shows that prematurely born children, particularly males and particularly left-handed males, are often developmentally delayed in their readiness for schoolwork. This lag may mask high intellectual potential, creating an incorrect impression of average or low intelligence. In spite of its impact, parents often forget to mention premature birth, and educators often overlook it in school placement.

Given a choice of sending a student into school several months younger or several months older than the average age in the class, both common sense and current research indicate a greater chance of overall readiness in the chronologically older child. Time alone will not immunize against school problems, but the readier the child, the greater his chance of success.

SOCIAL-EMOTIONAL MATURITY

Social-emotional maturity allows the child to approach learning with the expectation of success and provides resilience in times of stress. An observant adult can make a useful estimate of a student's social-emotional level by noting how easily he makes friends with others his age. The child who likes himself finds it easy to like others, and if his level of social-emotional development matches his classmates', friendships will come automatically.

It is important to assess the child's social-emotional maturity in large group activities as well as with one or two other children. Some young children can seem socially well developed in an intimate setting, but become silly, babyish, or wild when more children are involved. Others, intelligent and emotionally well developed, need time to watch before participating. The enlightened observer sees social-emotional maturity in the restraint of "look before you leap," distinguishing it from the self-doubt of the child who always seeks safety on the sidelines.

INTELLECTUAL LEVEL

We can assess a child's intellectual level by using direct observation and formal and informal screening instruments.

In direct observation we need to watch for the child's understanding of concepts and not be fooled by mere facility in rote recitation. For example, five-year-old Marnie can say the numbers from one to one hundred. She sits on her grandfather's knee and entertains him by counting to one hundred, but when she looks at the buttons on her sweater she sometimes tallies up six, sometimes nine, or ten. Marnie is not a budding mathematical genius. She is a sociable little girl who memorizes easily and likes to recite.

Ella, another five-year-old, enjoys playing with attribute blocks and making patterns with colored beads. She likes to see whether her older brother can continue her patterns. Her most recent was three red beads, four blue beads, five red beads, six blue ones. Ella is not a particularly good memorizer, but she obviously enjoys thinking.

Formal and informal screening highlight children who may be at risk for formal academics, illustrating some reasons for their potential difficulty and, by inference, indicating the specifics of preventive or remedial help. The section Principles of Good Practice, later in this chapter, gives examples of tasks included in well-known, reliable screening tests.

READINESS FOR FIRST GRADE

The ready child starts first grade with four abilities. He can postpone gratification, sit still and concentrate, manage symbols (with a pencil as well as verbally), and separate reality and fantasy.

These four abilities unfold as part of the developmental process; they are to be encouraged, not forced. If they are superimposed prematurely, they are like splints and crutches instead of skeletal structure.

The child who can *postpone gratification* can tolerate the inevitably slow pace and methodical nature of introductory learning, accepting preliminary drudgery for the sake of future enjoyment.

The child who is able to *sit still* can be physically at peace while learning, and being able to *concentrate* allows him to practice his newly acquired skills. A short concentration span will disrupt the practice he needs for consolidation.

The child who can *manage symbols* is ready to learn the abstractions of letters, numerals, and printed language. The child whose pencil is a saboteur instead of an ally has trouble writing symbols and is at risk for problems in handwriting, spelling, and pencil-paper math.

The child who can separate fantasy and reality, and has established a firm boundary between the two, can sort himself out from the creatures of his own imagination and deliver himself to the tasks at hand. Separating reality and fantasy helps the child distinguish between the probable and the improbable, sharpening his perceptions of cause and effect and helping him predict the consequences of his own actions.

Ironically, smart kids may develop these abilities later than other children; clusters of the ten traits of giftedness discussed in Chapter 1 may get in the way. Postponing gratification may seem a waste of time to the instant learner who "just knows things." Sitting at a desk may be confining to the child who wants to explore mathematical patterns. Printed symbols may be an annoying hindrance to the high-energy hands-on learner. Heightened perceptions and divergent thinking make it hard for the highly imaginative child to establish the boundary between fantasy and reality; he has a greater supply to manage. Katrina de Hirsch, a pioneer in theories of child development and learning, calls such children *superior immatures*.

The advanced verbal skills of superior immatures can often camouflage unreadiness. The child who can talk a good game at an early age deserves our skepticism of his readiness for schooling ahead of schedule. When adults push children into formal academic situations prematurely, they are behaving as if schooling were a train about to pull out of the station with not another one in sight.

To prevent unnecessary school problems, many superior immatures profit from taking an extra year before going to first grade. They need what Louise Bates Ames, of the Gesell Institute for Human Development, calls "the gift of time."

What happens if the school finds a child developmentally unready and wants to give him more time, but the parents want to move him ahead? The educators involved should use their strongest powers of persuasion, while also recognizing that parental endorsement of the decision is critical to its success.

GRADE PLACEMENT

Grade-placement questions may involve an unready child, a child who is ready in some ways and not in others, a ready child in a restrictive curriculum, an underestimated or an overestimated student, or a different learner in a standard curriculum. See the effect of grade placement decisions on these smart kids.

EMMETT

Emmett was a classic superior immature, whose aggressive father thought it would "grow the boy up" to be the youngest in first grade rather than waiting for the following year to be among the oldest. Emmett was a street-smart, wiggly little boy with a streak of sweetness that didn't show in the classroom. He couldn't sit still in first grade, and he used his pencil as a pretend gun or rocket instead of an instrument of communication. He was often sent out into the hall and frequently asked to be excused to go to the bathroom.

In second grade Emmett started having stomachaches in the morning before coming to school, where his teacher frequently kept him in from recess for uncompleted work. The resource-room teacher diagnosed him as learning disabled, having both "an attentional deficit and a weak visual memory." But Emmett was just a seven-year-old trying to do eight-year-old work.

In third grade Emmett was placed in the remedial reading track, which, because of scheduling, automatically placed him in the slow math group. This boy who had scored at the top of the class in the quantitative section of the Metropolitan Readiness Test at the end of kindergarten, who had loved numbers since he was three and had understood complicated math concepts easily, was confused at feeling smart and being placed dumb.

In fourth grade, he was disciplined for decorating the boy's bathroom with graffiti and is now considered a disciplinary as well as academic problem. Academic frustration fuels increasingly rebellious behavior. The mismatch between his developmental level and academic demand began in first grade and continues to cause trouble. Emmett has a school-created learning disability.

DAVEY

Davey seemed ready in some ways and unready in others. His parents asked a colleague of mine to evaluate his readiness for first grade. Davey had squeaked into kindergarten just under the cutoff date, and seemed doubly young for his class because, when there had been a question, most parents of his classmates had chosen to give their children extra time rather than starting them off early.

By midkindergarten, Davey still hadn't decided which hand to use for writing. He ate with his right, threw a ball with his left, and used both for block building and digging in the sandpile. At home he was a self-reliant, contented child who could amuse himself for hours. He played the piano by ear extraordinarily well for a child his age and was fascinated by the natural world. He carefully mounted his leaf collection and made constant, ambidextrous use of the junior microscope he got for his birthday. Whereas his self-reliance seemed adult at home, it was considered an indication of immaturity at school.

On the playground, Davey was shy and likely to play by himself. He was afraid of some of the bigger boys and cried easily if one of them took a plaything from him.

In spite of his obvious intelligence, Davey reverted to baby talk when formal reading readiness instruction was introduced. And, although he continued to be conversationally fluent, he frequently misunderstood such linguistic subtleties as dependent clauses and passive constructions when he heard them in conversation.

Because learning differences frequently run in families, my colleague was interested to learn that Davey's grandfather and two uncles are successful businessmen who had trouble with reading in school, and, as adults, seldom read for pleasure.

She recommended that Davey take an additional year in kindergarten. Although his musical ability, his interest in animals, and his general level of thinking indicated high intelligence, his language skills were weak, there was a family history of reading problems, and he responded negatively to formal classroom instruction. Both school and parents agreed he needed more time.

For his second year in kindergarten, the school planned a strong multisensory reading readiness program to help him learn his letters and sounds. This approach emphasizes the reliable relationship between sounds and letters. Students use their eyes, ears, and hands as they see a letter and make its sound, hear a sound and write the letter. Multisensory training, originally designed for dyslexic students, benefits all beginning readers and writers. Regular classrooms that use this technique show a significant drop (as much as 30 percent) in the number of students requiring remedial help. It is called by various names: *Orton-Gillingham, Slingerland, Alphabet Phonics, Project Read,* and *Recipe for Reading* to name a few.

Davey's teachers emphasized social development and gave him the opportunities for cooperative play he so clearly needed. Being at the older end of the class gave him a better shot at the success his family expected of him.

During that second kindergarten year Davey made friends, really learned to enjoy stories, and even developed a certain facility in telling them. He entertained at the year-end school fair as a magician in cloak, top hat, and spectacles. He delighted his audience with the "Step right up, ladies and gentlemen, and . . ." patter and the simple tricks he had learned in the Saturday morning Young Magicians' Workshop sponsored by the community college. As my colleague watched him exercising his power, she thought, "Yes indeed, magic." But a main part of his magic was the invisible magic of time.

ISABELLA

Isabella was a ready child in a restrictive curriculum. "I'm going to be a space settler and a doctor," said Isabella confidently, "and when I get there I'm going to grow the first vegetables and flowers they have. Where I live in Space is going to be really pretty. Do you want to see a picture?" Five-year-old Isabella held out her drawing. There, indeed, was a rendering of a domed space station, complete with a house for Isabella and her family, a lush garden of multicolored flowers and vegetables, a sign reading NO WEEDS IN SPAC, and Isabella herself, surveying the scene, smiling broadly, stethoscope slung casually from her neck.

Isabella goes to the local kindergarten. She has a math workbook, a reading workbook, and a workbook for something called concept development in which she does such exercises as drawing lines from pictures of objects to the rooms in which they belong. Each day the teacher and the teacher's aide correct the workbook pages during the morning, and any errors must be corrected at recess. Last Thursday Isabella spent recess at her desk wondering what she needed to fix on page 37. The teacher had said, "You have made a thinking mistake. Stay at your desk until you find it." By the end of recess, she was still puzzling. "Look," said the teacher, "you've drawn a line from the piano to the bedroom." "But that's where it is in our house," Isabella replied. "No," said the teacher, "that's not the correct answer. The piano belongs in the living room. Don't be stubborn, Isabella."

During art period Isabella and her classmates color predrawn figures on ditto sheets, and once a week children who wish to may copy a short poem from the blackboard, mount it on colored construction paper, and hang it on the bulletin board.

Attempting to balance out the negatives, Isabella's parents have found an afternoon modern dance class at the Y, and her mother is showing her how to play simple melodies on the piano—in the bedroom. Her parents keep plenty of paper, pencils, crayons, felt-tip pens, and clay on hand, and they give her time to use them. They have resisted the temptation to overprogram her every moment with formal enrichment programs. Isabella goes to Children's Story Hour at the library every Saturday morning. Her parents read aloud to her and her little brother every day without fail. Her father lets her wear his stethoscope and has shown her how to use it.

Isabella is as ready for intellectual exploration as she is eager to go into space. She is a smart kid with a school problem because her imagination and originality are cramped in her present setting. Acceleration by skipping a grade would only intensify the mismatch; Isabella would be separated from her peers while facing increased amounts of paper-pencil work. Isabella's wise parents will continue to encourage the intellectual and aesthetic exploration missing, to date, in her formal schooling.

AURORA AND ANDY

Meet an underestimated and an overestimated child. Some highly intelligent first and second graders, often male, are ready to learn concepts but are uninterested in the mechanics of the three Rs. Because they appear to be at the bottom of the class, their academic potential is frequently underestimated; they are the *pseudo-limited*. First and second graders whose mechanical skills develop rapidly may be placed in the top group, and their conceptual abilities overestimated. They might be called the *pseudo-gifted*.

Aurora, a tidy little girl with well-kept workbooks, disdained Andy both in the classroom and on the playground. Her socks were always clean and pulled up; his were rumpled and sometimes even disappeared into his shoes. While he was dropping his pencils; she was sharpening hers. Her hair was groomed and shiny. His was unruly and sometimes clumped in sweaty spears by the end of recess. They were in the same class for three years of mutual revulsion. She tattled on him whenever she could. He ignored her to the best of his ability. In first and second grades, Aurora was at the top of the class. She seemed to be a smart kid with no school problems; whereas Andy was in the bottom reading group and his papers were never displayed on the bulletin board.

Imagine her chagrin and Andy's amazement when he passed

her in third grade on his way to the very top of the class! He who, pockets full of Lego, had made boats, written about boats, drawn boats, and spent his recesses pretending to cross the Atlantic or fend off pirates—in short "that DUMB boy"—was the one who solved the math stumpers and the mind-benders. His poem about storms and his short story about fog were chosen for the school magazine.

In spite of some early reading and spelling difficulties, Andy's first- and second-grade teachers kept his spirits up. His first-grade teacher put Andy in charge of a three-ring notebook titled "Important Boats," which she kept on a shelf at the front of the classroom. Whenever Andy finished his required work, he was allowed to go and work in "the boat book." The teacher encouraged him to invite a friend to work with him on particular pages. Often the friend would write the words while Andy labored over the illustration. When Andy got discouraged about spelling or handwriting lessons, his teacher would say, "You'll be able to use this in the boat book. It's going to look fine!" She honored Andy's interest while acknowledging his difficulty. She brought his passion right into the schoolroom and found a way to integrate it with the required mechanical work.

In second grade, Andy's teacher wisely encouraged the continuation of his previous interest, but also required him to branch out. When the class studied American Indians, she designated him the resident expert on trapping, tanning, and leather. He learned thoroughly and eagerly.

Meanwhile in third grade, Aurora grew increasingly impatient with open-ended questions, yearned nostalgically for her flash cards, and asked to be the keeper of the class calendar. She recorded daily weather and each month filled in the class birthdays, trips, and holidays.

It was important for the educators to readjust their estimates of these two students' abilities and to recognize the influence of developmental patterns on academic achievement. They needed to convince Andy's parents that their son's slow start had been no indication of his scholastic potential. Andy's parents were initially skeptical of the good news, but relieved and joyful. Aurora's parents needed several conferences before they really understood why their daughter was no longer the star student. Their first impulse was to hire a tutor, their next was to blame the teacher, but finally they were able to adjust their expectations and accept her as she is, a competent, but not creative student.

THOMAS

Thomas is a different learner in a standard curriculum. One February day in kindergarten he dashed off a hillside snow scene, complete with evergreen trees, shadows, children on sleds with their scarves flying, dogs romping, and a father blowing on his hands to keep them warm. It was chosen for the permanent collection of children's art at a major museum.

Yet on that same day he could not recognize one single sight word or give the name of any letter. He could produce whole shapes with his pencil, but he could not read words by their overall design. He could draw fine details, but could not remember letters. Socially, emotionally, and conceptually he was ready for formal academics, but he had trouble with all the verbal symbols of our language. His different learning style masks his developmental readiness.

It is hard to create a comfortable setting for the developmentally ready student with a learning difference. Extra time can help if it is used for preventive training. Educators can recognize learning differences through screening instruments such as those we shall investigate in the Principles of Good Practice section. Using this understanding, they can anticipate mismatches and head off trouble for the developmentally ready, intellectually curious different learner.

PRINCIPLES OF GOOD PRACTICE

OBSERVATION AND SCREENING

Understanding developmental criteria, recognizing readiness for first grade, and making appropriate grade placement depend on observation and screening. The first part of this chapter explored observation. Following are examples of subtests and tasks culled from screening instruments that have proved trustworthy over the years. They may be helpful as foundations for observation or for developing informal tests within a school. A skillfully constructed, administered, and interpreted screening often reveals the patterns of academic talents and limits that underlie the paradox of smart kids with school problems.

Caution! A parent who is tempted to try testing his or her own child runs the serious risk of getting inaccurate information, making a child inappropriately familiar with material that could otherwise be used for accurate evaluation, and giving the child the unspoken message that something is wrong with him. If the parent weren't worried, he or she wouldn't test. The wise parent will want accurate evaluation from a professional and will do nothing to cloud the clarity of the picture that the parents, the child, and the school deserve.

Pencil-and-paper work. Most three-year-olds can make a single circle, most four-year-olds can copy a square, most five-year-olds can make a recognizable copy of a triangle. Students who are comfortable with these tasks will probably be adept in forming letters and numerals and spacing them appropriately on the paper.

Visual match. Most five-year-olds can find (not read) the two matching words in a group of four. Children who are skillful at matching overall visual configurations are frequently nimble sight readers. Children who can match accurately by analyzing letter sequence are often careful readers and orderly spellers.

Visual memory. Most five-year-olds can remember the names of some letters of the alphabet. They can look at an unfamiliar geometrical shape and, when shown four alternatives, can select from memory the one that matches the one they saw. Children with a strong visual memory are quick to recognize letters and sight words.

Auditory discrimination. Most five-year-olds can listen to a pair of words and tell whether the two are the same or different. They can discriminate between similar initial consonants, vowels, and final consonants (examples: *bit/lit, sat/sit, cap/cab*). Students with keen auditory discrimination usually perceive the sounds of words accurately and learn consonant and vowel sounds with relative ease.

Auditory memory.   Most five-year-olds can remember and re-peat word for word a simple sentence such as "Sam wants to eat a big hamburger at the picnic." Students with good auditory memory remember verbal instructions and explanations well.

Auditory analysis.   Most five-year-olds can hear and mimic a compound or two-syllable word and then repeat it again, omitting one of the two parts. Example: "Say *sandbox*; say it again but leave out *box*"; or "Say *magnet*; say it again and leave out *mag*"; or "Say it again and leave out *net*."[1] Students with a strong capacity for auditory analysis will probably use phonics successfully for both reading and spelling.

Naming (both letters and pictures).   Most five-year-olds can name many letters of the alphabet and can give the specific names of such common objects as keys, telephones, pocketbooks, combs, toolboxes and tools, or flashlights. Students with a good supply of labels have precise expressive tools, and also a good linguistic supply on which to draw when trying to match printed symbols to words in their own vocabularies. This ability to match visual and verbal symbols underlies competent reading, as we shall see in greater detail in Chapters 3 and 6.

Verbal reasoning.   Most five-year-olds can complete a simple verbal analogy involving such concepts as opposites: "Fire is hot, ice is . . ." They can explain why people do things: "People wear shoes because . . ." Students who are skillful in verbal reasoning have the capacity to enjoy abstract academic work.

Nonverbal reasoning (puzzle assembly).   Most five-year-olds can complete a simple ten-piece jigsaw puzzle. Students who enjoy nonverbal spatial reasoning frequently have the capacity to excel in mathematics and science.

Sequence.   Most five-year-olds can put three to five picture cards in the correct order to tell a story. Students who can establish a sequence show an understanding of the temporal relationships that govern narrative, history, and some kinds of mathematics.

Story recall.   Most five-year-olds can hear, remember, and retell a simple ten- or twelve-sentence story. Students who can hear and retell a story have the capacity to understand conversation and narrative and are usually strong in reading comprehension.

Math (counting and patterns).   Most five-year-olds can tell you how many pencils you are holding in your hand if you are holding five or fewer, and can tell you what would happen if you took two away. They can also analyze and continue a colored-cube or colored-bead pattern involving three colors. The student who can count and subtract is showing the ability to understand what a number represents. The student who can analyze and continue a pattern is showing an awareness of repetition and interval that augurs well for understanding mathematics, music, and some kinds of science.

Screening results can be used in deciding grade placement and in recommending specific help for individual children. Often some extra training in kindergarten can shore up minor weaknesses and prevent the growth of subsequent problems. A student whose scores are high across the board is ready for formal academic work. A student who is low in all the subtests has either low intellectual endowment or a low developmental level (or both), or he may have been coming down with chicken pox the day of the testing. A child with a low or erratic screening profile needs further evaluation. A student who is high in some areas and low in others is showing the kind of discrepant function associated with learning differences. The next five chapters are designed to shed light and offer ways to help.

Whether learning differences are tolerable or grow into disabilities depends on the *degree* of the discrepancy, the *flexibility* of teaching methods and materials offered by the school, and the student's *ability* to develop *alternative* learning strategies.

A CASE HISTORY: IAN

Ian is the youngest of four children in a family with a tradition of high academic standards. He grew up around books, paper, pencils, and school paraphernalia.

Ian was a sociable child who missed his brother and sisters when they were in school. Although he has an October birthday, he seemed so eager for playmates that his parents enrolled him in a nursery school program for three-year-olds even though he was only two when school began.

The following year he entered the program for four-year-olds and, although he was eager to set off for school in the morning, he was often weepy by lunchtime. His teacher said he particularly enjoyed the story hours and preferred playing with one or two children to playing in larger groups. She complimented his imaginative use of a large and varied supply of general information and said he was proud of learning to write his name.

Approaching his fifth birthday, Ian entered kindergarten at his siblings' school. He felt very grown-up to be a student in the building where he had previously been a visitor. During that year, he learned his letters and sounds and even discovered how to decode and encode simple words and to recognize some words by sight. He also started wetting his bed.

At the November parent-teacher conference, his teacher reported that although intelligent Ian was keeping up, the effort to keep up was taking its toll. He hated making errors and didn't want to have his workbook corrected. He was happiest in art projects, the costume corner, and drama. Socially, he had two close friends in the group, but he liked to play with them away from the other children. If they joined the group on the playground, Ian watched them from the sidelines.

In January, the learning specialist gave each kindergarten child a screening test, and Ian's parents were called in for a conference. They were told he had done well on all the screening subtests. His overall performance put him at the high middle of the class. Why the meeting?

The learning specialist said that Ian had been very tense and apprehensive throughout the testing, constantly asking, "Am I right?" and "Did the other kids do this?" During one difficult subtest the tears had welled up in his eyes, and when a few spilled down his cheeks, the examiner had given him a tissue, saying, "Don't worry, you're doing fine." Ian had bluffed, "I have a cold . . . a new cold . . . my Daddy says it's a cold."

When the educators said they wanted to give Ian another year in kindergarten, his parents were appalled. "We've never had anything like this in our family," they said. "Our kids are all good students and smart kids. Ian is too." "He'd die if he got left back," and "He's kind of spoiled being the youngest. School will toughen him up."

As the conference progressed, the educational team tried to emphasize the positive aspects of Ian's taking another year. They reiterated that he was putting enormous pressure on himself to live up to his own expectations. They pointed out examples of his intelligence but also his increasing reluctance to take risks. They described his timidity on the playground and in the gym. Ian's father, who had been very quiet throughout the meeting, said, "I was the youngest all the way through school, college, and medical school, and I always felt as if I were there by somebody else's patronage instead of by my own merits. I was near the top of the class, but I was always scared, and I never felt part of the group. I think we ought to give this idea a lot of consideration."

Ian's mother asked to help out with the forthcoming class trip. Afterward she said, "I saw things that help me with this decision. I noticed the way the other kids walk; they stride right along; Ian still kind of hops up and down. The other kids have lost the baby fat on their cheeks and hands; Ian still has his. Next to them, he looks really little."

At the second conference everyone agreed that Ian was an intelligent, inquisitive, sensitive superior immature who needed another year in kindergarten. They planned ways to keep him from being bored, agreed that if he were eager to read he would be given instruction, and that no ceiling of any kind would be put on his intellectual development.

Although Ian was initially embarrassed at the prospect of "staying back," his parents explained to him that they had started him in school too early, and that this was the time to put him with people his own age. They explained he was not "being left back"; he was "being given a whole year." He and his siblings took their cues from the parents, who were confident about the decision. Ian bloomed.

The next year Ian was screened again. His approach was joyful and carefree; his performance was superior. He made a minor error, said, "Oops, I goofed," wrote a correct answer over the mistake, and said, "Well, it looks a little messy, but that's okay." Willing to take chances and content with himself, Ian began a journey through formal education that proved stimulating and successful. Is there a doctor in the house? There soon will be. Ian has just been admitted to a combined program in liberal and medical education at a prestigious university.

3

VISUAL
LEARNING

Through the visual learning system, the child or adult recognizes objects, distinguishes sizes and shapes, perceives depth, notes color, and uses visual spatial awareness to estimate where he is. His visual system helps him organize the concrete realities of daily living and also to understand their symbolic representations; he recognizes his grandmother when she comes to his house and also recognizes her in a snapshot. When the child starts school (if not before), he will learn to see, interpret, and remember such printed symbols as letters, words, and numerals.

THE COMPONENTS OF VISUAL LEARNING

In school, visual learning underlies such varied disciplines as reading, mathematics, science, art, and athletics, but in this chapter we shall concentrate on the connections among visual learning, reading, and writing. To understand the paradox of a visually strong smart kid with a reading or reading-related school problem, let us consider three components of visual learning: vision, visual perception, and visual memory.

VISION

The ability to see ranges from blindness to perfect acuity. Someone with normal eyesight can see clearly at different ranges and is able to maintain or shift focus. If there is any question about a student's visual acuity, his eyes should be checked. Parents, teachers, and the students themselves, hoping for quick solutions, often pin high hopes on a trip to the eye doctor. Sometimes a pair of glasses does the trick, but more frequently than not, trouble persists.

Although good eyesight is handy, it is not a prerequisite to reading. I once taught a second grader with two weak eyes, each of which needed different and powerful corrective lenses, whose favorite pastimes were reading and baseball. Arnold Gold, M.D., pediatric neurologist at Columbia Presbyterian Medical Center, makes this distinction: "You see with your eyes, but you read with your brain."

VISUAL PERCEPTION

Accurate visual perception allows human beings to organize and understand what we see in the following ways:

Recognize visual images, remember their connotations, and distinguish the familiar from the unfamiliar. In daily living we probably recognize and understand such visual images as traffic signals and know whether a particular trademark is familiar. In reading we recognize the letters and words we have been taught and we know whether or not we have seen such symbols as abbreviations.

Discriminate among similar visual images. We can tell Fred, Jim, and Robert apart even though all three are six foot tall nineteen-year-old boys with brown hair and brown eyes. In reading we can distinguish *b* from *d* and *could* from *cloud.*

Understand the relationship of parts to wholes. We probably realize that single bricks combine to make a wall, and we see how they are arranged to form the complete structure. In reading, we understand that the word *do* is contained in the word *undoing*.

Distinguish between figures and their backgrounds.   Looking over a harbor we know which images are boats and which are water or sky. We can read black letters on white paper, white letters on a blackboard, green letters on yellow paper, generously spaced or dense print.

Maintain object constancy.   We recognize a fork as a fork no matter whether it is lying on a table, standing upright in a dishwasher, or jumbled in with other cutlery in a crowded kitchen drawer. In reading, we know that a *C* is a *C* no matter its size or color, just as we know the configuration of *t-h-e* as the word *the* no matter the style or size of print.

Interpret spatial relationships.   Standing in a room we know which pieces of furniture are closest and can tell where there is space to walk. We understand why a large airplane looks small in the sky. We can read both large and small print, relate uppercase letters to their lowercase counterparts, understand the directional difference between *b* and *d*, and the sequencing difference between *god* and *dog*.

Endow visual images with meaning.   We could probably get around a foreign airport by following the international symbols for baggage, rest rooms, restaurants, or buses. As beginning readers, we endow letters with sounds, see the relationship between a cluster of letters on a page and a word in our oral vocabulary, and gradually learn to absorb information by moving our eyes from left to right along successive lines of print.

VISUAL MEMORY

Having a crisp, reliable visual memory is analogous to having a good mental photocopying machine. The grocery shopper can visualize the misplaced list; the traveler may say, "We're about to come to the intersection where we turn right." In reading, the student with a strong visual memory may need only one or two exposures to lock a word into his sight vocabulary. His visual memory will also help him proofread his spelling. He fixes the word that "doesn't look right."

Paradoxically, reading problems can beset intelligent people whose visual system works well, or superbly, outside school. Their three-dimensional visual skills are as pronounced as their difficulties with two-dimensional printed symbols. If the student's vision is normal, the problem may lie either in visual perception, or in visual memory, or in or both.

Visual perceptual confusion is responsible for *strephosymbolia*. This term was coined by the pioneering neurologist Samuel T. Orton in the 1930s to describe the reversal or transposition of phrases, words, or letters or of any symbols. Afflicted readers may confuse such letter pairs as *b/d*, *p/q*, *y/h*, *m/w*. They may reverse the sequences of letters in a word, reading *was* for *saw*, or, as we shall see later, make as poignant an error as seeing *All Rights Reserved* as *All Rights Reversed*. They may make similar mistakes with numerals, confusing *6* for *9* or saying *17* for *71*. They may interchange words of similar visual configuration, confusing *house* for *horse*, *could* for *cold* or *cloud*, *palace* for *place*. One third grader asked, "What's rye beard?"

Some readers with visual perceptual confusion may omit or misread interior syllables in multisyllable words, mistaking *vacation* for *vaccination*. Others may have figure/ground trouble. They may have an easy time with a book made of dark, clear, generously spaced print on opaque paper but be undone by a pocket-size volume of Dickens lightly printed on onionskin paper. Still others with either obvious or residual visual perceptual weakness may be able to read accurately for a short time but then fall apart.

A weak visual memory can produce *wordblindness*. The term was coined by the same Dr. Orton to describe the phenomenon of the intelligent person with good vision who does not remember printed words. Many smart kids with school problems have a weak visual memory for symbols: letters, whole words, numerals, symbols for mathematical processes, or chemistry formulas. De Hirsch says it is as though they are trying to make an imprint in very loose sand. The problem does not vanish with childhood. William James (1842–1910), author, philosopher, psychologist, and brother of the novelist Henry James, was an intellectual giant with perfectly normal eyesight. Yet he said, "I am myself a very poor visualizer and find that I can seldom call to mind even a single letter of the alphabet in purely retinal terms. I must trace the letter by running my mental eye over its contour in order that the image of it shall have any distinctness at all."[1]

VISUAL LEARNING AND READING

Before we can help the student with a reading problem, we need to decide, what is reading? and how do people read?

WHAT IS READING?

Reading is a visual, aural, linguistic process through which the reader takes meaning from print. A reader uses his eyes to recognize in print the same language he has recognized with his ears in speech. To convey meaning, print must represent words the reader understands. It profits little to string the letter sounds *d-a-m-p* together if the word *damp* is meaningless. Although the more sophisticated reader learns some new words from reading, they stick only if they have some element of familiarity: either containing recognizable roots, or representing a concept already understood, or being so vividly descriptive that they convey an instant image.

Reading is a highly integrative process, which draws on all the learning systems, and in which people use varieties and combinations of methods, unconsciously choosing whichever fits the moment. The more methods readers have, the greater their facility. People read by *phonics*: associating letters with sounds, and blending the sounds into words; *look-say*: recognizing whole words; *structural analysis*: combining recognizable chunks of words such as affixes, roots, and syllables; and *inference*: guessing a word from verbal context, from an illustration, or from a linguistic hunch.

HOW DO PEOPLE READ?

To understand smart kids who struggle with reading, those of us who read easily need to recognize the arbitrary nature of the complicated symbol system we take for granted, sometimes explaining points that seem obvious.

Students may need to be shown that just as a spoken word is a unit of combined sounds, a written word is a unit of print, and each cluster of letters on a page represents one word.

Impaired readers often do not realize that there is more than one way to figure out words. When they discover that there are several ways, they still may feel that the method stressed in their classroom is the only proper way and that others are either inferior methods or some form of cheating. Their teachers and parents need to free them from this restrictive approach.

Students who have experienced the instant learning we explored as one of the traits of giftedness in Chapter 1 often feel that being able to read is a lucky accident of fate like having blue eyes, curly hair, or inherited wealth. The instant learner who can't yet read may need to be convinced that reading is a teachable, learnable skill. A former first grade teacher tells the story of the child who said to her, "I can read now. I can read ANYTHING!" She said, "Joey, that's wonderful. How did you learn?" "I didn't learn," he said. "The letters just whisper to me."

All students can be taught to read, at least at a rudimentary level. Although many conundrum kids will never read for pleasure, they can learn to decipher the code.

Caution! There was a time when people hoped that exercises and visual perceptual training would cure or alleviate reading problems. It seemed so logical. However, research shows that this is not so. At this writing, there seems to be a resurgence of quasi-professionals offering a quick fix. Beware of shopping mall charlatans. See the restatement of policy by the Ophthalmologists' Association, developed by the Ad Hoc Working Group of the American Association for Pediatric Ophthalmology and Strabismus, and The American Academy of Ophthalmology, May 7, 1981:

Indeed, children with dyslexia or related learning disability have the same incidence of ocular abnormalities, e.g. refractive errors and muscle imbalance (including near point of convergence and binocular fusion deficiencies) as children without. There is no peripheral eye defect that produces dyslexia and associated learning disabilities. Eye defects do not cause reversal of letters, words or numbers. Indeed recent studies suggest dyslexia and associated learning disabilities may be related to genetic, bio chemical and/or structural brain changes. Further controlled research is warranted.

No known scientific evidence supports claims for improving the academic abilities of dyslexic or learning disabled children, or modification of delinquent or criminal behavior with treatment based on:

Visual training, including muscle exercises, ocular pursuit, opr tracking exercises, or glasses (with or without bifocals or prisms);

Neurologic organization training (laterality training, balance board, perceptual training).

Furthermore, such training frequently yields deleterious results. A false sense of security is created which may delay or prevent proper instruction or remedial therapy. The expense of such procedures is unwarranted, and appropriate remedial educational techniques may be omitted. Improvements claimed for visual training or neurologic organizational training typically result from those remedial education techniques with which they are combined.

VISUAL LEARNING AND WRITING

The visual learning system also includes visual-motor integration. In daily living, visual-motor integration allows us to walk across a room without bumping into the furniture. In schoolwork, many visual-motor tasks involve eyes, hand, pencil, and paper, requiring both analysis and execution.

Copying, a school survival skill, is an example. Young students practice letter formation by copying single letters and then words. Older students copy spelling patterns from the board, they copy early drafts to final drafts on paper, they copy examples of arithmetical processes from textbooks, from blackboards, and from worksheets. They copy geometric shapes in geometry and laboratory experiments in science. They need to copy homework assignments quickly and accurately. The student who writes "read pp. 65–56" will not make forward motion on the assignment.

The first step in copying is analysis. The student either recognizes the object as a whole or analyzes its components. Once he knows what he needs to write, the next step is to carry out the plan: execution. For example, I could copy this page easily because I know each of the words and remember whole sentences. But I couldn't copy a German translation of my page that same way because the language and some of its written characters are unfamiliar. I would have to reproduce each word letter by letter, struggling to put the letters in the correct sequence, learning to put umlauts over vowels but never over consonants, and being careful to leave spaces between words but not inside them.

If I tried to copy a Chinese translation of my page, I might be able to analyze which characters come in which order, but I might not be able to form them correctly. Or I might be able to analyze and execute the character formation adequately as long as the original was there for reference, but not if I had to do it from memory. My errors might be in analysis, in execution, or in both.

Similarly, smart students who have trouble with visual-motor integration may have trouble with either analysis or execution, or in some instances, both. Some students have trouble seeing the small components of a whole design, or word. Others see the bits and pieces perfectly well but cannot make their pencils obey. Some children have trouble with both analysis and execution, whereas others can perform very nicely if the stimulus remains as a reference but be unable to reproduce the configuration from memory. To give appropriate help, we need to know where the problem is.

Students with visual-motor integration problems need to practice their handwriting until the motions are completely automatic. They need short frequent sprints: long sessions for these children means "practice makes worse." They should write on lined, not blank, paper and be taught to use the lines for spatial organization.

PRINCIPLES OF GOOD PRACTICE

Visual learning colors a student's entire academic career. Problems of visual acuity need diagnosis and a corrective prescription followed by regular checkups. Students with problems in visual perception or visual memory need specific training and must be shown how to strengthen their weaknesses with support from their other learning systems. Good training will show the weak visual learner how to manage his problem. It won't go away, but he can survive in school in spite of it.

A teacher or parent can evaluate the student's visual skills in light of the information in this chapter, noting which visual tasks the student does well and which give him trouble. It is important to collect representative samples of work for the master file and to review the student's performance with the overseer, whose role we explored in Chapter 1.

A reminder: fatigue, anxiety, or time pressure will invite the reappearance of past problems. A brilliant professor, who thought she had outgrown troubles similar to the ones in this chapter, was giving a seminar. By the end of the session she was tired and running short of time. Summing up a point she went to the blackboard and, trying to write the word *blackboard*, produced *balckbred*. She was oblivious to her error until everyone had left and she turned around to collect her belongings. Mortified, she erased the evidence and fled.

The student who has been helped to understand and surmount (or circumvent) his difficulty may be able to be as philosophical as William James in the quotation earlier in this chapter. Without such help, the student's self-concept takes a continual battering. A wounded person may direct his inevitable anger inward, deciding he is stupid or generally unworthy, or he may focus his anger on the society that has established requirements he cannot meet. Not surprisingly, there is a strong link between reading failure and juvenile delinquency.

It is never too late to get help. Many people who have hidden their illiteracy well into their adult lives have learned to read through approaches similar to those described in this book. Recent figures show that functional illiteracy (the inability to read beyond a sixth grade level) afflicts some 30 million adults in the United States. Those who do not yet know how to read need reassurance that teaching is available and learning is possible. See the Resources section for materials and programs for older nonreaders (pp. 244, 245).

Folklore says, "There's more than one way to skin a cat." Similarly, there's more than one way to read a word. Smart kids whose school problems are related to disordered visual learning need instruction and practice in each of the following approaches. The smarter the kid the more he needs alternative reading strategies for understanding print, which can nourish his emotions, enhance his aesthetic appreciation, and stimulate his intellect.

We can show students how to read by using a part-to-whole approach: phonics, a whole-to-whole approach: look-say, a whole-to-part approach: structural analysis, and an inferential approach: context clues.

A PART-TO-WHOLE APPROACH: PHONICS

Knowing the sounds of individual letters allows the student to blend them into words. This decoding approach to reading (and its complement, the encoding approach to spelling) works beautifully for many students. According to the 1985 National Institute of Education report, *Making a Nation of Readers*,[2] phonics is the preferred introductory method. Although using it is slower than reading by whole-word recognition, the student who knows phonics always has a reliable strategy to figure out a new word.

A WHOLE-TO-WHOLE APPROACH: LOOK-SAY

Recognizing whole words is the most efficient way to read, and good readers who begin with phonics should learn sight words as soon as possible. However, students with poor visual memory who have tried to learn through look-say have probably felt like unwilling participants in Russian roulette: "Maybe I'll know it or maybe I'll be dead."

In a seeming paradox, students with a weak visual memory who have trouble learning such high-frequency words as *the*, *one*, *would*, *was*, *of*, or *where* may exemplify what my colleague calls the *Tyrannosaurus rex* phenomenon. Although he misses the common words, he always recognizes *Tyrannosaurus rex*. Its size, shape, and length distinguish it immediately. This seeming contradiction bears on the whole-to-whole approach in two ways. First, it underscores that the little words are frequently the hardest to learn. Second, words that catch the student's interest may be the easiest to learn.

A WHOLE-TO-PART APPROACH: STRUCTURAL ANALYSIS

Figuring out words by going from whole to part is neither more nor less noble than going from part to whole; it is simply a reverse procedure. But students who have trouble with one approach are not always shown its opposite.

The easiest way for some children to learn to read is by finding whole words in recurrent patterns of sentence structure. Such readers may find the "key sentence" technique helpful.

Write out a key sentence such as "Who is here today?" The student parrots the sentence and answers the question. The teacher or parent writes out each answer.

Key sentence: "Who is here today?"

Johnny: "Who is here today? Fred is here today."

As the student reads the key sentence he identifies the words in the recurrent pattern, adds his own contribution, and sees it being written. Then the adult asks the student to find the word *who* or *today* or someone's name. As the reader becomes more proficient, the teacher expands the length and complexity of the key sentence.

Some students learn individual words by looking at the whole and then analyzing its parts. For example, a teacher might show the child his whole name: *Tommy*. "This says *Tommy*. What's the first *sound* you hear in your name? Yes \t\. Where is the letter that makes that sound? What letter makes the \o\ sound you hear in the middle of your name? What letter makes the sound you make when you keep your lips together and hum?" Then the teacher might say, "I am going to make one of the sounds in your name. When I do, I want you to write the letter that makes that sound. I will leave the card with your name on it right here for you to look at if you need to give yourself a hint."

When students master the early levels of phonics and look-say, they are ready to expand their reading powers through *structural analysis*: learning to recognize and isolate such chunks as *ing, ed, re, un*. If they learn to recognize affixes as units of meaning, they can read new unfamiliar words by covering up the familiar chunks, decoding the remainder, and then uncovering the chunks.

Here are some common prefixes: *un, mis, non, re, pre, uni, bi, tri, tele, micro.* Using the "cover up the familiar part" system students could easily read *uncover, misled* (not mistaking it as I did for years as mizled), *nonsense, restore, preview, unicorn, bicycle, tricycle, television,* or *microwave.*

The ability to recognize and isolate affixes both at the beginning and end of a word makes it possible for a young reader to decode such large words as *unforgettable*, making them accessible rather than unmanageable.

AN INFERENTIAL APPROACH: CONTEXT CLUES

Using pictures, inference, linguistic hunch, or a combination of all three, readers establish a context that saves them from having to figure out each word individually. Some students for whom reading is laborious are afraid that this kind of contextual intuition is a form of cheating.

Students should be encouraged to make informed guesses, but as a parallel strategy, they must also be trained to go back at the end of the sentence and check the guess by asking themselves, "Does my word make sense?" and "Are these the letters that spell my word?" A student who guesses the word *election* when the actual word is *electrician* is in for a shock at the end of the paragraph.

It is tricky for parents to try to teach a child to read, and the minute emotional negatives appear, performance will disintegrate. The student, particularly one who is struggling, deserves as much privacy as possible, but still needs to unlock the code of print. The Resources section (pp. 245–46) lists materials that can be used by a teacher, tutor, or parent if necessary.

As we shall see in greater detail in Chapter 6, "Language and

Learning," the richer the student's vocabulary, the more likely he is to anticipate the writer's words, and the less likely he is to be fooled by his eyes. Even habitual adult readers make visual errors. Today the front page of my morning newspaper had two pictures: one of a soldier and one of a ballet dancer. Between the pictures was a headline. At first glance, I didn't know whether it read FATE OF BATTLE UNDECIDED or FATE OF BALLET UNDECIDED. I had two options: I could either read the confusing word by syllables or I could scan the text for a clue. When I saw the words "graceful leaps," I knew the word was *ballet*.

Because I had both the decoding skills and the internal language to correct my error in visual sequencing, I was luckier than my high school sophomore student, alluded to in the beginning of the chapter. Looking at the copyright notice *All Rights Reserved* he asked, "What does it mean . . . All Rights Reversed?" What indeed? Perhaps it means that letters like *b* and *p* that face to the right get reversed to *d* and *q*. Or perhaps it means that his rights, his privileges, such as knowing how to read with all its attendant benefits, are reversed, meaning denied.

A CASE HISTORY: EDNA

Sixth grader Edna wrote: "I wont too du su orsid. I dot kar if I dy. I rid my bik fast so mabe I get hrt, and I klim to the hiist prt of the tre mabe I wil fal an kil misellf. I dont car. i hat been so dum." (I want to do suicide. I don't care if I die. I ride my bike fast so maybe I [will] get hurt, and I climb to the highest part of the tree. Maybe I will fall and kill myself. I don't care. I hate being so dumb.) The paper was returned marked "F. For the last time FIX YOUR SPELLING!"

Her next story said: "I did. I wen up to the ruf an I climd the chimee, an I sed godby an I jumt of. It is betr been ded I dot cy enemor." (I died. I went up to the roof and I climbed the chimney, and I said good-bye and I jumped off. It is better being dead. I don't cry anymore.) This paper was returned marked "F. The dead don't write about it."

Oh yes they do. She just did.

Edna lived in a rural area of Maryland where she entered school as a happy kindergarten child who enjoyed outdoor activities, animals, people of all ages, and numbers.

In first grade left-handed Edna did not learn to read. Each day the teacher would hold up look-say word cards, saying the words for the children to repeat in unison. After going through the new words for the day's lesson, the children would open their books to the assigned page and take turns reading orally, child by child, line by line.

Edna dreaded her turn. She couldn't remember what the words were supposed to be, and she had trouble keeping her place because she couldn't follow what the other children were reading. She would guess words she thought sounded like part of the story and try frantically to remember what words she had heard the teacher read from the cards, but she usually made mistakes. Edna would feel her cheeks get red and hear her own voice tremble.

In second grade, Edna was good in math but her reading difficulties continued. She tried desperately to memorize the words on her spelling list and sometimes could get them right on the test, but when she tried to use them later she forgot what they looked like.

Third grade seemed like paradise; there was no more reading aloud. She would take out her book, run her eyes around the edges of the page, study the picture, see whether she recognized any of the words in the text, and, after what she deemed a suitable time, she would turn to the next page and repeat the process. At discussion time she would listen to the other children's comments and make her own contributions in the form of questions she thought up from the pictures. "Why were Indian canoes always brown?" she would inquire innocently. "What an interesting question; what do you think, boys and girls?" and Edna would be off the hook for another morning.

She slipped through fourth grade, but not fifth. When the math teacher saw that Edna couldn't do the word problems, she uncovered the secret. Edna was a virtual nonreader.

Edna's father was an industrial engineer and her mother was the dietitian at the nearby hospital. Both parents were interested in the scientific aspects of their work, loved the out-of-doors, and loved Edna. They hadn't known about her trouble partly because she disguised it well and partly because they had no warning to be on the lookout. Nonreaders become masters of camouflage.

With the shameful secret disclosed, Edna was scheduled for reading lessons with the second-grade teacher four times a week during recess. The teacher got out the same word cards and basal reader she was using with her own class and tried to teach Edna. But that method had already failed once, and it just made matters worse. Not only was Edna kept in from the playground for lessons, but all the other children knew it, they knew why, and they knew she couldn't read what the second graders were reading. Her classmates were merciless. The second-grade teacher, who had taught many children to read by using these same look-say materials, grew impatient with Edna, and frequently there was a sarcastic undertone to her superficially friendly comments.

By sixth grade Edna's teachers described her as stubborn, uninterested, rebellious, stupid, inattentive, worried, and tearful. Her family didn't understand why she couldn't read and were frightened and ashamed. Edna wrote the two stories about suicide at the beginning of this section. When her mother saw them, she knew she had to act.

She took Edna to the pediatrician, who suggested her eyes be examined. They were perfectly normal. He gave her a comprehensive physical examination. She was perfectly normal. But she didn't feel normal.

Reaching out for comfort, Edna's mother telephoned her sister Martha, a nurse at Johns Hopkins Hospital in Baltimore, Maryland. She wept out the story of Edna's problems, her own anxiety, and the whole family's feeling of being literally and figuratively at a dead end.

Martha had heard about similar situations at the hospital and gave Edna's mother the name of a doctor to call. The rest is history. Edna went to Baltimore for an evaluation. The results are as follows. Her visual acuity is perfectly normal, her visual perception is imprecise and disorderly, and her visual memory is very weak. Her auditory acuity, perception, and memory are strong, as are her general language skills. Her spatial powers are extraordinary, and her scores in reasoning and thinking are in the ninety-ninth percentile.

This is how she was helped. In the seventh and eighth grades, Edna was tutored four times a week in the early morning before leaving for school. Using a multisensory method, her tutor taught her to read, write, and spell, but she was not expected to use these newly developing skills for her schoolwork. Instead, her mother or father read her assignments aloud to her; she listened to stories and books on tape, and she took her tests on the tape recorder.

These modifications of the regular school program were specified by the doctor who had evaluated her, and by the educational consultant who interpreted the test results and, acting as Edna's overseer, drew up the particulars of Edna's educational help. Because they came from a medical doctor's office, the school accepted them just as they would have accepted a plaster cast or a course of penicillin.

By ninth and tenth grade Edna was ready for a new level of tutoring. Although she completed much of her homework on her own, she received help with lengthy reading assignments and was coached in strategies for working with complicated polysyllabic words. She also needed help with her introductory course in Spanish. The doctor had said a foreign language would be hard for her and indeed it was.

In eleventh grade Edna discovered the joy of literature courtesy of the Brontë sisters. She anguished over the thwarted love of Jane Eyre and Mr. Rochester, she imagined Heathcliff on the hills surrounding her town—and she decided to apply to college.

On the advice of the doctor in Baltimore and her educational overseer, Edna requested and received permission to take specially administered SAT and college board exams. (There is considerable information on the hows, whys, wheres, and whats of this in Chapter 9, "Maturation and Higher Education: Getting It All Together"). She was admitted to the state university and plans to become either a psychologist or a medical doctor. When asked why, she said simply, "I know how it feels to hurt."

4

MOTOR FUNCTION AND SCHOOL ACHIEVEMENT

Smart students with mild small-motor weakness can end up with major, school-generated disabilities if their early problems go unnoticed or untreated. Yet the teaching of handwriting, a fundamental small-motor skill, is woefully neglected in many schools. Asking (or requiring) students to use handwriting as a vehicle for expression without giving them sufficient training and practice invites disaster; a student who tries to support strong conceptual work with weak mechanical skills is heading for a full-blown school problem.

"Children who read well but have diminished output or productivity may be misunderstood by parents and teachers, who may not be aware of the possibility that subtle developmental dysfunctions can impair productivity. As a result, a child's chronic failure to complete homework or exhibit enthusiasm in school may be attributed falsely to a poor attitude, a bad home situation or a primary emotional problem."[1]

LARGE- AND SMALL-MOTOR FUNCTIONS

In exploring motor function and school achievement, first we shall consider large- (frequently called gross-) motor function: walking, running, jumping, throwing, bouncing, skipping, batting, tackling, diving, or dancing. Then we will look at small- (frequently called fine-) motor work: cutting, pasting, braiding, knotting, tweezing, whistling, winking, buttoning, coloring or writing.

Both large- and small-motor function depend on muscles, coordination, and memory. These three have direct parallels to the components of visual learning we investigated in the preceding chapter. We might line them up this way:

vision	muscle
perception	coordination
memory	memory

MUSCLE

People need muscles for movement the way they need vision for sight. Just as some people have particularly keen eyesight and enjoy visual activities, some are naturally active and enjoy the feeling of movement. Others, equally intelligent, may be sedentary by choice or because of handicaps. Just as some people need to wear eyeglasses, others may need muscular supports. My aunt was a brilliant psychoanalyst who was crippled by poliomyelitis in her childhood and had to conduct her entire practice from a wheelchair. Muscle power and intellectual power are not synonymous.

COORDINATION

Coordination involves the organization of both large- and small-motor function and thus is parallel to perception in the visual system. Coordination includes spatial awareness, anticipation, and control. A person first learns to control himself or herself in space and then to do the same with materials or objects.

For example, the accomplished tennis player doesn't lunge around the court trying to catch up with the ball. He anticipates where his opponent will aim it and moves there to be ready. He plans where he will hit his return and coordinates his eye, racket, and ball to carry out his plan. Large-motor accomplishments such as these require a high degree of visual-motor organization; the pairing of the two systems is called *visual-motor integration*.

Small-motor organization works the same way: spatial awareness, anticipation, and control. A surgeon uses visual–small-motor coordination to transplant a heart or repair the damage to an injured limb, knowing where to cut, what to watch for, and how to guide his cutting or sewing implements with precision. The same spatial awareness, anticipation, and control are the visual-motor integration skills that produce easy, attractive handwriting.

Poor motor coordination plagues many smart kids and adults. A leader in the field of economics said of herself, "Watching me run is like watching a cow try to fly." Eva, the professor whose success story appears in Chapter 10 (pp. 215–27), still has barely legible handwriting.

MEMORY

Just as a powerful visual memory allows a reader to recognize whole words rapidly and accurately, motor memory permits precision, rhythm, and speed.

Once the motor memory for an action is established, whether it be for serving a tennis ball, for knitting, or for writing, the practitioner can perform the basic operation automatically. Until the motor memory is established, conscious effort must go into learning the necessary motions and arranging them in proper sequence. For example, after my right shoulder was surgically reconstructed several years ago, I had to develop a new large-motor plan for my tennis serve, and I still need to talk myself through the motions: "position, cock, toss, lean, hit." If I don't recite the steps in order, I get partway through my former pattern, realize I can't execute it, try to make an adjustment, forget where I am in the new sequence, and hit my shot out or in the net.

Motor memory opens the way to precision and rhythm, which in turn open the way for speed. Without precision and rhythm, speed is useless; speed built upon them is beautiful. Look at Olympic figure skaters or think of my elderly aunt who knits in the movies. An avid mystery fan, she has knit and purled her way through many a feature film, neither dropping a stitch nor missing a clue. When I told her I thought she was a wonder, she replied, "Nonsense! It saves my money and my waistline . . . you can't eat popcorn when you're knitting."

Many smart kids don't have a strong motor memory for letter formation, yet handwriting that involves no conscious sequence of motions is essential for school success.

MOTOR SKILLS IN SCHOOL

Smart kids with good motor skills bring well-developed large- and small-motor *muscle, coordination,* and *memory* to school, combining them with the visual system. They get on and off the bus without accident, navigate their way through crowded hallways without injury to themselves or others, organize themselves and their possessions, take off and put on their innerwear and outerwear, and claim or challenge the top of the jungle gym. Younger children enjoy cutting, pasting, bead stringing, block building, coloring, and writing.

Older students revel in such visual–gross-motor skills as skating, throwing, catching, running, jumping, or dancing, not to mention the ability of a tardy, well-coordinated adolescent to turn what is normally a three-minute journey into a forty-five-second dash—up the stairs, through the cafeteria, around the corner, into the classroom, and onto the chair before the bell rings. These students play on varsity teams and feel successful.

The fortunate older student will be able to extricate a pencil or pen, open a notebook to the appropriate page, take legible notes, and hand in a paper containing clear thoughts in good penmanship or an exam whose tidy appearance is in harmony with the quality of the content. This lucky soul will use the science lab materials skillfully, function accurately on a computer keyboard, and eat an entire meal without spilling his food or knocking over a glass of milk.

His physical behavior will convey an accurate picture of an intelligent, worthwhile human being.

Smart kids with motor problems are in bad trouble. Because students are called on to use motor skills in their very earliest school experiences, those with either large- or small-motor difficulties suffer blows to their self-concepts at particularly vulnerable moments. The clumsy child meets scorn on the playground as well as in the classroom. As the psychologist Erik Erikson says, school-age children have internalized the judgment "I am what I can make work." The smart kid with a wide discrepancy between his motor competence and his intellectual capacity has nowhere to hide. Curriculum requirements force him to make a public display of his weaknesses, which create an unfair and often inaccurate impression of stupidity.

Fine-motor ease in handling materials has a powerful influence on school success, on the impression a student makes on teachers and other students, on adults outside the classroom, and on a student's opinion of himself. The student who has trouble manipulating materials, be they books or beakers, calculators or keyboards, or, particularly, paper and pencils, has a hard time getting a high grade.

Teachers frequently equate tidy-looking papers with accurate content and clear thought; a messy paper may earn a low grade despite good ideas. Orderly written expression predisposes teachers to give higher grades in English, foreign languages, math, science, and history, namely those fields that carry the greatest academic weight.

Many times the student with poor handwriting, who is clumsy with small-motor tasks, is very skillful in combining large-motor function with spatial awareness. The athlete sprints through a chink in his opponent's defense; the actor or dancer uses movement and space to tell a story; and those with social skills use body English clearly and keep appropriate distances between themselves and others. But although these are skills the world admires, and that enhance the overall quality of life, sports, the arts, and social skills are generally thought of as "the extras." They may highlight the Good Joe or earn a student a varsity letter or certificate of commendation, but they seldom influence a grade-point average.

In fact, the student with good large-motor spatial skills and poor small-motor spatial skills is often treated unjustly by teachers or parents who say, "If he can be that precise on the football field (or stage or political rally), he could hand in a presentable paper (write a decent-looking exam) if he only tried."

Meet six smart kids with different types of unusual motor function.

JAKE

Jake is a big boy from a big family. Perpetual motion is the order of the day; Jake and his siblings clamber up and down the stairs of their house, toss balls, sling Frisbees, jump on bikes, pop wheelies, score goals, slide on slides, swing on swings, jump rope— and run!

As an infant, Jake was a rapid creeper and courageous climber. He walked at ten months, and once he got his feet under him, he kept going. His idea of torture is to sit still indoors. Figuratively, his motor is on and running.

Jake enjoyed all the active aspects of his kindergarten year: the playground equipment, the big block corner, the art activities, the singing, and the other children. He was a happy, energetic, popular student.

First grade was a disaster. Jake's handwriting was large and irregular, and he was embarrassed by its appearance. His spelling and reading were very poor. He was often kept in from recess to make corrections or to complete pieces of unfinished work. As the year progressed, his smile faded.

Matters were even worse in second grade, where he lagged far behind his classmates. Jake's letters were poorly formed, his words were illegible, and his numerals drifted out of their columns. He resented sitting at his desk, and his sadness turned to anger.

In preparation for parents' night, Jake's third-grade teacher gave a dictation, planning to hang the children's papers on the wall. The sentences were about a deer. Jake was an animal lover, but he couldn't remember how to spell *deer*, he mixed his *b*s and *d*s, and he left out two key words because he couldn't keep up. He was so discouraged he threw his paper away and was the only student who had no paper on the wall that night. He stopped trying. He began getting into fights on the playground, and the other children became frightened of him. He was big and strong; he became rough and angry. His classmates were wise to be afraid of him.

By fourth grade his work was the poorest in the class, and in November he had to be suspended from school for breaking another child's nose in a playground fight.

In junior high, he became involved in vandalism, and he finally dropped out of high school.

What irony that his motor system, which had brought him such happiness as a young child, was also the system that separated him from his work, from his friends, and ultimately from fulfillment in life.

KEN

Oafish is the only word to describe sixth grader Ken's appearance. He is heavyset and dark-haired, and his corduroy trousers stick in embarrassing places when he gets up from his chair. A boy of very few words, he is sure to bump into at least one desk in any trip down the aisle, his shoes are usually half off, and tatters of paper fall from his pockets like leaves falling off trees in an autumn wind. He wears layers of ill-fitting clothing to protect himself from the cold of the northwestern winters. His eyes are deeply set, giving him the appearance of a perpetual squint, but his visual acuity, perception, and memory are fine.

His teachers complain about his clumsiness and his messy homework papers. He jams them into his desk or book bag without regard. Even though some of his ideas are well thought-out, his handwriting is hard to read and the papers are usually either wrinkled or torn.

Ken needs to be shown how to minimize the effects of his clumsiness. He should keep his papers intact by putting them in notebooks for different subjects, arrange his desk and locker to accommodate them, and have an uncluttered surface to work on. Although his clumsiness makes him look stupid, Ken is actually an extremely intelligent boy who needs help.

Although he cannot move his own body around without collisions, his understanding of spatial concepts is immense and he outstrips many adults in his ability to anticipate and reason: he is chess champion of the entire county. He moves his bishops and knights carefully, he can move his queen with triumph, but he cannot move himself without disaster.

EMILY

Emily was only in the fifth grade when she wrote this beautiful fairy tale.

THE TRAVELER

There was once a traveler on horseback . . . weary, thirsty and with no prospect of shelter. He rode along and along until through the shadows of the early evening he saw the shape of a castle ahead. Comforted, he guided his horse in that direction. When he arrived, he tethered his horse and walked inside. No one was there. It seemed spooky but he was glad to be indoors where he could relax, and so he fell asleep.

When he woke up it was midnight and there was wild revelry. Hags, vultures and creatures were dancing to a wild tune. The traveler looked and was afraid. He looked for the door but for a long time he couldn't find it. Then he found it but it was locked and there was no knob on the inside. He was trapped. Again he was afraid.

Then came the dawn. Through the dusty window came a sunbeam. It looked like a road to the traveler and so he stepped on it, and walked on it out through the window and to his tethered horse which he released, and they rode away together.

This child who could guide her pencil through such intricacies and her characters through such scenery was so poorly coordinated that she did not learn to pump a swing until second grade, and so knock-kneed that getting up and down stairs between classes was a challenge. Gym classes were torture to her, and recess was a nightmare.

Other children isolated her because her motor problems were so obvious. Most of her teachers pitied her but did not think to look beyond her conscientious performance in routine daily schoolwork. When she submitted the fairy tale to the school magazine people were amazed. Emily needed the kind of adult help in finding a showcase for her talent we discussed in Chapter 1. In light of her own motor problems, it is poignant to note the powerful action in her story and the rhythmic quality of the traveler's escape.

MARSHALL AND MICHELLE

Marshall is a tiny first grader with huge ideas. He can read anything and has an immense vocabulary, a wry sense of humor, and original thoughts about the human condition. Although he is highly verbal, he has a noticeable articulation problem that slows his rate of speech, and his large, awkward handwriting makes it hard for his hand to keep pace with his ideas. If he concentrates on his thoughts, he forgets how to form his letters; interchanges *b/d*, *m/n*, and *i/e*; and intermingles upper- and lowercase letters. Letters that should drop below the line (*g, j, y, p, q*) float around as if filled with helium, *i* grows taller than *t*, he forgets to put spaces between words and sometimes puts spaces inside them instead. As a result, his output looks awful and is hard to read.

The parallel between Marshall's speech and handwriting patterns is a common one. Speech is the motor component of spoken expressive language; writing is the motor component of written expressive language. Those with trouble in one kind of motor expression are likely to have equal trouble with the other. This relationship is called a "bocca-lingual-grapho-motor link," from *bocca* meaning mouth, *lingua* meaning tongue, *grapho* meaning write, and *motor* meaning motion. Marshall needs a great deal of extra practice in handwriting until he can form his letters effortlessly. His speech patterns are a symptom of extra vulnerability in his expressive motor system, thus he needs additional reinforcement.

Marshall's classmate Michelle is his opposite. Although it took her a long time to internalize sound/symbol correspondence, she has it now, but resists being rushed. She wants the time to form her letters slowly, deliberately, and exquisitely. When asked to write quickly, she becomes frantic, perfectionist, ritualistic, stubborn, and angry. Rather than hand in a paper she considers substandard, she will throw it away. As a result, she has many pieces of uncompleted work. Although her teacher finds her one of the most interesting thinkers in the class, they are at loggerheads over the pace of her small-motor work.

Like Marshall, Michelle needs a great deal of handwriting practice to get up to an acceptable rate of speed.

ELLEN

Although left-handed Ellen, a first grader, had a difficult time learning to form her letters, she is extremely talented with her paintbrush, her drawing pencil, and her scissors, displaying an uncanny talent for origami. If asked to make an origami Indian tent, or turtle or princess (it didn't matter what), she would tip her head to one side, half-squint, take a piece of paper, fold it in various shapes and layers, make a few cuts with her scissors, and unfold it to reveal whatever had been requested. But when she tried to write letters and words, her hand changed from ally to saboteur. She was fortunate in having a teacher who understood the needs of left-handed students, Ellen in particular, and provided extra instruction, extra practice, and plenty of scope for Ellen's artistic talents. At the end of first grade, with the problem nicely disappearing, Ellen wrote and illustrated this metaphoric autobiography:

"Once there was a terofiing [terrifying] bull. All the men could not kill him, but one girl could fight anything. She bet that she could fight the bull, and she wun the batul. Then she became the queen. The End"

All six of these smart students needed extra attention because of their motor function, and five of the six needed additional training in handwriting. There are many like them in classrooms everywhere, many whose potentially crippling problems are misunderstood or ignored.

The Russian neurologist A. R. Luria coined the expression *kinetic melody* to describe an easy harmony between rate of thought and rate of pencil movement. Having kinetic melody can make the difference between enjoying and dreading written work. Among those who dread it are the avoiders who ask, "How long does it have to be?" Their sparse, sterile product earns a low grade. Others whose labored handwriting gives them good reason to dread writing

get caught up in ideas anyway, but their lag-behind ha.
word endings, whole words, phrases, or even sentences.

Let's look at some common patterns of handwriting instruction,
noticing why certain approaches aggravate, or even create, school
problems.

Kindergarten children learn letter formation, but formation is
frequently haphazard. Unchecked, beginners make some letters from
the bottom, others from the top, some from the right, some from
the left, and intersperse upper- and lowercase letters indiscrimi-
nately. In many kindergartens, children write their names and practice their letters on unlined paper and therefore don't learn the
relationship of letter to line.

First- and second-grade teachers may emphasize decoding for
reading, but often teach spelling separately and give handwriting
instruction at still a different time of day. Time is short, there is
much to do, and if the general level of handwriting looks fairly
respectable, many teachers inadvertently omit formal instruction.
This neglects a magnificent opportunity: first, second, and third
graders are keenly interested in learning to form their letters well.
Whereas fourth graders may think messy is macho, younger students
enjoy precision. Consistent instruction during these years, which
can easily be integrated with spelling and reading (as we shall see
in Principles of Good Practice), trains *muscles*, develops *coordination*, and builds motor *memory*.

In third grade, reading and writing shift from being the goals
of the curriculum to being its tools. Students are expected to have
an easy familiarity with letters and words, writing them to express
thoughts and feelings. This expectation is fine for the child with
well-developed expressive language who has a natural ease with a
pencil, but there is a sizable group of smart students who aren't yet
ready. Many of them are boys: some are left-handed, others are
developmentally immature, some were developmentally unready to
make good use of the training presented in earlier grades, and others
never received any training. These strugglers and stragglers are still
trying to remember how to form certain letters, or where letters
belong in relation to the lines, and are not ready to think and write
simultaneously. When these third graders are also asked to transfer

from manuscript to cursive writing, as is standard in many schools, they face an overwhelming combination.

Fourth, fifth, and sixth graders have an increasing flow of abstract ideas and are expected to write with mechanical accuracy and cohesive organization. But at the same time, handwriting instruction is either deemphasized or discontinued. The student whose attentional energy is still drained by the mechanics of handwriting, or whose hand tires quickly because of an awkward pencil grip, is hampered, to say the least. Resource room help, if available, generally centers on reading, and sometimes spelling, but rarely on handwriting, and, anyway, these are the years in which conceptually strong students would rather be dead than suffer the embarrassment of going for extra help. Their after-school hours are consumed by extracurricular interests or just "hanging out." Handwriting, then, is a skill that is required but not reinforced.

From grade seven on, increasing demands for volume and speed are superimposed on expectations of mechanical accuracy and well-expressed content. The student with handwriting problems is in real trouble. In day-to-day work, he is expected to listen, learn, take notes, and copy from the board and simultaneously absorb new ideas. He becomes overloaded. In pop quizzes or exams, his hand lags behind his thoughts, and he doesn't get his ideas across. For all his subjects he has different teachers, most of whom give weight to both content and mechanical accuracy in grading papers, and his marks suffer accordingly. By now the smart kid who started out with a minor problem is in major trouble.

Stephen is an example. He had two undiagnosed problems, each of which was minor in isolation and only mildly troublesome in the elementary grades. But, as he progressed through the educational system and as academic demands grew increasingly complex, his handwriting difficulty, combined with a weakness in auditory memory, caused serious setbacks.

For instance, although he was a conceptually powerful mathematical thinker, Stephen floundered in math class, and he was failing ninth-grade algebra. He said, "The teacher stands up at the board, explains something new, and we're supposed to listen, take notes, and do examples. I get behind in the writing, I have trouble reading what I've written, then while I'm trying to figure out what

I've written on my own paper I realize I've missed some important step in the explanation, I ask him to say it again, he gets mad, and by then I'm so far behind, it's hopeless and I give up. I guess he's right: I'm dumb."

We can often prevent such school problems from developing by including handwriting in the curriculum in the early years of school and being sure to continue the training through the sixth grade, or beyond in special cases. If we don't, difficulty begets avoidance; avoidance destroys the opportunities for practice, which could help correct the situation; poor performance leads to active distaste, to discouragement, poor grades, and a feeling that the whole problem is overwhelming.

Strategies for teaching handwriting are available and inexpensive, as we shall see in Principles of Good Practice. Strategies for large-motor skill development are also available, but it should be emphasized that the research shows no transfer from training in large-motor coordination to academic skills. The student who improves his throwing, catching, or balance-beam walking will enjoy athletics more, and may improve his self-concept as a result, but these exercises will not help him become a better reader or improve his handwriting.

PRINCIPLES OF GOOD PRACTICE

Many students need help with these handwriting skills: forming letters and numerals, developing small-motor muscles, holding the pencil appropriately, placing the letters, gaining accuracy and speed, producing an attractive product, and taking notes.

FORMING LETTERS AND NUMERALS

Because muscle memory for handwriting travels from the large- to the small-motor system, it makes sense for students to begin by using their large muscles in large spaces. In multisensory training the student learns the letter name, sound, and a verbal description of how to form it: "This letter's name is *o*; its sound is usually \o\.

O starts the way *c* starts and then closes the circle. Try it in the air. Hold your writing arm straight out, at right angles to your body, and write the letter in the air while you say its name and sound. Good."

When the student can write his letters in the air, he is ready to use the index finger of his writing hand to form them on the table or desktop, in a box of salt, tray of sand, or on the floor. He should start with large letters, about twelve inches high, and keep reducing the size until the letters he makes spontaneously are the appropriate size to fit comfortably on generously spaced lined paper. No matter the age of the student, the principle is to move from large-motor to small-motor.

DEVELOPING SMALL-MOTOR MUSCLES

When the student can perform the tasks described, he is ready to use his small-motor muscles. He should be given a pencil and lined paper and taught the correct formation of each letter and numeral, always with a verbal accompaniment such as the one cited previously, as well as the letter name, and a sound association·to help him attach meaning to the symbol.

HOLDING THE PENCIL APPROPRIATELY

A proper pencil grip is only mildly important for single-letter formation but vitally important for rapid manuscript or cursive writing. An ice-pick grip should be changed to an proper one. We can prevent the development of a hook in left-handed children by angling the paper so the lower right-hand corner of the paper points to the student's belt buckle. (Do the reverse for right-handed students.) If necessary, use masking tape to make a right angle on the desktop as a spatial guide for the paper. This will assure proper paper placement each time, with nothing left to chance.

PLACING THE LETTERS

The student needs to make peace with these four aspects of spatial organization: orientation on and between lines, directionality, letter size, and arrangement of rows and columns. Visual cues help, verbal cues help, but visual-verbal cues really do the trick.

Orientation.   Students can learn orientation on and between lines by the Traub designations of attic, house, and basement.[2]

_____	
_____	attic
_____	house
_____	basement

Directionality.   To teach directionality, have the student put a green dot (for go) in the upper left-hand corner of each paper and a red dot (for stop) in the right-hand corner. This is traffic light language for where to begin and end and gives a point of orientation in describing the directionality of letters: "*b* starts in the attic, comes down through the house space, goes back up through the house space, and swings away from the green dot"; "*q* starts in the house space, swings toward the green dot, goes down through the basement, and makes a little line toward the red dot."

Letter size.   To help a student with letter size, the teacher should first ask him to write out the alphabet, then ask him to draw an upright rectangle around all the tall letters, underline all the short letters, and draw an oval around those letters that go below the line. The student should practice each category.

Arrangement of rows and columns.   Students need to make accurate use of rows and columns in math. Those who need extra support lining up their numerals will be helped by using graph paper or by turning regular lined paper sideways so the red margin line is at the top and the blue lines become column markers. A simple mnemonic device to remind the student which is a row and which is a column is that the top piece of the letter *r* in *row* is horizontal, as is a row. The *l* in *column* is vertical as is a column.

GAINING ACCURACY AND SPEED

Most students receive handwriting training in letter formation, small-motor practice, pencil grip, and spatial orientation of letters, but instruction frequently stops there. The unhampered student can manage on his own, but the student with handwriting problems is shortchanged without extra training and practice. He needs this maxim: work in short spurts. Three ten-minute periods are far more effective than one of thirty minutes. As the hand tires, practice makes imperfect.

PRODUCING AN ATTRACTIVE PRODUCT

First, second, and third graders care very much about the aesthetic appearance of their written work. As students grow older, particularly girls in fourth and fifth grade, they are likely to want to miniaturize their handwriting. Tiny is cool. The problem is that tiny is hard to read and cramps the hand. We are well advised to reward larger letters.

TAKING NOTES

Those whose handwriting has become effortless can use their hands and eyes to help them remember what they hear. A young friend of mine, an outstanding college student, takes copious notes at all lectures. She says, "I listen carefully, write down key phrases and ideas, look at my notes as I take them, and in between I look up at the professor. At the end of the lecture, I look over the notes for a few minutes, and almost never look at them again, but the act of simultaneously hearing, thinking, writing, and seeing seems to imprint the stuff in my mind. When I'm thinking back trying to remember something, I'll remember where it was on a page of notes and the phrases will pop to my mind's ear. It makes studying for exams a snap. Years later, I'll hear one of those phrases and see where I had written it. I really remember the things I learn that way."

From kindergarten on, schooling places increasing loads on the student's handwriting, and as the levels get harder they require increasing motor proficiency. If the motor system is weak or un-trained, it will cave in under increasing demands to combine looking, listening, thinking, and remembering.

In spite of fine training, some smart kids will still struggle with handwriting. It is important to explore manuscript versus cursive writing; mechanical aids: typewriters, word processors, tape recorders; and alternatives to written reports or examinations.

MANUSCRIPT VERSUS CURSIVE WRITING

The battle rages over whether to teach students to print, to write in cursive letters, or to teach first one method and then the other. Some schools teach only cursive, a few teach only manuscript, and most start with manuscript and make the switch to cursive at third grade. Each system has its advocates, its advantages and disadvantages.

Advocates of manuscript say that the letters look more like the letters students see in books; therefore, learning to write manuscript reinforces learning to read print. They say that students find it easier to read their own early attempts at writing in manuscript than in cursive. They say that young students whose hands tire easily can write longer words when forming only one letter at a time. They also point out that printed labeling is a valuable skill for science, for other disciplines that require cataloguing or display, and for everyday life.

Advocates of cursive say that it is easier for a student to learn rhythmic handwriting when letters are connected. They also say that reversals and inversions are much less common in connected letters than they are in manuscript. They claim that students develop a clear sense of the overall shape of a word and an accurate idea of where one word ends and another begins, thus avoiding many spatial errors. Advocates say that students who start out with cursive begin with the system they will always use; therefore, there is nothing to unlearn and relearn.

Advocates of the two-step system claim the advantages of teaching manuscript at the same moment children are learning to read, and making the switch at the same time children need to increase the fluency and volume of their written output. They see the advantages in the students' knowing both systems. The smart kid with handwriting problems should be permitted to choose the style he finds easier, and then receive help to bring it to an effortless level.

MECHANICAL AIDS

Mechanical aids may help the student who has handwriting problems. They include typewriters, word processors, and tape recorders.

Typewriters. They have helped countless numbers of intelligent thinkers with poor handwriting encase their thoughts attractively, but it is important to recognize one truth and explore two concerns.

Smart kids with poor handwriting will certainly benefit from learning to type, but they still need to know how to write legibly with good speed to take telephone messages, write directions for getting to a friend's house, jot a marketing list, or take rudimentary or comprehensive lecture notes.

The two concerns focus on developmental levels. If typing is presented prematurely, the student may find it as laborious as handwriting, developing an aversion to a skill he will really need later. Each child is different, but my experience shows me that the summer between fourth and fifth grade is the earliest it makes sense to begin formal typing instruction, particularly with a student who has small-motor–visual imprecision.

The second concern is that students who develop their own hunt-and-peck systems may have trouble unlearning those motor memories and replacing them with the correct ones, which would be of genuine help. As increasing numbers of young children use typewriter keyboards for computers, we shall discover whether this concern is well founded.

Word processors. In spite of the proliferation of software, a growing body of elementary school teachers are turning away from computerized reading and writing programs for students in kindergarten through the second grade.

Detractors of computer language arts programs for young children say that first and second graders are eager to learn to write with pencil and paper. They feel it is unwise to lure students away from something that interests them, which they will need in later life, just to give them early training on a machine that will be waiting for them when they are older, and for which they may be physiologically, intellectually, and developmentally unready.

Most educators and parents agree that word processing is a technological gift for the middle-school child, the high school and college student, the postgraduate student, as well as authors of any age. A word of caution, here, too, however.

People with good small-motor muscle coordination and memory may pick up keyboard skills quickly. But the conundrum kid who lacks dexterity, and who has had trouble remembering sound/symbol correspondence, may need extra time and overlearning to master the keyboard and the specific commands of his word-processing program. Such students need a block of time to learn to operate the word processor before being asked to use it for writing or editing.

Tape recorders. An exam taker with labored handwriting receives invaluable assistance from a tape recorder. If a high school or college student with an acknowledged handwriting deficit begins the semester by explaining his problem to his teacher, asking permission to tape-record the answers to exam questions, and offering to answer harder questions than those on the regular test, administrators and faculty members may agree. The willingness of some highly competitive colleges to accept college board scores earned from alternatively administered exams has gone a long way to breaking down the thought that this is a form of mollycoddling. Chapter 9, "Maturation and Higher Education: Getting It All Together," offers examples of alternative ways to take tests, such as extra time allowance, having a reader, or relying on a scribe.

The tape recorder can appear to be a friend to the high school or college student who has trouble taking notes quickly. "I'll just get all those lectures on tape and never have to worry again."

But this ease is an illusion unless the student has enough self-discipline to sit down at the end of each lecture and transcribe the tape into notes. Few students (of any age) anticipate the need for this step; consequently, most find themselves with a handy thirty-six hours of recorded lectures to review for a test or exam—too much for anyone to absorb!

Another illusion is that a smart kid with weak handwriting skills can simply tell his story into the tape recorder and transcribe it afterward. This works only if the student has planned the organization of the story or essay very precisely. If so, the tape recorder will be his friend. But if he has organized it carefully enough to be successful on the tape recorder, he has probably researched and organized it well enough to write it out, so long as he is not under pressure of time. Trying to transcribe loosely organized thoughts is harder, not easier, than writing from scratch.

ALTERNATIVES TO WRITTEN REPORTS

Theodore Sizer advocates "exhibition" in place of written exams or reports. Sometimes teachers behave as if writing is the only way of proving comprehension. Nonsense! The conceptually keen student with poor handwriting deserves to be liberated from this restrictive point of view and helped to find alternatives. Just as some people learn more easily from seeing a demonstration than they do from reading a manual, some people do a better job of sharing their knowledge and concepts through painting, pantomime, cartoons, sculpture, dioramas, models, or oral reports.

A CASE HISTORY: PHILIP

Philip was a normal child born to normal parents in a normal delivery following a normal pregnancy. But he was not an average kid.

From his earliest years he was fascinated by science, math, and history. He would pore over the books in his family's extensive library and, oddly enough for a small child, was particularly interested in their three-inch-thick, eleven-pound book on the works of Leonardo da Vinci. He would spend hours looking at the anatomical and architectural drawings the way other children his age would spend hours with a Richard Scarry book about trucks.

Imagine his and his family's great surprise and frustration, then, when he started school and could not learn to read or write.

Not only could he not distinguish between *b*s and *d*s, *p*s and *q*s, he couldn't even recognize the letters in his name. This boy who could understand Leonardo's design for an airplane, which he called Birdman, couldn't tell the difference between the words *Philip* and *Edward*, his brother's name. He spent first grade as a reasonably content nonreader, in a relatively undemanding school with an unsophisticated teacher who didn't understand the significance of what he could and could not do.

In second grade he was as perplexed by his classmates' facility with schoolwork as he was annoyed by his own difficulties. His parents were concerned, but because his teacher wasn't alarmed and they knew Philip was bright, they didn't panic.

It was not until they moved and he changed schools in third grade that they discovered the severity of the problem. The head of his new school required that he be given a thorough, individual psychoeducational evaluation, part of which was the Wechsler Intelligence Scale for Children, Revised (the WISC-R). We shall explore such tests in Chapter 8, but for now we shall simply note that Philip's demonstrated ability in verbal reasoning was at the top of the scale but his ability to manipulate unfamiliar symbols quickly, with pencil and paper, was well below the national average. Clearly, here was a conceptually brilliant child with a severe mechanical deficit.

He was assigned to the resource room for reading, writing, and spelling help five mornings a week for thirty minutes a morning with a teacher who was both understanding and demanding. She said, "Yes, you have a difficulty, but it is in mechanics, not thinking. I'll help you overcome your weakness, but because you are so intelligent, I'm going to make you work even harder than other kids." Using a multisensory approach, she taught him the interrelated skills of reading, writing, and spelling. As is customary, reading fell into place first. His teacher gave Philip a phonics workbook, which he found both difficult and boring, but she also went to the library and got a copy of a book of Leonardo's drawings to keep at school. The agreement was "Phonics, handwriting, spelling, dictation, then Leonardo. No skills, no Birdman."

By the end of sixth grade Philip was reading at grade level. His teachers (and by now he had a different one for each subject) didn't know about his earlier problems, so they took his reading for granted. They were keenly appreciative of the conceptual levels so evident from his participation in class discussion, and they were equally appalled at the unacceptable quality of his handwriting and spelling. These, as is customary, lagged far behind his reading despite good, consistent help. His difficulties were aggravated by any kind of pressure, particularly timed tests or exams. The severity increased as academic demands expanded and as his rate of ideas accelerated.

In seventh grade he got caught in a perfect example of academic irony. For his science project he chose to investigate and illustrate hibernation, incubation, and migration. He used his own fund of general information and located new information in the library. The way he wove the old and new facts together into these three categorical headings was extraordinarily sophisticated. For each category he made a series of meticulously drawn illustrations and fastidiously correct labels. It was a stunning work of art as well as a thorough piece of investigative science. He handed it in in December and received an A.

In late January, he failed his science exam. Across the top of the blue book the teacher wrote "F: I cannot read one word of this exam."

In an exam, under combined pressures to remember, to reason, to explain, and to hurry, his handwriting reverted to its most primitive levels. He interchanged lowercase and capital letters, his letters floated high up and crashed down, he wrote with no regard to lines on the paper and left no spaces between his words but lots inside them. For example, in spite of his interest in the concept of hibernating and his familiarity with writing the word, when he tried to use it in the exam, he wrote "h nti ng." Spatial confusion resurfaced to obliterate his recently acquired but not wholly internalized manual skills.

When Philip had the time to work slowly at home, he could write legibly. He enjoyed putting his brilliant thoughts together in novel combinations. In a classroom, he contributed his ideas to group discussions, he was faithful about handing in his homework assignments, and he didn't complain about the amount of time they required.

In tenth grade, Philip took a remedial-level typing course and mastered the skill. When it was time for college boards, Philip was given permission to take untimed tests and to give his answers to an amanuensis, a scribe who wrote down what he said.

Philip was admitted to a highly prestigious northeastern university, where he was permitted to use either an amanuensis, a tape recorder, or a portable word processor to take his undergraduate exams. He graduated with high honors in biology and is now in graduate school training for a career in genetic engineering. The weakness in his mechanical muscle and memory is insignificant compared to the contribution he will make through his conceptual muscle and memory. Both will be with him always, but effective compensations or substitutions break the power of the weakness.

5

AUDITORY LEARNING

LEARNING TO LISTEN,
LISTENING TO LEARN

"Listening—even smart kids don't know how!" is what I hear from elementary and high school teachers when I ask them where their students have trouble.

Many school problems in intelligent older students are extensions of minor or unrecognized auditory distress from earlier years. A look at auditory learning in infants and young children will help us understand how the system works.

The young child with an intact auditory system absorbs the sounds of his environment, gradually connecting them to what he sees, identifying the source, meaning, and implications of each. An infant learns to recognize the voices of the people in his family and responds by looking in the direction of the speaker. He distinguishes his mother's voice from his brother's. He learns that the sound of the door opening at the end of the day followed by approaching footsteps heralds Daddy's return.

The word is the infant's introduction to verbal abstraction. This miracle occurs the first time he isolates a cluster of sounds from the running stream of speech, recognizing it as a unit with consistent meaning. Although the word may arise in different contexts or be spoken by different voices, the child learns to recognize the cluster of sounds as a consistently reliable representation of a person, thing, or action. Using hearing, auditory perception, and auditory memory, the child learns to listen and then listens to learn.

Last summer I watched and listened as eighteen-month-old Luke, a city child, discovered the beach. I did a double take when I realized he was doing exactly what I was writing about: he was identifying the sources and implications of unfamiliar environmental sounds, gradually relating them to new words that he learned to understand and then tried to imitate. By attaching the new sounds and words to what he was seeing and doing, he developed a whole new set of concepts.

He looked up from his digging at the sound of the engine of the approaching lobster boat, pointed, and responded with his own engine noise. I said, "lobster boat," and when I repeated it later, he looked out across the water to where the boat had been. He listened and watched as the water lapped against the rocks and the little waves rolled up on the shore. He looked up at the sound of splashing. I pointed to where some boys were jumping off a raft, told him what they were doing, and he moved his hands up and down the way he does when he splashes in the tub, saying his own approximation of the word *splash*.

He was absorbing the vocabulary for new objects and activities and responding with his own umbrella term, "sand-a-wadda" (sand and water), which he used in various inflections depending on intent. Declarative sentence: Sand-a-wadda. Question: Sand-a-wadda? Victory: Sand-a-wadda! He issued an imperative from the breakfast table, sand-a-wadda, and crooned a memory from his crib, sand-a-wadda.

It seemed so simple until I realized how many new words he was learning from listening, and how accurately he was absorbing them despite their similar sounds: *sand, sand and water, shovel, shell, seashore, sea gull, surf* (with its synonym *waves*), *seaweed, sailboat, lobsterboat, pail* (with its synonym *bucket*). Luke, the baby beachcomber, like other children with good auditory systems, was learning a whole new vocabulary. He was discriminating similar-sounding words (*big/dig, shovel/shell*) without confusion; he was hearing and combining what he heard with previous and present associations; developing concepts about water, sand, and holes; and storing his experiences and words away for subsequent reflection and use.

He was doing just what older learners do: using his hearing, auditory perception, and auditory memory to label, catalogue, and interpret his environment. A smart child with any malfunction in auditory processing is at risk not only for comprehending schoolwork but for understanding life as a whole.

AUDITORY LEARNING

Normal auditory learning incorporates *hearing* for the reception of sounds, *perception* for organizing and understanding them, and *memory* for storing their messages. These are analogous to the components we investigated in the visual and motor systems:

VISUAL	MOTOR	AUDITORY
vision	muscle	hearing
perception	coordination	perception
memory	memory	memory

It is important to stress, again, that although learning systems are interdependent and mutually reinforcing, we need to explore them separately.

HEARING

Just as visual acuity ranges from blindness to excellent eyesight, auditory acuity goes from deafness to excellent hearing. Normal acuity allows the listener to hear sounds of different volume, in different pitch, at different distances, and from different directions.

The smart kid with depressed hearing acuity may seem stupid, stubborn, or unfriendly, and, frequently, hearing-impaired children develop unpleasantly loud voices themselves. In cases of suspected hearing problems, the child should have a complete audiological examination.

Later in the chapter, we shall explore some reasons for the increasing incidence of hearing loss in young children, and its impact on learning.

AUDITORY PERCEPTION

Through normal auditory perception the listener learns to recognize words and extract meaning from speech. The poet W. H. Auden said, "I like hanging around words listening to what they say."

Inaccurate auditory perception undermines every kind of learning, including reading. A smart kid's school problem may originate with poor auditory perception of single sounds, words, syllables, phrases, or concepts.

Single sounds. When sounds are indistinct, words lose their meaning. Jim had trouble discriminating between the sounds \th\ and \f\. In the early days of reduced airline fares there was an economy ticket called No Frills. Returning from a weekend trip to Florida, Jim reassured me, "Don't worry, it wasn't too expensive; our family flies 'no thrills.'" To him, the sounds were the same, and since he didn't care much about either word, he was unaware of the substitution. Pity anyone who doesn't know the difference between a frill and a thrill.

Words. Word substitutions are cute in little children; in older students they are gateways to ridicule. Annette told me she was going to take her sick dog to the vegetarian.

Friendly listeners intuitively understand the speaker's intention and eventually don't even notice the errors. Annette is safe with her family—and with me—but not always with her peers. Trying to impress a group of other fifteen-year-olds at a restaurant, she put on her most sophisticated air and, meaning gazpacho, ordered a bowl of gazebo. She was mortified when everyone laughed. Gazpacho and gazebo were all the same to her. Ridicule hurts.

Syllables. Students prone to misperception of syllable sequence may say they eat "bizgetti," look at "mazagines," or admire the "ephelant" at the circus. Such errors aren't limited to little children.

Jane Holmes, a neuropsychologist from Children's Hospital in Boston and Harvard Medical School, was giving a lecture in which she made frequent reference to graphomotor skills. Fatigued toward the end of her talk, she delivered her punch line on "the vital role of grotomapher skills."

Dr. Holmes's slip revealed an underlying proclivity for which she usually compensates very well. Fatigue or anxiety, however, frequently revives old patterns.

Students who persistently tangle syllables in speech are showing unsteady perception of sound sequence that will probably hamper their ability to read polysyllabic words and to sequence their sounds in spelling.

Phrases. Auditory perceptual confusion can distort whole phrases. In administering a phrase repetition test I asked a nine-year-old boy to repeat "sheets and pillowcases" three times. He obliged: "sleeps and pillowcateses." When questioned, he said, "Yes. Sleeps. You put them on the bed where you sleep. In our house the sleeps and pillowcateses are different colors for different rooms. My Mom says it makes it easier to sort the laundry."

Concepts. Inaccurate auditory perception can skew whole concepts. A listener with imprecise intake stores sounds, syllables, words, or phrases in incorrect mental categories and therefore retrieves inappropriate pieces when trying to build concepts. Smart kids with imprecise auditory perception, who do not read enough to have their eyes teach them the concepts their ears have misinterpreted, may make ludicrous spoken or written errors, particularly when they use figures of speech or when they try to show off. Tenth grade Martha said, "I don't like big parties. . . . I get lost in the shovel." A high school senior trying to sound impressive in a college application essay wrote, "The character suffered from an edible complex."

These errors differ from ordinary slips of the tongue because they reflect the student's thinking. For people with poor auditory perception it as if a prankish homunculus is running between their ears and their minds, making confusion of what should be clarity.

AUDITORY MEMORY

The smart student who has trouble remembering verbal explanations or following directions deserves our sympathetic understanding for a legitimate difficulty that can cause horrendous and heartbreaking school problems. Reading and writing are language laid out in space, always available for another look. Listening and speaking are language laid out in time, there for an instant, but then gone for good.

Anyone who has ever stopped to ask directions and after following the first two (turn left at the corner of Maple Avenue; go three blocks to a blinker and . . . and . . .) forgets what comes next knows what it feels like to have an auditory memory lapse. An adult can simply hail the next pedestrian and ask again, but smart school kids are stuck. They are often scolded, ridiculed, or punished for "not listening," "not trying," or "acting spacey."

Often an annoyed adult makes the kid feel ashamed. Here's a classic scenario. The teacher says, "Today we will continue our study of the Middle Ages. Please collect your textbook, three pieces of lined paper, a pencil, and two colored markers." When the student with a weak auditory memory misinterprets the instructions or says "What?" the adult glares, and says, slowly, "Listen. Get your textbook (pausing to hold up a copy), three pieces of lined paper (holding up three fingers and a piece of lined paper), a pencil (waving one at the student), and two colored markers" (gathering two in her hand). Unwittingly, but often with sarcasm, she has provided ideal memory support; she has broken the task into small steps and provided visual accompaniment. When the student finally follows the directions correctly, she may say with exasperation, "If you'd only listen, you'd get it right the first time."

SIX FACTORS THAT INFLUENCE AUDITORY LEARNING

To understand the general level of auditory skills in today's classrooms (from nursery school through college) we need to investigate the implications of six seemingly unrelated factors prevalent in our current culture. Smart kids, those whose auditory skills are perfect, and those with problems ranging from minor to severe, are, directly or indirectly, influenced by these factors, which singly or in combination may create or aggravate auditory problems. They are ear infections, allergies, day care, non-English-speaking care givers, weary parents, and multimedia stimulation and instant gratification.

EAR INFECTIONS

A series of ear infections in infancy and early childhood may be the unrecognized cause of learning and behavior problems that wreak havoc in later life. Because middle-ear infections (otitis media with effusion, or OME) can cause intermittent, fluctuating, or permanent hearing loss, they may lower the child's acuity or disrupt his perception, causing him to miss or misinterpret individual words, verbal explanations, or general conversation. Diminished auditory function can have a devastating effect on the child's vocabulary development and the acquisition of general information and concepts that are the foundations of his developing intelligence. However, the hearing losses or fluctuations that frequently follow middle-ear infections often go unnoticed by the child's parents or pediatrician at the time, and their deadly effect is only understood in retrospect.

The parent and pediatrician of a child with an earache are concentrating on the acute pain and fever phase of the illness and not looking ahead to school and behavioral or learning problems. If the child is comfortable and seems to be functioning normally after the acute phase has subsided, no one may notice temporary or fluctuating hearing disruption for months, often years. Hearing disruption has no visible symptoms: no rash, no limp, no scar to act as a danger flag. It is a silent crippler.

Ear infections, one of the most common childhood ailments, need to be seen as acute-phase illnesses whose secondary consequences may have serious long-term implications for later learning and school. Research studies such as those reported over the past few years in *The Journal of Learning Disabilities* show increasing incidence of the causal link between middle-ear infections and problems with behavior as well as learning.[1]

> children with otitis media exhibited more maladaptive behaviors such as high dependency, short attention span and weak goal-orientation (observed by psychometrists). Significantly more mothers of the otitis media subjects described their children as restless, fidgety, destructive, not liked by other children and often disobedient.[2]

Understanding the impact of recurrent ear infections is important for two reasons. First, students with resultant learning and behavioral patterns will be a negative influence in their classrooms. Their distractions and short attention spans often disrupt other students with minor problems who find it hard to focus and learn in the presence of distraction.

Second, children who are (or were) susceptible to ear infections, whose Achilles' heels are their ears, need a thorough audiological examination to determine whether their hearing is normal in each ear individually and when both ears are used together. It is important to decide whether treatment is indicated or special accommodations are needed in school. For example, if a student has normal hearing in his right ear but depressed acuity in his left ear, he should not sit on the right-hand side of the room beside the window; he should sit so the teacher can speak to his right side.

In cases of significant hearing loss the student may require medical treatment or a hearing aid. But help must not stop there. He should have a language evaluation to discover the specifics of any resultant language impairment or gaps. These should receive remedial attention as soon as possible so that missed patches can be caught up.

ALLERGIES

Allergies, along with colds or flu, can disrupt learning and school behavior in similar ways. Allergic reactions are commonly respiratory, affecting ears (and therefore hearing) as well as throats, noses, and eyes. In addition to hearing poorly, the allergic student may be distracted from intellectual work by his overall physical discomfort. Furthermore, the medicines given for allergies have systemic as well as specific effects that often impede learning. For example, many antihistamines given to relieve sneezing and itching make the student drowsy, and cortisone and cortisone derivatives frequently affect energy levels, emotions, and appetite.

Teachers and parents understand how colds or flu inhibit learning but often underestimate the effect of allergies. Let us see how allergy seasons intersect with the rhythm of the school year.

September is time to establish the rules of the classroom, lay out the plans for the coming year, and review skills and concepts in reading, writing, spelling, and math. Much review is presented orally. What happens to the student whose hearing is fluctuating, depressed, or missing in whole or part, on one or both sides? What happens to the child who is restless and has a hard time concentrating either because of allergies themselves or the medicine given to relieve them?

From mid-October through March or April, the prime season for presenting and developing new concepts, the windows in the school building are generally closed, dust balls grow in the corners of classrooms and halls, blackboard erasers send off clouds of chalk dust, hamsters multiply among the cedar shavings in elementary school classrooms, and woolly sweaters with hairy souvenirs from Spot and Puff spill out of cubbies and lockers. What happens to the student who is allergic to dust or animal dander?

The spring term brings review, exams, and pollen.

Allergies have a direct and an indirect effect on all the students in a classroom through the distractions they inflict on the victim and the onlookers (onlisteners). Students with minor difficulties in hearing, attention, or concentration may work much less efficiently and require extra support and structure during allergy season. It is as if they are allergic to allergies.

As mentioned in Chapter 1, neurologists are noticing the frequent coexistence of allergies and learning differences or disorders. In trying to understand the paradox of smart kids with school problems, we must recognize that some students have an allergy that causes school problems, a single set of cause and effect. Others are doubly vulnerable. They have both allergies *and* learning problems; double cause and double effect.

DAY CARE

Any thorough discussion of auditory learning should explore the effects of day care on the listening skills of small children. We know that auditory learning develops through sustained, individual conversation. Listeners learn labels, nuances, and cadence of language; they expand their vocabularies and absorb models of correct usage of increasingly complicated language. As Luke did at the beach, they learn to listen and listen to learn.

The primary obligation of day care is to provide the greatest possible amount of physical safety and emotional security in a tolerable noise level. In spite of the best of intentions, the average adult/child ratio prevents sustained individual attention; opportunities for one-to-one conversation are limited. Day-care center directors wrestle with frequent staff turnover, and it is very difficult for them to train (and then retain) a staff to give a high priority to such an invisible skill as listening. Day-care wages are low, and workers, although dedicated and kind, are seldom highly trained.

Because of constraints imposed by space, time, and adult/child ratio many of the labels, phrases, and sentences children hear in day care are those that simply govern routine: "Time to go outside," "No-no," "Let's all have crackers and juice," or "Here's our story."

In addition, a group setting exposes its members to colds, flu, or viruses, which frequently turn into ear infections in small children.

Parents who use day care are well advised to pay particular attention to earaches. At the same time, they should take every opportunity to expand their children's listening experiences and conversational opportunities. Parents have a big role to play in early learning. Preschool, kindergarten, and first-grade teachers whose students have been in day care may need to leave extra time in their lesson planning for the development of accurate auditory skills.

NON-ENGLISH-SPEAKING CARE GIVERS

A child who is just learning to associate single words with the objects in his environment, and learning to understand connected speech, needs consistency in order to avoid confusion. Each language has particular sounds and rhythms as well as its own syntax and vocabulary. If the smart child who is just learning to understand speech hears one set of words, rhythm, fluency, and level of sophistication from a parent and then a different set from a non-English-speaking care giver, his language acquisition may be delayed, disorganized, or disrupted. The results may be devastating.

Although some young children manage two or more languages skillfully, a significant number cannot. The difficulty lies in predicting which children fit which category. Hindsight tells the tale fully, but after the damage has been done. Boys, who are generally later than girls in developing language, are particularly vulnerable to double-language distress, and instead of becoming bilingual, they may be semilingual.

To use Luke as an example again, suppose he had heard *sand, shovel, lobsterboat,* and *pail* from me on his introductory trip and then had returned to the beach with someone who had named those things for him in Spanish, German, or any other language. The labels would have been different, and in addition he would have heard the lilt and mechanically different speech sounds and constructions of a foreign tongue, one that perhaps puts verbs in different places and that attaches gender pronouns to objects as English does not.

Until the child's primary language has jelled, it is frequently overwhelming and destructive for him to hear conflicting linguistic messages. They are "double-talk."

There are three main groups of children whose early auditory learning is in more than one language: those whose families spend some time out of this country, those whose families have come to the United States from other countries, and those whose families employ non-English-speaking domestic help.

In the first category are children of military personnel, children of civilians in the foreign service of the government, children of those who work for organizations with plants or offices in foreign countries, and children of parents who want to live abroad and choose their jobs accordingly. In the second category are children whose families have come to this country for temporary or permanent relocation. In fortunate circumstances, these children become truly bilingual, but a significant minority are separated from their native language before they consolidate it. Even in seemingly trouble-free situations, highly intelligent bilingual students frequently need extra work in reading comprehension.

In the third category are children whose working parents use domestic help instead of day care. In many cities, the pool of domestic help is non-English-speaking, or uses English as a marginally developed second language, or speaks an English dialect. There is usually a big wage difference between those who speak English well and those who do not. Even though young working parents who use domestic help rate child care as one of their highest expense items, as well as highest priority, many, even those with two incomes, may feel able to afford only the lower wages of a non-English-speaking care giver.

A preponderance of children whose auditory learning has been in two languages tips the balance of a class, necessitating extra and different help from a teacher. In considering auditory learning in students of all ages we need to understand the direct and indirect effects of language confusion on all the teachers and learners in our schools.

WEARY PARENTS

In more and more two-parent families both parents work (the current figure is close to 60 percent), and almost all single parents work. A working parent is tired at the end of the day, and it takes enormous energy, self-discipline, and understanding of child development for a weary adult to converse with a preverbal or newly verbal child. It's much easier to give a kiss and a hug, to give something to eat, to be physically demonstrative and physically nurturing than to be verbally engaged. The temptation is to let them watch more television. This is particularly true of parents who are not overly verbal themselves.

Margaret said this: "I leave Mark at day care at seven-thirty and get the train to work. I have to be ready for action as I cross the threshhold; that's the way my job goes. I either have lunch with a colleague, or I eat a yogurt, and exercise at the health club. On the way home I read the paper and try to sort out the day's experiences. Then I pick up Mark, and usually have to stop and do some sort of errand, even though I try to do all the grocery shopping on Saturdays. By the time we pull in, I'm shot and we're both hungry. I talk to him as much as I can, but sometimes when I think I'm listening, I know I've been daydreaming and just saying 'Mmm.' I cook something for both of us, feed him, and have my own bites in between. Then I give him a bath. That's one of the best times. He loves the water, I love to watch him play, I love toweling him and putting him in his pajamas. He looks so cute. I sing him a song or sometimes we look at a book, and then he's down for the night."

Mark has been a cooperative, healthy, well-adjusted little boy, and Margaret is clearly a conscientious, loving mother, but there's not much opportunity for verbal exchange, for learning to listen and listening to learn. And now there is a new problem.

As all children do when first exposed to groups of other children, Mark is picking up the current bug of the week. In his case it often starts in his nose and throat and works its way around into his ear. He has had four ear infections in the last five months. The head of the day-care center says that ear infections are the most common cause of illness among her charges; that would not surprise any experienced nursery school teacher or parent of young children.

Mark's auditory learning is in triple jeopardy: he has recurrent ear infections, goes to day care, and has a weary parent. He is a deeply loved, intelligent child who may be accumulating the invisible seeds of school problems. In Utopia, his financially secure, professionally fulfilled, energetic, verbal parents would play and converse with him, guarding his health and monitoring his hearing. But Mark doesn't live in Utopia; he lives in Rhode Island, where his divorced mother is doing her enlightened best.

She has scheduled an audiological examination. She has bought some story and song records for him and is going to make a special effort to talk with him about the things they do together, attaching words to what they see and do on their weekend outings. She has talked with Mark's father about the importance of conversation, reading aloud, and verbal interaction. He has promised to reinforce her efforts when Mark is with him.

The young child's auditory nourishment has a profound effect on his vocabulary growth, concept development, and academic achievement. The smart school-age kid with insufficient auditory skills is hampered himself and indirectly affects the others in his class.

MULTIMEDIA STIMULATION AND INSTANT GRATIFICATION

Ours is a heavily visual, increasingly alingual culture of instant gratification. From the home computer to the videocassette recorder to the television, visual messages appear rapidly in response to the touch of a button. We want, we press, we receive. Young children, and students of all ages, are now accustomed to having visual imagery provided for them through television or films and are soon crippled in generating their own imagery. They have trouble digesting oral presentations in the classroom partly because they are used to motion pictures (instead of words) for imagery, musical accompaniment for mood, and canned laughter for setting a frantic pace. Although they respond to the cues that govern the watching-and-listening routine, they are seldom learning to listen or listening to learn. The effects of this dependency reach into every classroom in the country.

When they do listen, what do they hear? Contractions and fast-food lingo: "uh-huh," "waddyawant?" "wudja-gunna-get?" or "'s up?" Students whose intake consists predominantly of such verbal short-cuts have trouble understanding sentences containing negatives, passive constructions, or dependent clauses.

A recent research study charted the average sentence length in television scripts as being between four and six words. If this is the bulk of what our students are accustomed to hearing, it is no surprise that they have trouble when trying to comprehend whole paragraphs of information.

In other times and cultures, musical lyrics were interesting, intricate, or poetic. W. S. Gilbert, Cole Porter, Oscar Hammerstein, and Stephen Sondheim, more recently, put fresh vocabulary and imagery in the ears of their listeners. But most of today's popular music lyrics either are repetitions of single words or phrases or are submerged by rhythm.

Our culture reinforces dependency on pictures and music as accompaniments to words while also promoting the habit of nonlistening. The high level of environmental noise (jackhammers and horns in cities, or other students' stereos in college dorms) means that survival lies in tuning out or at least tuning down. So students learn to watch-listen to television and films, thump-listen to music, or tune out completely. Because school learning requires real listening, the student is caught in a push me–pull you of cultural habit and academic requirement.

All students can be affected by any one or any combination of these factors. The more the child has to bear, the greater the chance of his being impeded in learning through his ears. If this is true of children who have no inherent trouble with auditory acuity, perception, or memory, what happens to the student with genuine auditory processing difficulty? He lives in a culture that requires auditory skills but doesn't teach or reinforce them, and he receives diminished help in his area of greatest need. If, in addition, he has the bad luck to have a teacher whose preferred method of instruction is verbal explanation, he is in real trouble. How can he learn to listen and listen to learn?

PRINCIPLES OF GOOD PRACTICE

First of all, adults need to be on the lookout, or on the "listen out," for auditory problems. It is all too easy to assume that a smart, healthy-looking kid is totally intact.

Second, in any case of suspected auditory problems, teachers, parents, and the educational overseer should consult (or establish) the child's master file, looking for recurrent patterns of distress in hearing, perception, or memory. Has the student been adversely affected by any of the six factors that impede auditory learning? It is important to do the following.

REVIEW THE CHILD'S EARLY HEALTH HISTORY

Look for patterns of respiratory difficulty or ear infections. When indicated, the student should have an audiological examination. This should be more than a small part of a general pediatric checkup. If there is, or has been, a hearing loss, the school should be notified and the student should also have a language evaluation.

CHECK FOR ALLERGIES

Try to eliminate sources of allergic reaction or request appropriate medication, noting any side effects.

EXPLORE THE CHILD'S EARLY LANGUAGE DEVELOPMENT

The language of his caretakers, his interest in hearing stories, and his ability to understand and remember them are indicative. Was it easy for him to develop imagery to accompany what he heard? Was he dependent on illustrations or film; could he listen to learn?

Here are some suggestions for helping students with weak hearing, perception, or memory.

SUGGESTIONS FOR PROBLEMS WITH HEARING

Smart kids with hearing problems need both medical and management help. First they need a medical diagnosis and prescription, which may range from surgery to a hearing aid. In severe cases, special schooling may be necessary. Mainstreamed students, or those with manageable or mild impairment, still need careful management in school: appropriate seat location, visual accompaniments to verbal explanations, and opportunities to learn through their eyes and their hands. Other students need to be told the reasons for what their intelligent hearing-impaired classmate can and cannot do.

SUGGESTIONS FOR PROBLEMS WITH PERCEPTION

Listening skills are demolished by perceptual problems that distort individual sounds, single words, syllables, and phrases. In order, here are some ways to help.

Individual sounds. To teach auditory perception of sounds

within spoken words, use Jerome Rosner's Test of Auditory Analysis Skills in *Helping Children Overcome Learning Difficulties*. The student is asked to hear and repeat a word, then to say it again, omitting one piece. Here are two examples, one from the earliest and one from the hardest levels.

"Say *cowboy* . . . say it again but don't say cow."

"Say *stale* . . . say it again but leave out the \t\ sound." Once the student's accuracy and level are determined, the teacher or parent can move to the appropriate group of Rosner's clearly explained, sequentially arranged exercises designed to develop this fundamental skill. Students enjoy them, and furthermore they work. (See Annotated Bibliography for Chapter 5, p. 240.)

Single words.   A smart kid can use his eyes and his language system to compensate for auditory-perceptual confusion of single words.

Not only is seeing believing: seeing can mean understanding. Many of the words these students hear are slippery and elusive; the words they see can become reliable. Think of the confusion implicit in Annette's conversational gaffes: taking her dog to the vegetarian and ordering a bowl of gazebo. Visual analysis (vegetable, *-ian*: "one who") might have saved her from humiliation.

For example, for three years I taught a talented young scientist and mathematician whose severe spelling and reading problem was tied to a fluctuating hearing loss caused by recurrent colds, ear infections, and an allergy to dust. He wrote *I sall* for *I saw*, *chrane* for *train*, *buckees* for *monkeys*, *I em* for *I am*, *rēn* for *reading*, and *lant* for *landed*.

We would often begin our lessons with my exhortation: "Blow your nose for better spelling." When his head was clear he could begin to connect letters with sounds and then arrange them in correct order. He could also clarify the reverberating words in his head by literally *seeing* their *sounds*.

Misperception of word endings, such little items as plural *s*, *ing*, *ed*, or *er*, distorts the meaning of an individual word, undercutting true comprehension of language. We shall discover more about this in the next chapter, "Language and Learning."

Because accurate anticipation, "word-hunch," helps the listener clarify incoming words, a well-developed language system is a boon to the student with auditory perceptual problems. But language development and auditory learning are partners. Trouble in one system affects the other. We shall learn more about this in the next chapter.

Teachers and parents of students with auditory-perceptual confusion are well advised to anticipate the content of each particular course and make a glossary for the student to preview.

Syllables. Smart students with imprecise auditory perception frequently omit, substitute, or transpose syllables in what they hear or say. To overcome this problem, the teacher or parent should say a word, then ask the student to listen, repeat, count the number of syllables, and hold up a matching number of fingers. When he can do this accurately, the adult should give him a word, ask him to repeat it, and then to pronounce only the first, second, or third syllable. When he can isolate and pronounce individual syllables, he can be asked to spell a designated one. For example, "Say *magnification*. Pronounce each syllable in succession (*mag-nif-i-ca-tion*). Isolate and spell the fifth syllable." If necessary, let the student see the word as he is segmenting it. He should learn to use his eyes to help his ears.

Phrases. Smart kids with imprecise auditory perception should be taught figures of speech through their eyes, not their ears. This can spare them the ordeal of trying to "take the ball by the horns" "in the store that brought the camels back."

SUGGESTIONS FOR PROBLEMS WITH MEMORY

Help the student with a weak auditory memory bring his handwriting to the level of a reflex. As they grow older, students with auditory memory problems rely on note taking, but they need to save all their attentional energy for listening. None of it must be drained away in remembering how to form letters. Although it may sound strange to stress handwriting in a chapter on auditory learning, it is vital.

To help people remember what they hear, teach them to make a mental movie; repeat; use pantomime, draw a rebus, or write words; and request a graphic accompaniment.

Make a mental movie. Students in today's world have little generating their own imagery because television routinely ... standardized pictures for them. As is true with narrative, they need to practice getting a picture in the mind's eye to accompany directions like "Go to the next traffic light: turn left" or instructions like "In the blue math book, do the first three problems at the top of page 54." The mental image may be easier to recall than the vanished spoken words.

Repeat. Repeat the directions aloud: "Left at light, go three blocks."

Use pantomime, draw a rebus, or write words. When I am given traffic directions, I gesture with my hand (out of sight to save my pride) pointing left, holding up three fingers for three blocks, and so on. It works. Other people jot a personal pictographic shorthand of arrows, dots, or whatever is quick and easy. Others list key words. Any of these memory aids is a fine preliminary to full-fledged note taking.

The student who uses these strategies is already harnessing his other senses to assist his auditory memory. He develops a multisensory habit: hear it, see it (mental movie), say it (repeat), write it.

Request a graphic accompaniment. Many teachers use visual aids in their teaching. Charts, graphs, maps, and examples help the student with a weak auditory memory. Teachers who don't use such aids routinely are often glad to incorporate them if asked. A very verbal teacher often forgets. Most teachers are willing to write assignments on the board instead of simply dictating them. Many teachers, particularly in high school and college, give their presentations from an outline and are willing to share the outline with their students. Listening to a presentation while looking at an outline is an invaluable aid to a student with a weak auditory memory.

An older student should explain his difficulty to his teachers at the beginning of the semester *before* any problems arise: "Sometimes I have trouble remembering things if I only hear them. Will you give a graphic accompaniment as frequently as possible? Also if I need to have a comment or assignment repeated, please understand that I am not trying to be annoying."

Many students with auditory memory troubles do better with whole ideas that they can then break down into components than they do with little increments that they must assemble. But from phonics to history, much schoolwork is presented in parts for the student to build into a whole. When teaching and learning styles collide, educators are wise to scrutinize the method rather than calling the student "at risk," "at fault," or "disabled."

We can help smart kids by remembering and reinforcing the link between listening and language. Listening nourishes language; language facilitates listening.

A CASE HISTORY: STUART

Stuart, an eighth grader, has always been an agile runner and strategic soccer player, and on family camping and boating trips he has been outstandingly good with maps, charts, and compass.

Because Stuart seemed comfortable and ready, he started school early. He was a tall, competent child who loved the playground, the gym, art, music, the block corner, and the cooking projects but had trouble following directions. If the teacher said, "Please get a blue crayon, a red crayon, and a piece of paper and line up at the door," he would hotfoot it to the door, smile engagingly, and wonder why she was cross. When reminded, he'd say "Oh, okay," as if hearing the instructions for the first time.

He was a gregarious, verbal boy with a mild articulation problem, pronouncing \r\ and \l\ like \w\. One of his favorite songs was "Wed Wivoo Vawee."

In first grade he had a rigid teacher who used only one textbook series and one approach to teaching reading. Stuart couldn't string sounds together into words; by the time he finished saying *b-a-t* he forgot where he started. Trying to blend *m-u-s-t* he said, "stamp?" He spelled *dup* for *dump*, *hepl* for *help*, and *fst* for *fist*. He was in the lowest reading group and he did poorly on pencil-and-paper math, although he was good with money and counting at home. His teacher said that he was inattentive and that his handwriting was clumsy. By his sixth birthday Stuart considered himself a failure.

When he entered second grade, approaching seven, his fame had preceded him: his teacher assumed he would become a disciplinary problem, and he obliged, frequently disrupting the class with silliness and mimicry. He was a playground leader and his teacher's bane.

When he was in third grade his parents gave Stuart permission to walk to and from school alone. He was proud of his independence and navigated his way through pedestrian and motor traffic as skillfully as he wove through the opposition on the soccer field. At home and on the street he was wiry and winsome, but in school he continued to be restless. His grades were low and dropping. His only moment of glory came in the class play, where he played his minor role superbly. His report card read, "If only Stuart would give the attention to his academic subjects that he gave to the play, we would have a star student."

That summer Stuart took diving lessons, and after a hiatus in the fall to continue in his soccer league, he enrolled in an after-school diving program at the neighborhood Boys' Club for the winter term. He was an excellent diver, once again demonstrating his extraordinary ability to position his body in space.

In school he was excited about science and problem solving. In art class he learned to do macramé (the sailor's embroidery) and made a beautiful wall hanging. In reading and language arts, however, he was in the lowest group.

In fifth grade his classmates elected him captain of the soccer team, but the position was taken away from him because of his poor grades in reading and spelling. He was required to take extra work in those subjects in place of sports. Needless to say, he was angry, rebellious, and in no mood to learn, particularly because there was no attempt to vary the approach; it was just more of the same.

To save his sanity, his parents allowed him to continue the diving. By January everyone was concerned over his unhappiness and worried about his lack of academic progress.

His parents took him to the pediatrician, who found him normal. The reading specialist who evaluated him reported that his work was below grade level and suggested he should read for pleasure . . . an unlikely possibility! The psychologist who tested him found him an intelligent boy with low self-concept, at high risk for school failure. He also remarked on Stuart's minor articulatory difficulty and suggested a speech checkup.

Thus it was that Stuart arrived at a speech, hearing, and language clinic, where the evaluation showed significant auditory problems: his acuity was low, he had some perceptual confusions, his auditory memory was very weak, and in addition, he suffered from a chronic infection known informally as "swimmer's ear." With this discovery, the pattern became clear. He was a smart boy with superior visual-spatial skills and a serious auditory deficit.

Realizing that he had some catching up and patching up to do, Stuart and his family agreed that he should repeat the sixth grade and receive tutoring for four forty-five-minute sessions per week after school. The learning specialist assigned by the school to oversee Stuart's program said that the boy's retraining and remedial work would be very different from what he had received previously.

Stuart was eager to improve, eager for success, and afraid to try wholeheartedly in case the plan didn't work. It wasn't until January of the new year before he really began to trust himself and to see the strength he was gaining. Once he sensed that, the last ice of his resistance melted away and he made giant strides. That spring Stuart exhibited a piece of his work in the school science fair and was elected a team member for the group who entered Olympics of the Mind. He has continued his soccer and given up diving. His extracurricular hunch about his own intelligence has been confirmed in school. He knows he is smart, and so does the rest of the world.

6

LANGUAGE
AND LEARNING

INTELLECT, LANGUAGE,
EMOTION

Language disorders can paralyze smart kids in school, causing reading problems in word recognition, rate, fluency, or comprehension; blocked or scattered spoken or written expression; disorganized ideas, possessions, or work habits; trouble with word problems in math; unsatisfactory relationships with other people; psychological distress and poor self-image; impoverished concept development.

Yet because everyone uses language, and because it is invisible, many people take its sources, structure, and power for granted.

Leon Eisenberg, professor of child psychiatry at the Harvard Medical School, says, "Linguistic competence stands at the very center of what is crucially human in each of us. We are as we think, we think as we read, we become human as we understand each other through language."[1]

A look at the functions of language, and the normal progression of receptive and expressive language development, will help us understand what happens to learning when language goes awry.

LANGUAGE FUNCTIONS

The developing child joins the rest of us in using language for expression, for organizing, for mediation, and for reasoning.

FOR EXPRESSION

Through language people can express their ideas and feelings, share their insights, transmit and receive knowledge, and formulate questions, abilities unique to humans.

FOR ORGANIZING

Language is the great organizer, allowing us to sort our ideas, emotions, and experiences first for storage, then for retrieval, and finally for making useful or imaginative combinations. If we think back to the intellectual traits of gifted thinkers, we can understand why divergent thinkers who are alert to pattern, who have heightened perceptions, who delight in originality need to develop effective linguistic filing systems.

FOR MEDIATION

Language is the mediator between fantasy and reality. In early childhood, fantasy is a force that controls the child. At around the age of five, the child establishes the boundary line between fantasy and reality and gains dominion over fantasy by separating the two. He needs language to accomplish this vital task. As we saw in Chapter 2 the fantasy/reality border influences formal academic work, but more important it helps the child stabilize his universe, allowing him to distinguish between the probable and improbable, the likely and the ludicrous.

All of us use language to distinguish between the wishes and the oughts of life. Resisting a piece of chocolate cake, I said, "I talked myself out of it." Giving in, I said, "They talked me into it." When a small child is first learning to use language to control his own behavior, his actions and words may be contradictory. When our son, Angus, was at this stage I heard him in another part of the house emphatically saying, "No! No! No!" Following his voice, I found him shouting "No" while using a fat red crayon on a freshly painted white wall.

FOR REASONING

Language is a tool for reasoning, for the embellishment and extension of original thought, for disagreement with others, and for defense of opposing positions. Growing children who are trying to make sense of what they see around them need language to keep their assumptions on target.

When Angus the crayon criminal was three-and-a-half, I had an important appointment for him with a doctor in New York. The drive from our house to the medical center generally takes about an hour, but, as the day came nearer, my chronophobia made me fret about being late, missing the appointment, and having to wait another two months for the next one.

We left home at 8:00 A.M. and walked in the door of the medical center at 9:00, two full hours early. I had brought a big tote bag stuffed with animal crackers, toy cars, Richard Scarry books, and other paraphernalia and said to the innocent child, "Oh good, we can sit right here on this nice wide bench and play with the stuff in the bag." And we did.

People went in and out of the elevators across from the bench, and there was the general scurry and bustle of a big organization starting up a new day. Finally, with a bare forty-five minutes to go, I gathered up our things and said, "Okay, time to get in the elevator." He looked first at the elevator and then back at me and said, "No." Surprised, I said, "Yes," and the more I said "yes" the more he said "no." Finally, I asked why. "Don't you see?" he said, pointing to the elevator, "Everybody going in there comes out different!"

In our vigil he had watched people go in and seen the elevator doors close. When the doors opened again, Presto! there were different people . . . some of them in wheelchairs.

I had been too caught up in my own concerns to recognize that this country child didn't know that inside the elevator door was a moving box that would save us from climbing up thirty-three flights of stairs. Without the language of verbal explanations to lead him beyond his visual threshold, his observations told him it was a change-box.

LANGUAGE DEVELOPMENT

Language is both receptive and expressive, the relationship between the two being like that between seed and crop. Skimpy planting brings skimpy growth. Just as flowers and vegetables grow best with generous amounts of light and water in tilled, fertilized ground, the child's language crop grows best when it is cultivated and supported. Just as extremes of weather can damage plants, a harsh or cold emotional climate can wither language.

The lifelong process of language development begins as the developing child absorbs the rhythm and melody of the rushing stream of sound surrounding him, trying to imitate what he hears.

Gradually the child recognizes recurrent clusters of sound, identifying them as words. Adults consciously and unconsciously encourage the process. A mother talking to her baby spontaneously speaks in short sentences, repeating key words slowly and frequently. "Hi, Jesse. Hi, big boy. Jesse is a big boy! Let's play 'How big is Jesse?' 'Soooooo big!' Wow, Jesse, what a big smile!"

Sometime during the second year of life, the child learns to speak the single words he has absorbed. The baby who says "Dada" or "Mama" discovers he can stop the world!

The child first understands words and then uses them to communicate with himself as well as with others. In her book *The Magic Years,* child psychologist Selma H. Fraiberg talks about the child who has been put to bed and is heard chanting "Mama," "Mama," "Mama" in his crib. There is neither urgency nor petulance in his voice. He has discovered that by using the word *Mama,* the label for that all-important figure, he can summon her presence without her having to be there physically. This discovery, seemingly minor, gives the child instant access to every person, event, emotion in his experience for which he has a label. He accumulates vocabulary through his receptive language capacity, and through the abstraction of words he becomes the organizer of his own experience.

In every child, the growth of expressive language follows this progression: gesture; labels; two words; articles, pronouns, and affixes; word order; and semantics.

As the language learner progresses from one stage of expressive language to the next, he builds on the earlier, more primitive levels, incorporating them into his speech. Let us take them one by one.

GESTURE

The baby's first intentional smile starts him off on the road to communication. He smiles, and the world smiles back. The infant learns to hold up his arms to be picked up, to point or reach for what he wants, to purse his lips against unwelcome foods, and to flirt in peekaboo. Adults as well as children communicate through body English. From the stamping of a two-year-old foot, to the message of a wink or the comfort of an arm around a shoulder, expressive opportunities abound without reliance on a single word.

LABELS

Labels allow the language learner to catalogue his world. Once a child discovers single words or phrases within streams of sound, he begins to use them: *Dada, Mama, car, cookie.* He wants to find out what everything is called; the process becomes a passion.

The growing child learns actual labels and invents others to describe things he can't yet name. Three-year-old Amy showed her father a nearly invisible cut on the fat pad of her thumb, saying, "It's on my thumb-stomach." Sometimes the child's original labels are difficult for adults to understand. This same Amy would say, "Amy do the 'gwinner' " every time she approached the entrance to her house and would cry when her mother opened the door. It took several tearful episodes before her mother understood that Amy wanted to turn the knob and push open the door herself: "Amy *do* the go-in-er."

A single label, *gwinner,* can convey an entire concept, and, as is true with gesture, people of all ages use labels for verbal short-hand. Depending on inflection, the student may use the label *home-work* to express gloom (weary voice, "homework"), inquire about plans ("homework?"), vent outrage ("homework?!"), or accept the inevitable ("homework"). Labels used as epithets can extend the meaning of a word well beyond its dictionary definition, as in "Chicken!"

Later on we shall see what devastation comes of not being able to label.

TWO WORDS

The child's language capacity explodes when he discovers how to pair words with one another. The single word *ball* can become *red ball, my ball, Mommy ball, big ball, little ball, new ball, ball go, ball now,* or *ball bye-bye*. Nouns can pair with adjectives, other nouns, or verbs, and markers of such properties as size, color, and location, sparing us the impossible job of using a separate word for each possession, experience, or emotion.

ARTICLES, PRONOUNS, AND AFFIXES

So far so good. Most of us from the age of two to ninety-two can express ourselves through gesture, labels, and two-word com-binations. The next stage is the ability to use articles, pronouns, and such affixes as *s, er, er/est, s, ing,* and *ed*. This level, *mor-phology,* has a profound effect on the child's ability to understand what he hears and what he reads, the seeds of what he will say and write. Because many smart kids have unrecognized weaknesses in this language level we will give it extra scrutiny.

These little words and word endings are small and may look simple at first, and yet they build the base for comparison, cate-gorization, and analogy, the foundation of advanced intellectual ex-ercise. They help the learning child understand and express the language of space and of time, two vital concepts.

Comparing and categorizing. Articles and pronouns such as *a, the, this, these, that,* and *those* distinguish between singular and plural and indicate location in space: *a cat, the dresses, this apple* (here) and *these apples* (plural, or over there), *that box* (over there), or *those boxes* (plural, or in another place). Simple as they seem, these are tools for comparison, categorization, and spatial placement.

Personal pronouns mark the difference between self and others, distinguish among genders (masculine, feminine, and neuter), as well as indicate singular and plural: *I hope, you deserve, he went, she won, it was red, he fasted, they ate*. Like articles, they allow comparison and categorization.

The ending *s* changes a singular object to a plural: *cat, cats*.

The ending *er* can change an object into an agent: *paint, painter, farm, farmer* (but not *moth, mother!*), another tool of comparison and categorization.

The endings *er* and *est* establish degree: *fat, fatter, fattest; near, nearer, nearest*. When they are used to describe size and location they function as the language of spatial organization, another way of saying the language of mathematics: relative position, size, shape, interval, and ratio. These, too, are tools for comparing and categorizing.

Analogy. Articles, pronouns, and affixes, the language tools that allow comparison, categorization, and spatial and temporal organization, open the door to analogy, the foundation and the tool of higher-level abstract thinking.

Young children practice with such simple analogies as

> paint : painter :: farm : _____ (farmer)
> prune : prunes :: elephant : _____ (elephants)
> I : we :: you : _____ (us)
> taller : tallest :: more : _____ (most)
> jumping : jumped :: going : _____ (went)

The words in parentheses must be supplied by the student.

Higher-level students use more complicated analogy to explore history, literature, philosophy, religion, mathematics, science, music, art, political science, and economics.

Verb tenses and time. The endings *s, ing,* and *ed* are the language of present and past: verb tenses. They mark temporal organization: she jump*s*, the computer is runn*ing*, the plane land*ed*. Time, being invisible, is difficult to grasp. The child who understands the separation between the present and the past can store his experiences away for later reflection and sort them chronologically, giving himself a window on cause and effect.

The child who understands the difference between the present and the past can develop realistic anticipation of the future. The language learner who hasn't grasped the implications of verb tenses lacks the tools to organize the past, the present, and the future. He remains a prisoner of the present, and probably behaves accordingly, taking what he wants and filling the needs of the moment as they arise.

The ability to postpone gratification, a prerequisite to success in school as we saw in Chapter 2, depends on the child's ability to anticipate realistically. The child who understands the *will* and *next* in "You will get the next turn" can tolerate watching another child playing on or with something he wants.

Time is the language of sequence; sequence is the language of both memory and planning. College sophomore Eleanor laid out her study program for her political science course this way: "First I will read *The Federalist Papers*; then I will choose either Madison, Hamilton, or Jay as the subject of my term paper. Meanwhile, I will keep watching the evening news and see whether federalism is evident today."

Second grader Pete had a different agenda. "First I'll take out the trash and pick up my room. After I do that Mom will let me go over to Sammy's. We're going to put Lego motors on our space machines."

The language of time and sequence allows us to understand cause and effect. "If . . . then" depends on understanding a sequence. For this the student needs verb tenses.

Verb tenses and temporal markers put time into words. Without time and words students cannot explore the higher-level concepts that beckon smart kids.

Why do so many young people have trouble at this language level? Think back to the six factors disruptive to auditory learning that we explored in Chapter 5: weary parents, day care, non-English-speaking care givers, allergies, ear infections, and a culture of multimedia stimulation and instant gratification. Consider their potential impact on this level of language acquisition.

Weary parents keep their conversation simple and unembellished.

Day-care personnel have to limit their language to what most young children will understand quickly.

People who are just learning English, or who speak it poorly, may use verb tenses, pronouns, articles, and affixes incorrectly or omit them entirely.

The child whose hearing acuity is impaired, temporarily or permanently, from ear infections, allergies, or respiratory ailments may be unaware of word endings. If he doesn't absorb them in speech he will overlook them in reading and omit them in speaking and writing. If his perception is imprecise he may misinterpret them.

In our visually oriented, verbal-fast-food culture the linguistic niceties of this language level are often omitted or misused.

Although surrounded by noise, even by words, children who do not consolidate this level of language are cut off from important concepts. The smarter the kid, the greater the loss. If these influences affect the linguistically sturdy, think of their impact on a linguistically vulnerable student.

WORD ORDER

Word order, or *syntax*, refers to the rules that govern the order of words in sentences. Syntax changes a declarative sentence into a question: "The dinner is scorched again" "Is the dinner scorched again?" This syntax is uncomplicated and obvious. With complicated constructions it is not. The child who has absorbed rich syntax will be able to express complicated thoughts in appropriate constructions, but many children have not had this linguistic exposure. Think back to the six factors that inhibit auditory learning and consider their effect on this language level.

SEMANTICS

Semantics involves the way words hang together to make sense. A comedian talking double-talk uses real words in familiar inflections and cadence. The double-talker creates the illusion of intelligibility, but what he says doesn't make sense. Language without meaning is useless.

Not everyone reaches the highest semantic levels. Some smart kids whose gifts lie in working with their hands are comfortable with concrete language but stumble over metaphor and figures of speech. They may understand each individual word in "A rolling stone gathers no moss," but they don't understand what the phrase means.

LANGUAGE PROBLEMS

Difficulties in learning language, or in using language as a learning tool, can properly be called "the dyslexias." The singular form, *dyslexia*, has previously been used to describe one particular type of reading problem; however, language-based difficulties have more than one manifestation. Increasingly, neurologists, pediatricians, researchers, and clinicians use the plural *dyslexias*. As we saw in Chapter 1, the brain organization thought to underlie the dyslexias often also underlies great talent in such fields as science, the arts, and mathematics.

In his monograph *The Advantages of Being Dyslexic*, Richard H. Masland, the Columbia University neurologist, quotes Albert Einstein, who is commonly regarded as having been dyslexic: "The words of the language, as they are written or spoken, do not seem to play any role in my mechanism of thought. The psychical entities which seem to serve as elements in thought are certain signs and more or less clear images which can be voluntarily reproduced and combined. . . . Conventional words or other signs have to be sought for laboriously only in a secondary stage, when the mentioned associative play is sufficiently established and can be reproduced at will."[2]

We shall explore five types of language disability: receptive disability, coding difficulty, expressive disability, emotional interruption, and difficulty with abstraction or organization.

RECEPTIVE DISABILITY

Receptive language is intertwined with auditory and visual learning. It is nurtured by listening and reading, and what the reader has absorbed through receptive language determines the level at which he will read with ease and comprehension.

Young children normally absorb words from their surroundings, but the child with a receptive language disability (whose hearing is normal) does not understand the full meaning of language and learns to ignore it or tune it out. This child may have a hard time establishing rapport with other people.

People are not attracted to a child who seems uninterested in what they have to offer. Apparent coolness on the child's side makes others less inclined to seek him out. The child misses the feeling of being attached to the world through comprehension and conversation: explanations, admonitions, stories, jokes, the gift of big new words to keep and use. A sad picture emerges of a lonely child connected to the world around him by a thin string instead of a stout intertwined line.

Departures from the following general guidelines for normal receptive language development are warning signals.

By one year, most children understand gesture and such simple labels as *Mommy, Daddy, cookie, doggie, peekaboo.*

By two years most children understand and use two-word combinations. They enjoy being shown picture books and may "read" them independently.

By three years most children enjoy hearing a story and sit still to listen.

By the age of five, most children can understand articles, pronouns, prepositions, and verb tenses as well as passive and negative constructions. They can carry out a three-part command, "Please hand me a pencil, put the rubber toy on a chair, and go touch the window." Much of elementary schoolwork depends on listening to and following directions. The child who understands single words or very short constructions but cannot process larger chunks of language has trouble in every area of school life. He may appear to be listening, but when the words are finished and it's time for action, he may have to copy his neighbors.

By first and second grades most students learn to take meaning from print just as they previously learned to take meaning from speech. Receptive language is visual as well as auditory: reading is listening through the eyes. Through decoding words and short sentences ("The cat is black"), they learn to take meaning from printed symbols.

From third grade on, reading shifts. No longer primarily a conscious process of visual pattern decoding and recognition, it evolves into one of automatic linguistic recognition. Good readers take in whole phrases at once. People used to think that language growth was a product of reading, but current research tells us the opposite. Language must exist inside the child to give incoming information something to stick to. With language inside, the child connects the new information to his existing supply, and the two join together like two sides of a closing zipper.

Third graders use language as a social as well as an intellectual tool. They are more likely to argue than hit; they instigate and resolve their disputes verbally; they play with homonyms and tell riddles.

Fourth graders join language with numbers to solve word problems. Exercising and relying on the seemingly simple skills discussed in the section on articles, pronouns, and affixes, they experiment with the structure of language. From fourth grade through adulthood, readers (and listeners) are expected to remember facts, arrange events in sequence, absorb new vocabulary, identify main ideas, anticipate outcome, and understand inference as well as fact.

Because accurate, fluent reading is a result of anticipating what is to come, and then letting the eye match the probability, marginally developed syntax prevents a child from reading with rhythm and fluency and impairs his comprehension. Familiarity smooths the way, allowing the reader to "cast a linguistic shadow." Nancy has a receptive language difficulty and, consequently, poor linguistic hunches. Haltingly, she reads out, "Be quite, there's a hung elephant, wait for my single." Abigail, whose decoding is shaky but who has grown up drenched in stories, reads it correctly, "Be quiet! There's a HUGE elephant. Wait for my signal."

Here are comments from actual reports on students with receptive language disability.

Kindergarten: "Tim's a doer not a talker. He prefers blocks to stories."

First grade: "George has trouble following directions."

Second grade: "Ellen is a gentle, quiet child who lets others go first, watches what they do, and then tries her own hand."

Third grade: "Billie gets in fights on the playground and disrupts classroom discussions."

Fourth grade: "Barbara is so interested in everything that she just plunges in without waiting for instructions. A little more restraint would be helpful."

Fifth grade: "Mary does well in social studies projects but seems lost in discussions and explanations."

Sixth grade: "Allen uses the present tense in telling about his experiences. His vocabulary is small and he is a weak reader."

Seventh grade: "Jack could do good work if only he'd try harder. He is good with numbers but doesn't apply his knowledge to word problems."

Eighth grade: "Mark is failing French this term."

Ninth grade: "Francie has one of the lowest grades in this history class. She seems to have no sense of cause and effect and can't keep events in their proper order."

Tenth grade: "Unless there is major improvement, Terry should be seen by a psychiatrist."

Eleventh grade: "Charles is too old for this restless behavior."

Twelfth grade: "Tom's spelling is still dreadful." Comments such as these deserve red-flag attention.

CODING DIFFICULTY

Coding difficulty can make trouble in either decoding (reading) or encoding (spelling) or both. Few difficulties frighten parents more than a reading problem. Often they panic, wondering whether they themselves are to blame, whether the child is stupid, and whether there is any hope.

As we know from the preceding chapters, there are several ways to try to crack the code that connects written and spoken words.

The dyslexic who has trouble with decoding may reverse or invert letters (*b/d, p/q, h/y, n/u*) or words (*on/no, was/saw, dog/god*) and may confuse words of similar configuration (*cold/could, house/ horse*). Obviously such confusions distort meaning. It is important to distinguish between "he was a god" and "he saw a dog." Similarly, "a cold house" and "a cold horse" require different remedies.

The student with encoding difficulties may forget which letters represent which sounds, and, once having remembered, may still be uncertain how to form them correctly. His handwriting may range from the unattractive to the illegible. His spelling may show incorrect sequence of sound order, missing letters, or omitted syllables.

It is important to separate the student's intellectual challenge from his training in coding. He needs both, but they can seldom come in the same lesson. Teachers need not pretend that phonics is intellectual enrichment, nor should they frustrate the student by offering tantalizing concepts in words he cannot decode.

EXPRESSIVE DISABILITY

We should consider the following expressive language difficulties: sparse output, incorrect pronunciation and spelling, conversational shyness and fear of writing, atypical rhythms in speaking or writing, and word-finding difficulty.

Sparse output. If sparse output results from a small vocabulary or unfamiliarity with complex linguistic constructions, the student needs opportunities and exercises in language development. He needs to hear well-developed language in conversation and in the classroom. Ideally someone will read aloud to him, individually or in a group. If this is not feasible his parents should be encouraged to involve him in story programs at the local library. Stories on records and cassettes are often available at libraries, and Books on Tape has many selections available for rental or purchase (see p. 245).

Inaccurate pronunciation and spelling. Many young children may lisp or have other forms of imprecise articulation until their second teeth are in place. The sounds for \th\, \l\, \r\ frequently present difficulty. For instance, many children as old as six say \y\ or \w\ for \l\: *yittu* for *little*. They may say *w* for *r*, *wuv* for *love*, *wed* for *red*, *vewy* for *very*. They may use \v\, \f\, or \d\ for \th\; *wiv* or *wif* for *with*, *du* or *vu* for *the*, *dis* or *dat* for *this* or *that*. These errors are within normal limits until age seven, and many children outgrow minor articulation problems. However, if the child has trouble making himself understood, he should receive language therapy as soon as possible. A smart child whose communication is blocked suffers profound frustration.

Spelling difficulties harm written expression, making the writer appear stupid. The student who relies on a weak visual memory may write *nieghber* or *niehgbor* for *neighbor*. The student with auditory confusion who tries to spell phonetically may write *dup* for *dump*, *kafyujan* for *confusion*, or *azgeti* for *spaghetti*. The pattern of spelling errors will dictate what kind of help is needed.

Conversational shyness and fear of writing.   Some students are reluctant to contribute their ideas to classroom discussions; other original thinkers who are just plain shy in verbal situations may do very well on paper. Conversely, many students who enjoy talking are intimidated by writing. They might be called "paper-phobes": the sight of a blank piece of paper waiting to be filled paralyzes their ideas. These may be students who spell poorly, who have poor handwriting, or who are simply untaught, unpracticed writers.

Atypical rhythms in speech and writing.   Slow speech may be a symptom of word-retrieval difficulty or it may be the hallmark of a speaker with a large vocabulary who selects his words carefully. In either case the speaker is likely to use fillers (and um, the um, you know) that make it hard for the listener to stay tuned in. Other speakers talk very quickly, their thoughts seeming to come in rushes that they spit out in rapid-fire clusters. Their speed sometimes makes them hard to understand. Fatigue or pressure will accentuate atypical rhythms.

Rhythms in speech are likely to be mirrored in written work. The careful speaker can often write a letter or paper on the first try. The rapid speaker often blurts his thoughts out on the paper and has to eliminate, reorganize, and rewrite.

Word-finding difficulty.   A subtle, common cause of expressive disability is frequently overlooked or misunderstood. It is word-retrieval difficulty, sometimes called *dysnomia* (from *dys* meaning poor or having trouble with, and *nomen,* to name) or *aphasia* (from *a,* meaning not, and *phatos* to speak). It disrupts all communication: speaking, writing, listening, and reading.

Anyone who has momentarily forgotten someone's name knows what dysnomia feels like. The dysnomic may have trouble retrieving the name of a person, the location of a battle, the title of a treaty, a date in history, or the label for a common object. The reader who has ever said "Hand me that thing" or "Look! There's a whatcha-callit" has used some classic dysnomia-dodgers. All of us have experienced this at one time or another. We are perfectly familiar with the object or person, but the label won't come out. "It's right on the tip of my tongue," we say. "I can't remember it right now, but I'll know it at three in the morning" or "When I tried to introduce him, I drew a complete blank!"

While the speaker (or writer) is still searching for the elusive word, its absence creates what William James called "an intensely active gap." No other word will quite fit in its space, and when it finally floats into grasp, it fits in the gap as snugly as a piece in a jigsaw puzzle. So far, it sounds like a mild social inconvenience, and for most of us it stays that way. But the afflicted student suffers in school, where many teachers do not understand the disability and its manifestations.

Monica studied hard in her eighth-grade history course. She understood the concepts and enjoyed her homework readings, but she had some trouble in classroom discussion, did very poorly on pop quizzes, and failed three important tests.

Recently I visited her class. Monica, conscientiously prepared as usual, took her seat. The teacher began, "I want to review some of the events in last night's homework that preceded the declaration of war. We know that the people on both sides were going hungry, we know that there was a boundary dispute and that there was a violation of a treaty. What was the name of that treaty . . . Monica?"

Monica froze. She had studied it the night before. In her mind's eye she could see the name in italics halfway down the left-hand page of her book, but she couldn't remember it. "Wait, wait, oh I know it," she said. "I knew it last night." The teacher interrupted, "Monica, if you knew it last night, you'd know it today." Penciling a mark in her record book, she turned to another student, saying, "Mark, how about you? Can you remem . . ." "Oh I've got it now," Monica blurted. "It's the Treaty of. . . ." The teacher cut her off. "Monica, how many times do I have to ask you not to interrupt? You had your turn. If you would study more carefully, you'd pass this course, you know."

The tears welled up in Monica's eyes. She *had* studied carefully; she just forgot when she was called on to answer quickly. When she got scared she forgot, and when the pressure was taken away, the answer came bubbling up.

Monica was struggling with dysnomia, a specific disability. It didn't trip her up when she was able to choose her own topics. Using familiar vocabulary she could express herself adequately. When she wandered further afield, she relied on time buyers and fillers, description, and function: "the—um—you know——the thing over the door" (she meant transom); and "the, the um, the . . . razor blade," "hand me that blue doohickey over there" (the blue photograph album on the chair); and "Let's get 'em with the watershooter" (the hose).

Single-word answers are hard for the dysnomic to deliver, but they are simplicity itself compared with trying to summarize or trying to write a test answer. For example, in recapping a short story, Monica's classmate said, "Maude, who was the main character, realized that unless she delivered her brother's parka to the hockey rink, he wouldn't have it for the trip. The team was due to leave directly from the rink without stopping back at school." In trying to sum up the same story, Monica said, "She tried to figure it out and stuff, but she didn't think she could get it over there, and if she didn't and he left, well, like, it would be really bad."

The problems created by dysnomia multiply when the student is required to write, particularly under time pressure, as in a test or an exam. Tension and anxiety are normal parts of test taking, but anxiety is the enemy of memory.

Students working in workbooks may do nicely when filling in

the blanks or when answering questions from multiple-choice answers. When they are asked to write extemporaneously, however, their work is either brief or disconnected or their papers are swiss-cheesed with erasures. When the workbook provides the word, there is no problem. But when the student has to retrieve, think, and write simultaneously he becomes overloaded.

Dysnomics are likely to be either poetic or rambling. For example, Harvard linguist Anthony Bashir uses the example of the high school student who, in writing an exam, was trying to refer to a migrating flock. Lost for the words, he wrote "a flying wedge." Metaphor is beautiful, but it may not earn a high grade on a science exam.

Dysnomia creates trouble in both listening and reading. The dysnomic listener forgets the words he has heard and often has trouble remembering oral directions accurately.

Dysnomia takes its toll in both early and more sophisticated reading. Reading means taking meaning from printed symbols. The reader who has trouble with word retrieval may look at a word, recognize its configuration, know that it represents a hairy four-legged creature who whinnies and jumps over fences, but have trouble retrieving the label *horse*. Whereas the reader with problems in visual learning may make a *horse/house* error, this reader may make a *horse/pony* error. His errors will be within categories instead of outside them. This is the reader who would read *salt* as *pepper*, in contrast to the reader with visual confusion, who would see *salt* and say "slat."

The competent reader actively generates language in anticipation of what's coming next. The reader who has trouble retrieving a target word is on the spot and may tire easily. Research by Denckla and Rudel has shown that such a student may retrieve the needed word the first or second time he meets it, the third try will be slower, and the fourth and fifth slower still and less accurate. This reader's retrieval ability is rapidly exhausted. It has no relation to visual perception, physical energy, native intelligence, or good attitude. It's as if he is driving a large car with a very small gas tank.

Of course not all people who forget names, speak slowly, or say "and um" or "like" are dysnomics prone to *horse/pony* errors.

All of us use time buyers and fillers, and we read inaccurately on occasion. The tip-off is frequency. If we know someone, particularly a child, who depends on gesture, inflection, a smile, time buyers, and descriptive terms instead of labels, we owe it to that child to probe for dysnomia. Once we understand, we can help. Until we do, we will continue to offer inappropriate remedies or fruitless threats and exhortations to "do better."

EMOTIONAL INTERRUPTION

Emotional difficulty can interrupt or block language development. In the metaphor of a staircase, the young language learner starts out with two feet firmly planted on the floor. As he begins his ascent from one language level to the next, it is as if he climbs a staircase. With both feet on one tread his linguistic balance is pretty secure. But, as he reaches for the next level, one foot stays on the familiar tread and the other is traveling the riser to the next level. One foot gives half the balance of two. If an emotional upset or interruption coincides with a transition from one language level to the next, the child's language may regress or not reach the next level as quickly as expected. What could cause this?

The child who starts school too soon may revert to earlier language levels as a signal that he is in over his head. Recurrent illness can encourage helplessness, which shows in baby talk. An older child who loses his place in the family hierarchy with the arrival of a baby or a set of step-siblings may regress to an earlier language level. The pain of parental separation, divorce, or remarriage frequently affects the developing child's or adolescent's language level. The budding orator may drop back to "factory outlet" expression.

A change in a child's language level is a warning signal. Regression needs to be met with patience and understanding. In cases of serious or prolonged difficulty a language clinician should be consulted.

Because we shall explore the effects of emotional difficulty on schoolwork in detail in the next chapter, "Psychological Availability for Schoolwork," here we only mention the way it interweaves with language development.

DIFFICULTY WITH ABSTRACTION OR ORGANIZATION

Many smart kids who are reaching out to learn new things don't take the time to distinguish main ideas from irrelevant ones in what they hear or read and may have trouble arranging their spoken and written thoughts. They need to allow the linguistic filing system to make its contribution. Orderly storage makes retrieval easier, thus helping the student organize his spoken or written output.

Students with trouble in abstraction and organization are often those who did not consolidate the preanalogy skills of comparison and categorization (see the section on articles, pronouns, and affixes, pp. 113–16) and don't really understand the concept of time.

Unfortunately, specific language disabilities aren't limited to one to a customer. An artistically gifted student may struggle with coding and also have word-finding problems. A young scientist with expressive problems may also face an emotional interruption. The more the conundrum kid has to contend with, the harder the task, and the greater the need for specific, on-target help.

PRINCIPLES OF GOOD PRACTICE

Many reading problems spring from a disorder in the language system and can afflict highly intelligent students.

When a parent or teacher suspects the existence of a language problem, the student should have a thorough language evaluation. Although learning specialists and psychologists are trained as testers, many have not been trained to evaluate the specifics of language development and are not tuned in to the academic implications of subtle language disorders. Therefore, this kind of evaluation should be made by someone trained in speech, hearing, and language. An evaluator can be found through the school system or the medical profession.

The child's pediatrician may make a referral, or help may be found by inquiring at the nearest large hospital. Many hospitals have a department of speech, hearing, and language staffed by people qualified to diagnose and prescribe. Failing these sources, The American Speech, Language and Hearing Association, 10801 Rockville Pike, Rockville, Maryland 20852, has regional listings of certified practitioners.

In preparation for the evaluation, parents should consult (or start) the master file described in Chapter 1 (pp. 18–19). It is important to reconstruct the child's history, noting the age at which he reached developmental milestones, particularly the onset of speech. It is also vital to note family history. If Great Uncle Ernie had a hard time learning to read and write, he may be casting a generational shadow. The teacher should contribute samples of current work and descriptions of classroom behavior, mentioning specific instances of success and failure. Cooperation among the student's parents, teachers, and the overseer whose role we probed in Chapter 1 (pp. 16–18) is essential.

The student needs to learn the reason for the evaluation in an age-appropriate way. It may or may not be helpful to refer to "the dyslexias." Some students are more comfortable having a name for their problem; others feel that the label is a confirmation of disease. An honest and positive approach goes a long way to banishing the student's spoken or unspoken fear that he is stupid. The gifted thinker who sets high standards for himself and struggles with learning problems may have difficulty understanding or using the words to deal with such fears.

If professional language therapy is indicated the clinician prescribes the particulars, but parents and teachers can make immense contributions too. Following the order in which we explored the language difficulties, here are suggestions for help.

RECEPTIVE LANGUAGE DISABILITY

To help a student with receptive language problems we may need to lighten the language load. Giving him more words, more quickly, or more loudly (the way some people shout at foreigners) only aggravates the problem.

Starting with gesture and labels, and moving through the other levels of language growth, we can determine which words have meaning for the child, how many he can handle, how long he can remember them, and whether he can transfer them from one context to another.

We can connect interesting vocabulary with his actual activities. Memorized vocabulary lists don't stick.

We need to use active and passive constructions and dependent clauses as he is able to understand them.

We should be sure he understands those little words that shift meaning: *if, unless, whenever, nevertheless,* and so on.

Always we can encourage him to generate visual imagery to accompany what he hears.

It helps if we use the terminology of time precisely: we shall be leaving *in half an hour,* or *right after lunch,* or *at 12:30.*

Of course we want to read aloud and get books on tape.

Probably we need to help him sort his vocabulary. He needs to hear and categorize words. He needs to be taught the meanings of figures of speech, idioms, and proverbs. He needs training in listening. The specific strategies in Chapter 5 on auditory learning will help. He needs short, frequent language stimulation, with change of pace. He needs specific training in reading comprehension. He needs to reinforce the link between language and mathematics.

Many outstanding mathematicians are weak in certain kinds of verbal work. Many highly verbal people are more skillful with words than with numbers. But students, and thinkers of all ages, need both words and numbers to use math for asking questions and solving problems. We need to be sure he understands such words as *each, diameter, circumference, area, volume, ratio,* and *every other.*

We should investigate his understanding of time, not just noticing whether he can read the face of a digital watch. We need to find out whether he knows the meaning of the terms *morning, noon,* and *evening* and why *afternoon* is called *afternoon;* the feeling of elapsed time: how long ago does your birthday seem, the worst day of your life, the first time you saw your baby brother, and so forth; the anticipation of elapsing time: whether he knows he is going somewhere in twenty-five minutes, whether he can be ready in time without looking at his watch; that human beings use the language of time to organize thoughts and experiences into present, past, and future.

Above all the student needs sympathetic acknowledgment that his difficulty is a legitimate one that others have had and overcome.

CODING DIFFICULTY

An intelligent child who has not learned to read or write in spite of exposure to traditional teaching methods needs something different. More of the same will continue to produce disappointing results: frustration or failure.

To help a student who has coding problems, teachers or parents should arrange for him to receive multisensory training. If this training is available in school, the student is fortunate. For the parent who is not sure how to ask, it may be described as Slingerland; Orton-Gillingham; Traub, *Recipe for Reading*; or Alphabet Phonics. If it is not provided in school, the teachers need to recommend outside help, and parents need to provide it much as they would eyeglasses, a hearing aid, or physiotherapy.

A smart kid struggling with coding difficulties is like a singer in a soundproof room or an athlete in shackles.

EXPRESSIVE DISABILITY

Here are some ways to help the student with word-retrieval difficulties.

Help the child use words with as many associations as possible: opposites, synonyms, categories, and so forth. A word stored alone has only one handle by which to grab it. A word stored in a pair has two. Storing in pairs, then, doubles the shot at retrieval.

Provide verbal accompaniment to label the items and experiences in the child's life: "Here, hold your mittens while I zip the zipper and tie the drawstring. I'll button my sweater, and put on my down vest. Then we can go on the sled" instead of "Okay, hang on, we'll get set, here, see? Okay, let's go."

Expose the child to different kinds of experiences, using the vocabulary for each. Language uses different sets of words for dif-

ferent purposes. Even young children can tell the difference be
tween the language of a television commercial, the language of a
bedtime story, the language of a scolding, or the language of a secret.
Each one has its own words. By helping the child (or student of any
age) to pay conscious attention to differences he understands subliminally, we expand the number of lexicons to which he has access.

Invite eye contact that makes a bond between the speaker and
the listener. It will buy time (and patience) from the listener.

Make special preparations for taking a test or writing a paper.
The dysnomic student preparing to write a paper, or take a test,
should sit down with his books beforehand to list the labels and
terms he thinks he's going to need. Generating the list is one more
way of underscoring and overlearning the words. Then he can leave
the list out on his desktop while he's writing the paper so the words
are all neatly captured.

He should prepare for a test in the same way. In the process of
compiling the list, he's actually sorting important from unimportant,
a valuable comprehension and study exercise. With explanation of
his difficulty and a sympathetic teacher, he may obtain permission
to take the list with him to the test or exam. Just knowing that
primogeniture, photosynthesis, or *Phoenician* is right on his card
will allay his anxiety about retrieving the term. He will be able to
spend his time thinking, instead of chasing through his own mind
with some verbal net trying to catch elusive words.

Open-book exams are a release for these students and are more
and more often used in high school history and English courses.

Foreign languages are particularly difficult for these students,
and high school or college students may need to try to have that
requirement waived or simplified. As we saw in the case of the
college student in Chapter 1 (p. 23) whose dean suggested she be
tested to effect such a release, understanding of the problem is
increasing.

EMOTIONAL INTERRUPTION

Although teachers and parents can help, the student whose
work and language are disturbed by emotional interruption needs

131

)m someone trained in mental health. This is no place
.. .neaning amateur.

The distinctions between the roles of educational and psychological therapist mentioned in Chapter 1 are important to bear in
mind. As Katrina de Hirsch points out in her monograph "Interactions Between Educational Therapist and Child," the educational
therapist allies herself with the student's intactness and reality, the
psychotherapist with the student's pathology and fantasy. We shall
explore this further in Chapter 7, "Psychological Availability for
Schoolwork." Meanwhile parents need to be aware of this distinction, understanding which kind of help is needed and what it is
intended to accomplish.

We shall explore how to help the student with emotional interruption more fully in Chapter 7.

DIFFICULTY WITH ABSTRACTION OR ORGANIZATION

The student needs to learn how to outline, using major headings, subheadings for successive topics, and subheadings to the subheadings: Roman numeral I, subheading A, subheading i, subheading
a, and so forth.

Conceptually strong students with poor organization or verbal
abstract thinking profit from "Supermarket School." There are
boundless opportunities for cataloguing, remembering, choosing,
comparing, selecting, and describing: in other words, putting language to practical use. Students who have trouble with the school
language they consider esoteric can often be lured, and then helped,
by practical language exercises connected with everyday experience.

Supermarkets provide endless opportunities for exercising receptive or expressive language:

Labels: oil, vinegar, dishwasher detergent, cantaloupe
Two words: baby carrots, fresh peas, french bread
Categories: starches, preserves, canned goods, fresh produce
Comparison: new potatoes, Idaho potatoes, frozen french fries
Analogy: plum : prune :: grape : raisin

Parents can help their children hone their organizational skills in
the supermarket:

We are doing our grocery shopping for the whole week. You

are the dessert king. Please pick out enough to last us until we return.

We are taking a picnic to the beach tomorrow. Please pick out enough rolls, hot dogs, relish, napkins, fruit, soda, plastic forks, napkins, paper cups, and plates for six people.

We shall have three age groups tonight: Grandpa, Aunt Edith, and second grader Sammy. Please find a snack for each of them.

All students, and particularly those who struggle with language problems, grow through being read to. In addition to enhancing language, reading aloud has other benefits that, although important to all students, are vital for intelligent students who struggle with the dyslexias. Reading aloud:

soaks the listener in complex language. Language is more caught than taught.

enhances concept development, delivers new information, and promotes opportunities for philosophical reflection. Through literature the dyslexic can meet the questions that have puzzled and delighted juvenile and adult thinkers throughout history.

helps the listener recognize the existence of, and differences among, such genres as biography, poetry, adventure, romance, and satire, to name but a few, and provides the comfort of bibliotherapy when needed.

gives the listener the feeling of belonging we explored in Chapter 1. In hearing a story, the young listener (or the adult playgoer) can identify with characters and share responses with others in the group, be it his family or a class in school.

A CASE HISTORY: LAVINIA

Lavinia, the youngest of three girls, admired her three male cousins. When she was three, one of them gave her an outgrown baseball cap, which became her trademark. She wore it whenever she could, or carried it around the way another child might tote a security blanket. She was a beautifully coordinated blue-jeaned tag-along who loved physical adventure.

Other people would catch their breath at some of her stunts, but her parents learned not to worry. Oddly, for all her physical daring, she had very few bruises, never broke a bone, and probably wore fewer Band-Aids than any other child her age.

In contrast to her talkative sisters, Lavinia was a quiet child who could entertain herself for hours playing with the blocks at her cousins', making things with clay, drawing, painting, creating collages, or making adventures for her stuffed animals.

Her passion for the jungle gym, the tricycles, the blocks, and the art corner flowered in nursery school. She was an active, hands-on doer. Her beloved baseball cap was with her always, pressing down on her curls but not concealing them.

Toward the middle of the year, however, her sparkle dimmed. She pulled her baseball cap down over her ears and became an unhappy, aggressive group member who hit and pushed whenever she didn't get her way. The other children began to pull away from her. They were afraid.

Late in the spring her class did a project with shadows, which culminated in the teacher's making life-size silhouette portraits of each child. Lavinia slashed hers with scissors. When reprimanded, she cried but wouldn't explain why she had done it.

In kindergarten she contributed little if anything to group discussions and pinched or found some other way to disrupt when the talking went on too long. Her classmates isolated her, and the lonelier she was, the more demanding and physically abusive she became. Her artwork lost its joyful quality. She pulled down the brim of the cap that had become her emotional barometer. The only time she was happy was when she was in gym. Academically, she had a difficult time trying to learn her letters, and, even though she was a whiz with money, she had had trouble with paper-and-pencil math.

The kindergarten teacher requested testing, and the first results were alarming. Lavinia's receptive language was above average, but her expressive language was far below the national norm, near the level of many retarded children. The second round of testing revealed another side of Lavinia. In all measures of nonverbal reasoning she scored in the highest possible range. Here was a child of immense nonverbal intelligence.

Her parents agreed to a language evaluation, and the results bore out the school's hypothesis that Lavinia was an extremely intelligent child with a genuine expressive language difficulty. Her natural inclinations had led her to block building, sports, arts and crafts, and away from words and abstraction. This had been fine during the early years of preschool, when the emphasis was on action, but when words became the medium of exchange, she was isolated. Competitive but unable to get to the top, she resented those who usurped what she considered her rightful place, and her anger took physical form. She had trouble using letters and numerals because they were abstract verbal symbols.

The discrepancy between her nonverbal and verbal reasoning was creating anger and pain. The gap between her comprehension and her output was forcing her into more and more antisocial behavior. The angrier she grew the more she needed a way to express herself, but her only way was through physical aggression. The greater the anger, the greater her need, and the greater her need the greater the anger at not being able to do anything about it.

Her parents agreed to take her three times a week for language therapy, and the miracle began. As her words came, her smile crept back. She pushed her cap back on her head so her face could be seen. As she found ways to explain her ideas, her feelings, and her plans, she began to take joy in her artwork again. Although she was hesitant about trying to make friends with her classmates, she made such good progress in her individual language therapy sessions that she was soon able to join a therapy group, in which she socialized with increasing ease.

Returning to Leon Eisenberg's phrase "we become human as we understand each other through language," Lavinia became human, and she became human through language. She learned how to ask for a turn, she learned how to invite another child to play, she learned to use *if*, that tiny powerful barter word: "If I give you this block, will you let me have the green clay?" She learned to use "Trade ya" as an offer instead of as a claim. Last week she said, "If you'll be my friend, I'll invite you to my birthday at my house and let you use my best bike."

7

PSYCHOLOGICAL AVAILABILITY FOR SCHOOLWORK

AROUSAL, ATTENTION, ACTION

Arousal, attention, and action are the Get Ready! Get Set! Go! of psychological availability for schoolwork. Just as the athlete gets ready by warming up, the student prepares by arousing himself physically and intellectually. The athlete tenses his muscles, poises his body, and gathers his energies to get set; the student gets set by focusing his attention. The athlete gets ready, gets set, and then goes into motion; the student converts his combined arousal and attention into the action of active learning.

Those of us who know how to Get Ready! Get Set! and Go! may be puzzled by others' difficulty, yet many smart kids with school problems cannot accomplish this seemingly simple sequence and are not psychologically available for schoolwork. In exploring why, we should bear in mind the intellectual traits of gifted thinkers and also the social-emotional needs we explored in Chapter 1.

In addition, we should be on the lookout for the impact of the factors disruptive to auditory learning discussed in Chapter 5 (pp. 91–100). We should recognize their power to prevent arousal, divert attention, or block action.

AROUSAL

Arousal is the first phase of attention. "I could teach him if I could only get him *with* me." The student who has trouble arousing himself is literally unavailable. His parents, teachers, or educational overseer should talk together about sleep, food, allergy and hearing, boredom, and emotional resilience.

SLEEP

Luther was an outstanding student until November of sixth grade, when his midterm grades dropped dramatically. His math teacher recommended tutoring, his English teacher threatened academic probation, and his guidance counselor suggested a comprehensive psychoeducational evaluation. Common sense and a conference found the cause and the cure.

It turned out that Luther's father had started a new job, which required frequent travel; his mother was taking evening graduate school courses; and the sitter-housekeeper was lax about discipline. Luther was watching TV until 10:30 or 11:00 P.M., and trying to do his homework on the bus on the way to school. Arriving tired out, and sitting in an overheated classroom, Luther found it hard to stay awake. When the facts emerged, TV was banned on weeknights, Luther's bedtime was reestablished, he was ready to learn again, and the problem melted away.

FOOD

It is virtually impossible for a hungry child to rouse himself to a symbolic task. This has always been true, but the number of children who come to school without breakfast is increasing to include many from affluent and middle-class families.

As the number of women in the work force increases, the number of traditional breakfast makers decreases. Independence is the mealtime theme, particularly in the morning, when family members rush to keep to their various timetables. The child is often expected to prepare his own dish of cereal, muffin, or whatever. If there are

several children and both parents, or the single parent, are trying
to get to work on time (sometimes with the added scheduling problem of dropping a younger child at day care), the schoolchild's breakfast habits may be overlooked. In many households that rely on
domestic help, the housekeeper who comes in for the day arrives
after the children's departure for school.

A child who goes to school hungry may be all right for the first
period or even the first hour and a half, but the two periods before
lunch are worthless. When physical energy wanes, psychological
availability wilts.

ALLERGIES AND HEARING

Allergies are the enemy of arousal for two reasons. First, the
allergy itself causes physical distress: stomachaches or upper respiratory ailments. A child whose physical well-being is disturbed
rarely has the energy left over to "get ready" to learn. Second, many
allergy medications cause drowsiness or lassitude. Allergic reactions
may also affect hearing acuity or perception, interfering with re-
sponsiveness.

BOREDOM

Sometimes, sad to say, lessons are just plain boring. Smart kids
are sedated by boredom, which may spring from genuinely unin-
teresting material or presentation, or from a mismatch between the
type of presentation and the learning style of the listener. It is hard
for the visual learner to stick with a primarily verbal lesson.

EMOTIONAL RESILIENCE

Although only a trained psychologist or psychiatrist can diagnose and treat an emotional problem, a parent, teacher, or concerned adult can often make useful guesses. Parallel to the questions
raised about his physical condition, we can ask, Does the student
seem psychologically refreshed or weary, nourished or hungry, irritated or at peace? In the section on Action we shall explore some

emotional factors that drain the student's psychological energy and block his availability for schoolwork.

Without arousal the would-be learner is merely a passive observer. The unroused child may be extremely intelligent, active in other types of situations or at other times of day, but he will continue to have school problems until he can "Get Ready" to "Get Set" to "Go." Educators and parents can plan appropriately if any of these conditions seems to be the cause of the problem. Often, as in Luther's case, the remedy is simple. If the cause is difficult to pinpoint, the student should start with a medical checkup.

ATTENTION

Adults are so aware of the student's need to *focus* his attention that they frequently minimize the importance of the flip side: the ability to *shift*. Unhampered students do both, but some smart kids can't.

In medically diagnosed cases of attentional deficit, medication can have a dramatic, positive effect on the student's concentration, but not all students need it. Some developmentally young children are interested in so many things that it's hard for them to settle on one. If these children are young for their grade level, smart but unready, they may be misdiagnosed by impatient adults. These children don't need medicine; time and training are the appropriate remedies.

Sometimes a smart kid can focus his attention but has trouble shifting it. If he is exploring a concept or project, he likes to pursue it to its outermost limits and resents interruption. As we know from the traits discussed in Chapter 1, sustained concentration can be a hallmark of gifted thinking. A student with this capacity needs free time for projects at home, he probably needs to strengthen his concept of time, and he needs to be teased into flexible thinking. Let's look first at *focus* of attention, and then at *shift*.

To focus his attention the student needs arousal, a filter, language, and appropriate work.

Arousal awakens the attention, which then needs to be focused.

A FILTER

A filter keeps out external or internal distractions. External ones may be sounds, sights, uncomfortable temperatures, hard chairs, or poor lighting.

Some students have a hard time filtering out sounds that others don't even notice. For four years I worked with Eugene. A brilliant thinker, he used his native intelligence and high motivation in trying to overcome his reading problem. Everything would be fine until a telephone would ring, the furnace would go on, or the maintenance crew would turn on the snow blower. Eugene would give a start, shake his head, and try to discern the source and meaning of the sound, and he would need to remark on it before he could settle back to work. His alertness to environmental sounds was paradoxical, considering his difficulty with phonics and blending sounds together to make words. He would say "s\t\a\n\d . . . stand? . . . Yes. Stand" and, in the same breath, "That's the third ambulance that's gone by this week."

Other smart students may have trouble filtering out visual distractions: someone walking along the side of the room, a piece of paper fluttering, or a simple environmental change.

Hughie is an accomplished fourth-grade mathematician who has trouble with reading comprehension. Last week his teacher gave him a sheet and said, "Hughie, here are the questions that go with today's reading. Read the questions first, think about them, then read the passage, and we'll work on the questions together when you're through." Halfway through the short passage Hughie looked up, saying, "Why did you move the red books to the other shelf?" Glancing up in the middle of his reading, he had noticed the change and needed to be told the reason for it before he could continue reading.

Eugene and Hughie are keenly alert to environmental detail, and would be great exploring a desert island or solving a crime, but in school they get in trouble because their filters aren't strong enough to screen out environmental distractions.

An effective filter also blocks out internal distractions: fatigue, hunger, the kinds of irritable sensation that accompany allergies, or that insidious thief of concentration, daydreaming.

Daydreaming is a silent, seductive interruption. In severe cases, the student should have a checkup by a psychologist or psychiatrist. But here's something to try first, which I learned from Katrina de Hirsch. Often the person isn't aware of the onset of daydreaming but, instead, comes to with a jolt, realizing, "Oops, I don't know what's been going on." When you work with a daydreamer, sit beside him. When you feel him slipping away, touch him and ask, "Are you daydreaming now?" If the answer is yes, ask whether he can remember what it felt like just *before* his attention slipped away. The first time or two, he probably won't be able to answer, but, simply through having had the question raised in a friendly, non-threatening way, he will begin to recognize the premonitory sensation. The student who understands his own warning signals can be on guard against daydreaming, the internal intruder.

LANGUAGE

Language organizes thought; organization allows the student to focus his attention. As we saw in Chapter 6, the language of time is a framework for planning: first, next, finally. The student uses language to break down a large task into manageable pieces, to anticipate cause and effect, to categorize and to sort ideas according to their relative importance. Some students who appear to have trouble paying attention actually lack the language to structure their work. They don't need pills or extra workbooks; they need language help.

APPROPRIATE WORK

Sometimes the label *attentional deficit* is applied to a student who is merely in over his head.

Sandy's second-grade teacher called his parents for a midyear conference and suggested he be taken to the pediatrician with a request for medication for attentional deficit. She said, "He's out of his chair, swinging around on the rows of desks, talking to his neighbor; he doesn't pay attention, and he disrupts the other children with his comments, jokes, and general restlessness."

In looking over his work folder, Sandy's mother found fourteen sheets of seat work (five pages of arithmetic word problems and nine of reading), all of which she knew were too hard for him to read. Sandy was chronologically young for his grade, had had chicken pox and two episodes of severe bronchitis in first grade, and consequently had missed a lot of instruction. Not surprisingly, his reading was quite far below grade level, and yet his work folder contained standard fare for second grade. Here was a young, insufficiently prepared child being chastised for being unable to solve problems he couldn't read and being a candidate for drug therapy to reduce hyperactivity when the root problem was a mismatch between skills and tasks.

SHIFTING ATTENTION

Language prods and helps verbal shifts. Students need to learn to use one word in two ways, either in homophones (*steel/steal*) or homographs (*present/present*).

Parents and teachers can encourage children by playing with riddles and puns. The student also needs to interpret figures of speech and metaphor, understanding both the individual words and overall meaning of "two heads are better than one."

Language prods and helps the student to shift attention as he increases his accuracy and speed in sorting, filing, and retrieving ideas. Awareness of different styles and rhythms of language helps him shift among categories of spoken or written messages, differentiating among television commercials, fiction, business letters, and journalism. Each has its own vocabulary. Parents and teachers can point out these differences, helping students become consciously aware of categories they recognize subliminally.

Here is yet another instance of how understanding the language of time influences behavior. To be willing to shift attention, students need to grasp the meaning of such words as *now*, *later*, *tomorrow*, *before, after, until*. People with a hazy grasp of time are understandably reluctant to leave something interesting; they are not sure when they can return to it. "Later" and "after math and science" may have no more real meaning for them than "in an hour." As we saw in Chapter 6, many smart kids are in this category.

ACTION

The student who can channel his arousal and attention shows psychological availability for schoolwork. Action, active learning, depends on willingness to take risks, acceptance of the error half of trial and error, and openness to ideas.

Action can be slowed or halted by fear, disorganization, depletion, helplessness, guilt, or depression. These operate like a sea anchor, as a brake below the surface.

It is important to remember that when one family member has a psychological problem, fallout spreads to the others. One family member's problem can flush up guilt, resentment, anguish, jealousy, despair, or bitter warfare among the others. As we consider psychological distress we need to think, then, of secondary as well as primary victims.

The Center for Preventive Psychiatry, White Plains, New York, offers the following Table of Trauma, listed in order from most to least devastating: (1) death of parent, (2) divorce, (3) separation, (4) visible deformity, (5) death of brother or sister, (6) jail sentence of parent, (7) remarriage of parent, (8) hospitalization of child, (9) involvement with drugs/alcohol.

Here are some blocks to active learning I have seen over years of teaching smart kids with school problems: fear of failure, disorganization, fear of depletion, learned helplessness, guilt, and depression.

FEAR OF FAILURE

Smart kids from high-achieving families sometimes become prisoners of perfection. When such a child enters school, the unspoken expectation might as well be chiseled over the front door: GO TO THE HEAD OF THE CLASS. A little child pleases his parents by smiling, walking, talking, and doing other expected things. Schoolchildren know that academic success pleases their parents and think that scholastic failure may cause withdrawal of parental love, a child's deepest fear.

As we know, smart kids have very high expectations for themselves, can anticipate the complicated nature of unfamiliar tasks, and hate to do poorly. When the stakes are academic success and parental approval, it is tempting to abandon a novel idea in favor of a sure shot.

Fear of failure can prompt either "If I don't try I can't fail" or "I'll only do it if I'm sure I'll get it right."

DISORGANIZATION

Clear organization is conceptual cartography. It requires being able to pick a starting point, aim for a midpoint, anticipate a conclusion, and create a mental map to get from one to the other. Whether the cartographer starts with lots of details and builds them into a whole or starts from the whole and assembles the parts, the goal is the same: organizing material to fit inside the contours of the idea or the project. In the absence of a mental map the reader, listener, watcher, interpreter—whoever—doesn't know which way to go.

It is hard for some students to think in an orderly way if their personal possessions are disorganized. A colleague in California said it this way: "So many of my students are from split-custody families. They're with their mothers on Mondays, Wednesdays, and Fridays, and their fathers the other days. They alternate weekends. These kids don't know where their sweaters and tennis rackets are, but worse than that, they sometimes can't seem to find their thoughts. It's as if their touchstones are in misplaced backpacks: not lost, not stolen, just not handy."

FEAR OF DEPLETION

I learned about fear of depletion at a medical lecture and felt as if each word were a brush stroke in a perfect portrait of a student I had never really reached. This is what I learned.

Some children who have suffered painful loss set up psychological safeguards against having to reexperience the feeling. They remember how they felt before "it" (whatever it is) happened. Now the loss has taken away a part of them, leaving a hole. Unconsciously they think, "Something valuable is gone. I don't want that hole to get any bigger, so I'm going to hang on to whatever I have left, including my ideas. If I share them, I might use up my whole supply and hollow myself out even more."

Children who have lost a parent through separation, divorce, or death are particularly vulnerable to fear of depletion, and as the divorce and separation statistics mount, so do the incidences of this fear and its effects on schoolwork.

These students are reluctant to share original thoughts in class discussion, to generate new ideas for written work, or take intellectual risks. A smart kid, adept at spotting patterns, a divergent thinker, one with heightened perceptions, has natural impulses to be inventive. When fear of depletion cripples his imagination, a paralysis that works against the child's nature and delays the healing of the original pain results.

Loss through death, though terrible, has a finality. Margo was a second grader when the car in which she and her father were riding was struck broadside at an intersection by a drunk driver. Her father was killed instantly. As the family tried to accept the shock, everyone remarked on Margo's ability to cope. She kept to her previous schedule, took care of her little sister, and was "a perfect little grown-up."

In a handwriting project she copied four poems out of a book and traced their illustrations. This, in spite of the fact that she had previously been an accomplished artist and creative writer. Her deportment was so considerate and tidy, and she seemed to have accepted the death so well, that it was a long time before her mother saw Margo's manners and coping skills for what they were: a deadening of emotion, a denial of grief over something she couldn't bear to accept, and a hoarding of ideas. She was happy to copy and recite but afraid to release original thought.

With the encouragement of a perceptive teacher, Margo's mother enrolled her in an after-school drama and arts program. She learned her lines quickly and well and began investing them with emotion and powerful body English. Margo discovered that the more she gave out, the more her power increased. She made the same discovery in her painting and drawing and finally began to contribute her ideas to classroom discussions. She found that replenishment came steadily, and she is now a vigorous contributor.

Loss through divorce may, paradoxically, be harder for the child to accept than sudden death because the coming and going of the absent person keep alive the hope of permanent reunion. Children of any age have trouble with "here today and gone tomorrow," and they may lay a burden of perfection on themselves, attempting to bring back the absent parent. "If I am better, Mommy will come home for good." "If I get all As, Daddy will be so proud he won't be able to stay away." This can add fear of failure to fear of depletion, doubling the problem.

LEARNED HELPLESSNESS

Martin E. P. Seligman, M.D., coined the term *learned helplessness* in his research as a clinical and experimental psychologist at the University of Pennsylvania. According to Seligman, learned helplessness develops in animals and people whose efforts have no impact on their circumstances.

For instance, if animal number one, placed in a water tank in danger of drowning, thrashes around and then is plucked from the water, he associates his own efforts with the rescue and will struggle again the next time he is in danger. Animal number two, also about to drown, thrashes around and is only rescued later, after he has stopped thrashing. He does not connect his rescue with his efforts.

The first animal learns that what Seligman calls the *locus of control* is inside him: effort brings rescue. The second animal learns that quixotic fate may be cruel (jeopardizing him to begin with) or benevolent (arranging the rescue), but that the locus of control is outside, beyond his reach. Animals who learn helplessness give up when danger comes; they drown quickly.

As Seligman illustrates, learned helplessness, unchecked, leads to passivity, depression, and, in extreme instances, death.

For some of our students it's not such a long step from the experimental drowning tank to the mainstream classroom. The student who has difficulty doing what others around him do easily can either thrash around or give up. When a child in difficulty thrashes around trying to save himself, but nothing changes, he "learns" that the locus of control is outside him.

Where is the locus of control in most school settings? The teacher plans the lessons; the student does them. The teacher sets the standards; the student must meet them. The teacher gives the assignments; the student completes them. The teacher grades the product and the effort; the student is measured. When the match is right, each success fuels the next endeavor. In a mismatch, who feels the pain? The student. Who struggles? The student. Who has the power to change the circumstances? Seldom the student.

Which children are particularly vulnerable to learned helplessness?

The child whose early health history contains major illness, hospitalization, or chronic poor health may develop a fundamentally passive approach to life. During the years he should be exploring and gaining dominion over his world, the ill child who survives by taking medicine, breathing oxygen from a machine, having transfusions, having things put into or cut out of his body learns that strength is external rather than something that can grow from within. The unhealthy young child survives and recuperates through obedience, rest, and restraint. These early experiences of helplessness can deplete psychological availability for schoolwork.

Once in school, the athletic child with a weak visual memory sinks in look-say reading instruction. The mathematically powerful student with slow visual-motor integration gasps for air trying to take dictation. The verbal reasoner with a weak auditory system drowns in words in classrooms that emphasize listening. The intelligent child with receptive language disability grasps at straws, trying to learn through reading. The poetic child with visual-spatial confusion loses ground trying to solve math problems by using manipulative materials. These are a few examples of students at risk for learned helplessness.

Smart kids with school problems who are powerful in areas that are not acknowledged in school live at two simultaneous psychological extremes: power and helplessness. Swings between such distant poles are confusing and debilitating.

What diminishes the risk of learned helplessness? Giving students a sense of control over their own learning. Students need to learn strategies more than they need to learn facts. If a struggling student is given tutoring in the facts that everyone else around him already knows, is given the "whats," he is receiving information that he feels he ought to learn independently. He sees his success as coming from the benevolence of his tutor; the locus of control remains outside. If, on the other hand, the student is taught strategies, the "hows," he can begin to take charge of his own learning. The locus of control moves inside.

With the locus of control outside, life teaches the lesson of learned helplessness. With the locus of control inside, life reinforces the lesson of learned competence.

GUILT

The preschool child sees the world as an extension of himself, believing that external events occur because of his internal wishes and emotions. As he grows older, the machinery of cause and effect becomes more apparent, and he trades omnipotence for common sense. While it is painful to relinquish total power, it is also a relief to shed its responsibilities. In normal development, the child makes the trade at around age five and goes on about his business, constantly learning "If I do this, such and such will happen" and "If I do not do this, such and such will or will not happen."

If a child suffers a traumatic loss through death, divorce, or separation when he is still an omnipotent thinker, he feels responsible for the event. If the little child says "I hate you" to a parent (as perfectly normal children do from time to time) and the parent subsequently packs up and leaves because of a marital problem, the child nevertheless feels responsible and therefore guilty.

If a father dies or leaves home at the height of a little boy's struggle to resolve an Oedipal complex, the child unconsciously feels guilty that what he wanted has come to pass.

The statistics show an increasing number of divorces and sep- arations among the parents of preschool children. Unconscious and inappropriate assumption of guilt can make the child afraid to explore questions of cause and effect. Who needs public confirmation of secret shame? Because active learning involves cause and effect, this fear can set up new learning problems or aggravate existing ones.

Erik H. Erikson says the child's psychological growth follows a preordained sequence of internal crises, using the word *crisis* to describe the tension between negative and positive forces. The res- olution of the crisis, negatively or positively, determines how the child will react to the next stage of his life and tips the balance for the outcome of the next "crisis." The infant's crisis is basic trust versus mistrust. The preschool child's tug-of-war is autonomy versus shame and doubt. The mounting statistics on parental departure during these years when the child considers himself omnipotent tip the balance in favor of shame and doubt, which has a powerful influence on the resolution of the schoolchild's crisis: industry versus inferiority.

DEPRESSION

Educators and parents need to acknowledge the phenomenon of childhood depression, recognizing it as a serious problem re- quiring professional care. Although a concerned adult can sense sadness or inturned anger, only the professional is qualified to con- firm the existence of clinical depression, only the professional should try to assess the depth and scope of the illness, and only the profes- sional should apply the treatment. Kind people with common sense are allies who must recognize their limits. Sigmund Fraud is a dangerous imposter.

The teacher and psychotherapist play separate and distinct roles. The teacher is the student's ally in the realm of reality and keeps him in touch with his own intactness by conveying "This is what you *can* do," "These are things you *have* learned," "Here are ways for you to help yourself." The student needs acknowledgment of his competent side in order to keep faith in himself. The psychotherapist meets the student in the realm of fantasy and pathology. Without pathology there would be no need of treatment. The child needs to know there is someone who will help, respect, and accept him in spite of his confusion. If the teacher, who is meant to hold the child in the realm of reality and intactness, glides over into the realm of fantasy and pathology, the child loses his guide. This is a profound betrayal.

Depression deserves volumes to itself, and any attempt to cover it in a chapter, or part of a chapter, would be both presumptuous and unprofessional. There are, however, two ways in which depression and school overlap that are particular perils to smart kids with school problems. One is mourning and schoolwork; the other is the chicken/egg question of school problems and depression.

A school-age child may mourn the death of a person or pet or the departure of a parent through separation or divorce. As mentioned, the reappearance of the separated parent may prolong the grief. Reappearance denies finality, yet the acceptance of finality is a prerequisite of true healing.

Children mourn, too, for less obvious losses. The child, particularly one with the intellectual traits of a gifted thinker, may mourn his own infancy and childhood when things seemed easier. He may also mourn his departing sense of competence or his access to those activities and areas in which he finds joy and success.

During a time of mourning, the student's schoolwork may suffer because of these symptoms: diminished powers of concentration, trouble with short-term memory, shortened attention span, and distractibility, not to mention sadness. Mourning children need reassurance that these symptoms are both normal and temporary. According to Louise Conley, Ph.D., a guidance counselor whose specialty is mourning through death, separation, and divorce, a healthy period of mourning takes roughly one year. Educators and parents need to understand the length, depth, and full effects of this healing process.

Depression can be either the result or the cause of school problems. Clearly, the smart kid whose heightened perceptions cast a terribly bright light on his own shortcomings, whose big dreams seem blocked by his own incompetence, and whose divergent thinking is being confined and forced down through the narrow end of a funnel is vulnerable to the feelings of anger turned inward and helplessness that fuel genuine depression. The anger at not being able to accomplish what others accomplish effortlessly, the anger at being asked to do what cannot be done must go someplace. It may go into depression.

As noted earlier, the smart kid with school problems may be angry with himself or at the society that imposes requirements he cannot satisfy. The depressed student's anger turns inward, putting him at risk for harm, ranging from deliberate troublemaking, to substance abuse, to suicide.

It is also true that depression can be the cause of school problems, affecting all three levels of psychological availability: *arousal*, *attention*, and *action*. As depression drains psychological energy it inhibits arousal. As depression prompts introspection it steals attention. As depression is the companion of passivity and pessimism it blocks action. The depressed student is not free to mine his own assets.

Recently I heard a guidance counselor from a competitive university lecture on the high incidence of depression among intelligent, attractive, affluent adolescents. He emphasized that "having everything" confers no immunity. In fact, material comfort may be a contributing factor to depression in a child who feels helpless, discouraged, or inadequate. Being showered with the benefits of someone else's competence can reinforce the passivity and learned helplessness from which certain depressions arise.

He explained further that many students with indulgent parents seldom face the consequences of their own actions: the boy who turns off the alarm clock and goes back to sleep is driven to school by a parent who doesn't want him to miss breakfast or be late. This kind of parent may write a health excuse note to explain away incomplete homework. The list goes on. The guidance counselor showed how some depressions have their roots in this pattern.

When the catered-to adolescent tries to rebel, his parents excuse, overlook, or cover up his attempts to strike out: "My Sammy was with a bad crowd that day," "Beer missing? No I didn't notice," or "Julia, we'll say you were with us if you'll promise never to do such a thing again." These responses to rebellion steal the adolescent's power, saying, in effect, "Your actions aren't worth my strong response," the extension of which is "I really don't care about you."

Depression and powerlessness go hand in hand. When indulgent parents try to spare a child the consequences of his own actions, they deny him the power to provoke, then reciprocally, the power to please. They reduce his assaults to flying marshmallows.

This counselor urged his listeners to expand their awareness of adolescent depression and self-destruction beyond suicide to include drug (including alcohol) abuse, withdrawal into solitude, and non-completion of work.

If the smart kid without school problems is vulnerable to depression and its serious fallout, his hampered counterpart is in double jeopardy.

PRINCIPLES OF GOOD PRACTICE

When a student is psychologicallly unavailable for schoolwork, the school and family should join forces to investigate possible physiological causes and should share anecdotal information with one another as well as with the child's doctor. Such symptoms as circles under the eyes, persistent congestion, bad breath, constant yawning, or restlessness need to be pinpointed and investigated. The school and family can help by offering specific examples: "After lunch, it is hard to get his attention," "Noises in the hall disrupt him easily," "He does better when he sits near the person who is speaking," and "Making eye contact helps him focus" are much more helpful than a generalized "He doesn't seem to stay with the group," "He never finishes anything." Be specific as to when and where the child has a particular type of difficulty.

In preparing for a joint conference, the parents, teachers, and educational overseer will want to review the master file, noting his strengths and weaknesses in the learning systems explored so far. A student with seeming arousal problems may not hear well, one whose attention wanders may have trouble filtering out visual distractions, another who doesn't hand in his assignments may have

trouble with handwriting or organization. Appropriate notations should
be added to the master file.

Much can be learned from a classroom observation. A teacher,
the learning specialist, the school psychologist, or, if none of these
is available, an adult who knows the student should sit in the classroom and observe him for a half an hour three times during a day,
with no other obligations during this time. It is surprising how much
information can be gathered by an observer who is free to focus on
one person, who has the time to notice the student's concentration
span, and the types of situations in which he is psychologically
available or unavailable. What is the thread? Where is the pattern?

If a student has difficulty with arousal, the alert adult will notice
when he laughs and when he relaxes. Knowing what he cares about
helps parents and teachers incorporate these interests into the activities in which he is lethargic, building a bridge from one to the
other. If he is interested in rock music, he can be asked to make
up a math word problem for each morning's math class about bands,
groups, hits, instruments, or whatever. If the student laughs over
riddles, he can be the master of ceremonies of the Riddle of the
Day. Real learning is active and energetic.

The student who has trouble focusing attention needs to learn
the strategies for listening outlined in Chapter 5 (pp. 101–105).
During explanations he should sit near the front and maintain eye
contact. When he is expected to work independently, he may need
a desk away from the window and door, perhaps even a carrel.

The student who has trouble shifting his attention needs var-
iations of activities. Mind benders, word problems, and logic exercises tempt smart kids. "What if" questions require flexible thinking.
Word play promotes it. Asking students to invent math word problems stimulates it, as does telling three-fourths of a story and asking
the child to invent an ending.

The old-fashioned parlor games I Spy and Twenty Questions,
which can be adapted to family or classroom use, are a quick way
to stimulate flexible thinking with a group. In I Spy, "It" selects
something in everyone's full view and gives one description: "I spy
something yellow." The guessers then try to identify the object by
asking questions with yes or no answers: "Is it in the left half of the
room?" "Is it bigger than a breadbox?" In Twenty Questions, "It"

thinks of a person, place, or thing that the guessers must identify by asking no more than twenty yes or no questions.

If a student has trouble with action, here are some suggestions to release the brakes.

To reduce fear of failure, parents and teachers can honor originality over conformity by offering open-ended questions, giving assignments that have no correct or incorrect answers, such as writing a poem, inventing a conclusion to a story, or building a diorama to illustrate a concept. Adults can try new things themselves with the students, teaching willingness to take risks through personal example.

To help overcome disorganization, teachers and parents should be certain the student really understands the language of comparison, categories, space, and time.

Adults can diminish a student's fear of depletion by engaging him in brainstorming exercises in which everyone thinks and shares: How many things can we name that are found in most kitchens? Let's get as many adjectives as we can to describe a fish. Discovering the feeling of replenishment, particularly if it is connected with laughter, will encourage the fearful student to let go.

Adults can help the student replace learned helplessness with learned competence by putting the locus of control within his reach. Teaching him strategies as opposed to giving him correct answers gives him a chance to direct his own attempts and makes a link between effort and success.

We can help students avoid some unnecessary guilt by verbalizing the causes and effects of events in daily living:

"I dropped the glass of milk because my hand was slippery from the soap."

"You hurt your toe because you were so busy trying to carry the box that you forgot to look."

"Your daddy is in the hospital because he hurt his shoulder on the camping trip, and the doctor needs to fix it there."

Educators and parents should be aware of the possibility of childhood or adolescent depression and seek professional diagnosis and treatment as quickly as possible. This is no place for amateurs.

Literature can lead people of all ages to psychological availability for learning. Rich stories allow us to play with elemental themes and questions with no verifiable answers. To find that other cultures and other peoples have wrestled with the ambiguities of the human condition is a reassuring discovery to everyone, and particularly to students in psychological distress.

Creative writing, at home or in school, can tweak arousal, capture attention, and channel action. Recently, during a three-day workshop for parents, administrators, and teachers of gifted children, I invited a large group of local students to participate in an exercise I had used in our school. We started with a brainstorming session on stars: where do we hear about stars in nursery rhymes, popular music, fairy tales, religion? What do they symbolize? Are they near, far, hospitable, dangerous, inhabited? Are they like one another?

Moving from Twinkle, Twinkle Little Star to pondering e. e. cummings's "I would rather learn from one bird how to sing than teach ten thousand stars how not to dance," to reading selections from Antoine de St. Exupéry's *The Little Prince*, we explored the students' memories and associations, comparing them to other authors' ideas. Then it was time for them to invent their own stars. One brilliantly original sixth-grade thinker, who had been hiding and hurting in formal academic settings, wrote:

"My star can be as cold as a stare, hot as hatred. It is located in the back of my mind, far as infinite but as close as a wink. You visit only when you fall asleep, leave when you awake. All speak strange, yet you understand them. You may find friends but may not. Anything can happen, limited only by your imagination. You never eat, drink, get hurt, or die. Those distant stars are my dreams. I hope they never burn out."

A CASE HISTORY: LARRY

Larry is the youngest of four children whose parents are frequently busy in the evenings, leaving him in the care of his older brothers and sister. If they have plans of their own, Larry is left alone. He is never quite sure who will be where, when. His brothers are strong and enjoy contact sports. Larry does not and reports being "scared of Eddie . . . he knocks me around." His sister considers herself "above" the male horseplay and doesn't intervene unless there is a bad fight.

Larry's nursery school teacher reported that he had trouble paying attention and following directions. "He's in outer space," she said, coupling his distractedness to his fascination with astronauts and space shuttles. He needed constant reminders about the simplest routines, and she would often have to call "Earth to Larry."

His spaciness continued in kindergarten, and in spite of his obvious intelligence, he seemed at risk for failure in first grade. Although he could build anything with his hands and had gathered extensive knowledge about the space shuttle from studying pictures and diagrams, he couldn't stay in his seat for more than a few minutes at a time.

In second grade, Larry had trouble with spelling, doing pencil-and-paper arithmetic, and following directions. His teacher said, "Larry is frequently silly, disrupting other children and distracting himself from his own work. His time-on-task record is very poor." His erratic work habits annoyed her and, truth to tell, she didn't like him very much. She tried to be more sympathetic in February, however, when he lost the index finger of his left hand in an accident.

He and a friend had been playing in Larry's yard on an old toy with spinning seats anchored to a center post. When it wouldn't spin, Larry put his finger down the center of the post to see whether anything was stuck. At the same moment, his friend started pushing the seat around by hand. Larry's finger was caught; the friend pushed again, hoping to free his finger but cut it off instead. No adults were home, and although the boys finally got help it was too late to restore the finger. Larry was terrified by the accident and ashamed of his hand.

He was in considerable physical pain for at least six weeks, and, to no one's surprise, showed little interest in his schoolwork for the rest of second grade.

In third grade Larry had serious problems with reading comprehension, his handwriting was sloppy, and although his understanding of math concepts was good, his columns drifted and he added the wrong numbers together.

His parents were impatient: "He's perfectly bright; he just isn't trying. . . ." His teachers were irritated: "If that kid would pay attention he'd be a top student." The school learning specialist said that he was disorganized, did not know how to tell time, misunderstood such spatial markers as *every other*, and showed spatial confusion in letter formation and placement. Her report read, "This seems to be an intelligent child who is not performing well in school. He should have a comprehensive psychoeducational evaluation."

Larry's scores on the testing showed very high abstract reasoning, barely average visual-motor skills, and sequential skills well below the national norm.

The evaluating psychologist wrote that Larry had a poor self-concept and his sense of physical intactness had been badly shaken by the accident. He was embarrassed by the appearance of his hand, felt abandoned by his parents, and was afraid of his siblings. He felt overwhelmed by the requirements of his schoolwork and didn't know how to ask for extra help because he couldn't tell what it was he didn't know. He had no idea how to organize either the problem or the solution. He said, "It doesn't matter what I do. I just can't do any of it."

With this information in hand, the psychologist and the educational team arranged a conference with Larry's parents. They also shared some of the results of the testing with Larry, who was surprised and proud to hear about his high reasoning ability. The educators and parents discussed the implications of the testing with the psychologist and planned appropriate instructional measures.

A private tutor, provided by the parents, met with Larry in school three times a week to work on his handwriting and review concepts of time and space. She gave him strategies to organize his materials, ideas, and homework. They practiced techniques for strengthening his reading comprehension, and gradually Larry's day-to-day work improved. He agreed to take a six-week summer academic skill-building program as long as he could be allowed to continue playing in the soccer league. Everyone knew that his athletic successes were important in helping him overcome the trauma of losing his finger.

His parents made some family rules: an older sibling was to be at home with Larry any time his parents were out. Bullying was prohibited. They also instituted a Saturday morning family marketing trip. Each week, each person was charged with collecting the necessary ingredients for one night's dinner and then responsible for preparing it. The one who cooked didn't have to wash the dishes.

Larry loved to fix pizza and salad, which turned out to be Eddie's weekly favorite, and the others enjoyed it nearly as much. Providing a way for Larry to make a contribution to family living was an example of confirming a child's worth not by praising him, but by depending on him.

Larry received a supportive combination of academic help, emotional support, security in his daily living, and appropriate opportunities for responsibility. It took a while for the benefits to show, but he bloomed.

8

TESTING
DEMYSTIFIED

SCORES, INTERPRETATION, PLANNING

This chapter is designed to demystify testing and to show how test scores can work *for* a conundrum kid. Many teachers' experience with testing is limited to the classroom. Some administrators are accustomed to looking at whole-class or whole-school test results and have less experience with assessing individual profiles. Most parents are bewildered by a collection of test scores and unfamiliar terminology.

Because we learn more from patterns than we do from any single score, the emphasis is on identifying *clusters* of strength, *types* of behavior, *kinds* of weakness, and *areas* of difficulty. Recurrent themes emerge when we join anecdotal material, school records, and the results of an individual evaluation.

But expecting the uninitiated to collect these different materials is as unfair as asking a hungry noncook to shop for the ingredients of a satisfying dinner. He may know he needs to eat; he wants a nourishing, tasty meal; but he doesn't know how to check the cupboard for what's already there, where to go to get what is lacking, how much of what to buy, which things are fine ready-made and which need to be made from scratch, how to combine the ingredients, when he can manage on his own, or when he needs to hire a cook.

THE TESTING PROCESS

We shall explore a glossary of testing terms, types of tests, reasons to test, hazards of testing, benefits of testing, and variables in testing.

A GLOSSARY OF TESTING TERMS

The terms are listed in the order most general to most specific.

Norms.   Norms are the results of the typical performance of the group of individuals to whom a test is administered when it is being standardized. National norms are derived from a nationally based population sample. Independent school norms represent scores attained by applicants to, or students in, independent schools. Local norms are developed from the testing results within a given school. Norms indicate average performance as well as degrees of deviation above and below the average.[1]

Percentile.   The term *percentile* comes from *percent,* meaning per hundred. A percentile shows where one student scores in relation to ninety-nine other students. The ninety-ninth percentile is the highest. Because this score shows relative performance, it is not to be confused with getting a score of 99, 69, or 31 on an exam.

Stanine.   Stanines are standardized scores that go from 1 to 9 in the sets of 10 between 1 and 100. The ninth stanine is the highest. A score of 7 would be in the first stanine, 14 in the second, 28 in the third, and so forth.

Mean.   Mean is an average. The mean score of 65, 76, and 84 is 75, derived from adding the scores together and dividing by 3.

Median.   Median is that which is midway between the highest and the lowest.

Standard deviation.   Standard deviation is the amount by which scores can be above or below the mean without major statistical significance. If the standard deviation is 10 on a test whose mean is 100, scores from 90 to 110 do not mark as major a difference as scores from 80 to 100 or 100 to 120.

Numerical score. The numerical score tells how many answers a student had right. If he had 73 correct on a test with 85 items his score would be 73, or 73/85.

Raw score. The raw score is the test taker's numerical total. Alone, it has no significance on instruments that have converted scores.

Converted scores. Converted scores are derived by putting raw scores into a conversion table to compare a student's performance with that of others of his age, sex, or grade level.

Grade equivalent. Some test results give a grade equivalent (GE). If a fourth-grade student has a GE math score of 8.5, it means he has performed on that test as well as a student in the fifth month of eighth grade. It does not mean that he is proficient in eighth-grade math.

Mental age equivalent. Some test results deliver a mental age equivalent (MAE). If the same fourth-grade student has an MAE of 17 on a particular test, it means that his performance matches that of seventeen-year-old students. It does not mean that he is ready to go to college.

IQ. These letters stand for intelligence quotient, a number derived from the student's scaled scores on a standardized test (defined in the next section). It is intended to measure how smart someone is.

TYPES OF TESTS

Standardized tests. A standardized test is one whose results are tabulated from criteria to compare students' performances. Scores are reported in norms, percentiles, stanines, and the other ways listed previously. They differ from teacher-made tests because they compare students from large groups.

Achievement tests. Achievement tests are standardized instruments that measure what the student has learned.

Aptitude tests.   Aptitude tests are standardized instruments that purport to measure the student's aptitude for learning. Theoretically, acquired knowledge doesn't enter in. Some disagree.

Intelligence tests.   Intelligence tests try to tell how smart someone is.

Diagnostic tests.   Diagnostic tests try to tell something about the student's learning style. Their titles are usually self-explanatory: Slingerland Pre-Reading Screening to Detect First Grade Academic Needs, Wepman Test of Auditory Discrimination, Beery-Buktenica Test of Visual-Motor Integration. Projective tests are psychological diagnostic tests.

Group tests.   Group tests are given to whole groups at once.

Individual tests.   Individual tests are administered to each student individually.

Timed tests.   Timed tests must be completed within a time established by the test maker, time being a factor in the test's standardization.

Pencil-paper tests.   Standardized pencil-and-paper tests require the student to mark his answers, usually multiple choice, in a test booklet or to mark an accompanying answer sheet.

Verbal tests.   Verbal tests measure verbal skills.

Performance tests.   Performance tests require a student to manipulate materials.

Quantitative tests.   Quantitative tests measure mathematical skills.

Multiple-choice tests.   Multiple-choice tests have questions that the student must answer by choosing one of the (usually four) answers provided. The student cannot offer his own answer.

Essay question tests.   The student provides his answer in his own words in essay form.

In most schools, students take a set of standardized achievement tests in reading and math once during each year. Some achievement tests include aptitude sections; others do not. The results report individual students' scores and the scores for each class as a group. They are recorded in norms, percentiles, stanines, and the other ways described previously.

REASONS TO TEST

Three good reasons to test are to find out something not already known, to confirm a hunch, and to support recommendations.

When a kid is struggling in school, the first suggestion often is "Let's get him tested." That may or may not be necessary. Look first in the file to see what's already there. This is analogous to checking the kitchen shelves before going out to shop for dinner. School files are filled with test results gathering dust.

When unknowns remain after checking the records, or when it seems time for an update, appropriate testing should be arranged. We shall explore the specifics shortly.

Sometimes a parent or a teacher has a hunch about a kid but would not feel responsible in making a diagnosis without objective or professional information. The teacher who is concerned about a student's hearing wants the verification of an audiological examination. The parent who is worried about developmental readiness wants clinical evidence to help with a school placement decision.

Sometimes numerical test results are needed to support a recommendation. Numbers talk.

"Mr. Smith, Johnny's teachers don't feel he's solid enough to go into first grade" is less effective in buying Johnny the extra year he needs than "Mr. Smith, although we all know Johnny is bright, he scored below the fiftieth percentile in all subtests of the standardized testing. With another year under his belt he could be at the top of the class."

HAZARDS OF TESTING

Dr. Seuss, the philosopher who writes books for children, wrote a poem for a class of college seniors: "The Art of Eating Popovers." It might as easily have been written for people who interpret standardized test results: "Do a lot of spitting out the hot air and be careful what you swallow."

For reasons explored throughout this book, many smart kids score poorly on standardized tests, creating an incorrect impression of low overall ability.

In today's cultural climate, test scores are taken seriously, but the tests themselves are often insufficiently analyzed. For example, one section of a well-known test is called Spelling, but the student is not asked to spell. He is asked to find the correct spelling from among four alternatives; this is proofreading. Some clumsily designed test items test two, or even three, separate skills within one question. Well-designed test items probe discrete areas separately.

Group-administered or "quick-to-give, easy-to-score" IQ tests are dangerous as well as inaccurate: the picture they give is shallow, and the result is usually a numerical score, which gives no indication of patterns. Many such tests require the student to read the questions. One of my students, an intelligent poor reader, received an IQ score of 74 (national norm 100). In this era of data banks, numbers that do not represent what they purport to represent are dangerous. Once a number is on a transcript there is no control over who sees it, what interpretation is given, and what use is made of the interpretation. Intelligence tests and diagnostic tests should be administered individually.

BENEFITS OF TESTING

Well-planned, well-used testing has many benefits. First, today's kids need to be familiar with the process. The sooner they start and the pleasanter the initial experiences, the more they will take testing in stride.

Standardized testing can protect creativity in the classroom. Being able to say "The students in Mrs. Smith's room, who do such magnificent projects, also score well above the national norms and even above the local community norms on their standardized tests" enlists support for the projects from even the most conservative onlookers.

A cumulative record of test scores is an invaluable addition to the student's master file. Historical perspective highlights patterns.

VARIABLES

Three variables deserve close attention. Changes in the child's external environment may influence his daily performance or his performance on a test. Changes within the child (as he moves from one linguistic, developmental, or psychosocial level to another) may influence his performance. Changes in the focus of the curriculum may influence the quality of his performance, as we have seen throughout the book.

A test measures a student's performance on one particular instrument on one particular day in one particular situation. If the results don't ring true, educators and parents should probe further and should not let test results own the student. He should own them.

INDIVIDUALIZED TESTING

If you, the adult reader, think the student should have individual testing, what do you ask for, where do you get it, when should you have it, what does it look like, how long does it take, what are the results, and how do you use them?

WHAT DO YOU ASK FOR?

You ask for a comprehensive psychoeducational evaluation, which should include the child's developmental history, current achievement levels, an IQ test, screening for learning disabilities, and psychological or neurological testing if deemed necessary by the examiner or examiners.

WHERE DO YOU GET IT?

You can arrange for testing through the school system or have it done by a private organization. There are advantages and disadvantages to each. If the student is in the public school system, the testing will be done by an evaluating team, which usually includes a school psychologist and/or a learning specialist. Testing will take place in school without extra charge. If you have faith in the school personnel, this is fine. If you, as a parent or teacher, feel that the student is not well understood, you may prefer an outside opinion.

If the student is not in the public school, but you are a taxpayer in the district, you are entitled to an evaluation, by the school team, without charge. However, you have no choice as to who will administer the tests. This is either risky or safe, depending on the district. Check. Because the evaluation will be the foundation of a great deal of subsequent planning, quality is vital.

If you choose to have this done outside the school, there are several ways of finding people to do it. Ask the guidance department in the school, check the pediatric or neurological departments of a nearby hospital (a teaching hospital if possible), or ask the student's own doctor. Failing these, you could contact the regional representative of The Orton Dyslexia Society, 724 York Road, Baltimore, Maryland 21204, to ask for the name of a doctor or psychologist near you. Remember the caveat: if the results don't ring true, probe further. The test results should mirror the child's performance. Because costs vary widely, it is impractical to address that question here.

WHEN SHOULD YOU HAVE IT?

Although some excellent diagnostic tests are available for use with preschool children, IQ tests are of dubious merit before the age of six. A smart child with school problems should have an individual diagnostic screening for learning disabilities at the first hint of trouble. A smart, healthy child, working under a good teacher in appropriate grade placement, who has trouble mastering what others are learning easily should have an individual evaluation, ideally before entering second grade.

An evaluation should be given as soon as the family, the student, or the school becomes concerned. If one was given when the student was in first grade, it is appropriate to have another around fourth or fifth grade, and perhaps again at around tenth. These suggested intervals are suitable but not mandatory. Although individual subtest scores may vary, the pattern of learning style within the test results usually remains consistent: fingerprints don't change.

WHAT DOES IT LOOK LIKE?

For older students as well as younger ones, it will seem like conversation, games, and puzzles with a friendly person.

HOW LONG DOES IT TAKE?

The examiner will probably schedule one intake session with the parents; two or three testing sessions with the student, lasting roughly one hour apiece; and then a final interpretative session. If not all three testing sessions are necessary, it is easy to cancel one.

WHAT ARE THE RESULTS?

Skillfully interpreted, they highlight not so much *what* the student has learned, but *how* he acquires information, and whether he can manipulate as well as acquire it. The scores will be reported in percentiles, stanines, norms, or in the other testing terms listed in the glossary.

The parents and school should request a written report to accompany or follow the oral, interpretative session. They should inquire ahead of time whether the examiner is willing to put the findings and interpretation in writing; if not, they should obtain permission to tape-record the session and write down any and all numerical scores. It is important to have the subtest numbers. Later in the chapter, we shall look at ways of using these numbers to understand the student's learning style and make some educational decisions. The interior, subtest scores are much more helpful than the numerical total.

HOW DO YOU USE THEM?

The results can form the platform for short- and long-term educational planning: choosing the best type of academic setting from the available choices, tailoring the combination of courses best suited to the student's learning patterns; and selecting areas of study which will exercise talents, shore up weaknesses, minimize frustration and failure while encouraging interest and success.

Let's look at one test battery, and one recently published book, which suggests an entirely different look at intelligence and measurement. They are the Wechsler Intelligence Test for Children, Revised (commonly called the WISC-R) and *Frames of Mind: The Theory of Multiple Intelligences*, by Howard Gardner (New York: Basic Books, 1983).

Why these? The WISC-R has stood the test of time, there is a great deal of interpretative data on each subtest, and interesting research shows new and additional ways of interpreting the scores. Because it is familiar to educational, psychological, and neurological evaluators everywhere, the results are transferable among disciplines.

In *Frames of Mind: The Theory of Multiple Intelligences*, Howard Gardner bases his hypotheses on work done in three areas. He works with victims of brain disease and injury at the Boston Veterans Administration Medical Center, he is an associate professor at the Boston University School of Medicine, and he is a codirector of Harvard Project Zero, in which he studies the artistic and intellectual development of normal and gifted children. He feels that restricting intelligence measurement to verbal and performance categories, or linguistic and logical/mathematical categories, results in rapid, prejudicial labeling of smart and dumb and gives an unfairly negative appraisal of many who, under different, expanded standards would be superior. A review of his book said:

> There is an increasing tendency to restrict the measure of students' intelligence to the numerical scores they can earn on standardized tests. The simplistic illogic that a high score equals an intelligent, worthy human being carries with it the fallacy that a low score equals an unintelligent, unworthy human being. When these ideas take hold, social critics, educators, and parents cry out for higher scores and the activities of young minds are restricted in response. In effect, students are pushed down through the narrow end of a funnel. Now, in contrast, Howard Gardner inverts the funnel, inviting an expanded and

benevolent yet scholarly and explicit model of human intelligence.[2]

Let's take a deeper look at each of these.

THE WISC-R

Although the WISC-R is an intelligence test that can be administered only by a licensed psychologist or tester, the scores may be interpreted in several different ways by specialists and nonspecialists alike who understand the significance of the numbers.

A WISC-R delivers a *full-scale number* representing the student's overall IQ. This number is derived from the scaled combination of two sets of subtests, Verbal and Performance. Each of these two categories has its own total, which is derived from the scaled combination of six subtest scores:

VERBAL	PERFORMANCE
Information	Picture completion
Similarities	Picture arrangement
Arithmetic	Block design
Vocabulary	Object assembly
Comprehension	Coding
(Digit span)	(Mazes)

VERBAL SUBTESTS

All verbal subtests are presented orally and are intended to be given in this order:

Information. This is a test of general information. Good readers and students with rich cultural background usually do well here.

Similarities. This subtest is often considered the most valid predictor of academic success. As the name implies, it requires comparison and contrast on an abstract level. Good performance here can indicate facility with abstraction and manipulation of concepts, poor performance the opposite.

Arithmetic.   This subtest is an oral presentation of counting and word problems. Students with weak auditory memory have a hard time, and anxiety works against good performance.

Vocabulary.   This subtest requires word knowledge and the ability to give definitions. Critics complain that it is culturally biased; also, auditory-processing problems may lower vocabulary levels.

Comprehension.   This subtest probes the student's knowledge of social conventions and the way the world works.

Digit span.   This exercise in auditory memory and concentration tests the student's ability to hear and repeat (forward and backward) a meaningless string of numbers. It is sometimes omitted and sometimes not factored into the verbal subtotal.

PERFORMANCE SUBTESTS

No performance subtest requires the test taker to read, and only Coding requires writing.

Picture completion.   The student must discover what is missing. A good score indicates sharp eyes, alertness to detail, and common sense.

Picture arrangement.   The student arranges a group of pictures to tell a story in correct sequence. Poor performance in this subtest indicates susceptibility to certain types of language and reading problems.

Block design.   This subtest is considered to be a highly accurate indicator of spatial intelligence. Students who do well here grasp spatial relationships and abstractions quickly, exercise good small-motor coordination, and often become talented engineers, scientists, and mathematicians.

Object assembly.   To score well, the student must put puzzle pieces together quickly and adroitly to form a picture.

Coding.   This subtest requires deft visual-motor integration. Students with strong visual memory have an advantage. Concomitantly, students with weak visual memory, anxiety, and difficulty with concentration or pencil manipulation are penalized.

Mazes.   This subtest requires the student to use a pencil to find his way out of a maze. This subtest may be omitted and is not required for a performance score.

Each subtest delivers a scaled score, which may range from 1 to 19, 19 being the highest and 10 being the national norm. In addition, each numerical score falls into both a descriptive category (dull-normal, superior, and so on) and a percentile. A perfectly normal profile (that is, the norm) would be 10 on each subtest, a verbal IQ of 100, a performance IQ of 100, and a full-scale score of 100, intelligence falling in the fiftieth percentile. But people are seldom so consistent. *Discrepancy* is the key word for conundrum kids. Witness Miranda.

The opening paragraph of her individual evaluation reads, "Miranda was referred for testing because of her uneven school performance. While she sometimes contributes sophisticated comments to classroom discussion, her written work is poor. Her teachers and parents question her overall endowment and wonder why her performance is so erratic."

WISC-R
Miranda X
Full-Scale: 122

VERBAL: *128*	PERFORMANCE: *109*
Information: 14	Picture completion: 13
Similarities: 18	Picture arrangement: 12
Arithmetic: 11	Block design: 15
Vocabulary: 15	Objection assembly: 12
Comprehension: 15	Coding: 5
Digit span: 12	Mazes: no score

Miranda received a verbal IQ of 128, placing her in the Superior range; a performance IQ of 109, or Average; and a full-scale IQ of 122, also in the Superior range. Of note is the 19-point discrepancy between the two categories. Of even greater note is the internal scatter, or discrepancy, among her performance subtests, which range from 5 to 15. And we see a span of 18 to 5 from her highest to her lowest subtest scores across the categories: 18 on the verbal Similarities and 5 on the performance Coding. Because a discrepancy of 3 points from the student's own mean (Miranda's would be 12.5 +) is considered significant, Miranda's scores are very revealing.

What do the totals tell us? Miranda's verbal house is in good order, and she is less adroit with performance tasks. Does the number 122 tell us very much? No. It is a much lower number than she would have had without the Coding score, but there is no little warning flag saying, "Watch out; this is not the whole story."

We can see a great deal by looking inside the totals. Miranda is a good thinker whose mechanics are weak. She is comfortable with abstraction (see Similarities and Block design), has a good understanding of the world around her (see Information, Vocabulary, Comprehension, Picture completion), and relative "freedom from distractibility" (see Arithmetic and Object assembly), but she has miserable visual-motor integration (see Coding). Her verbal strengths are easy to spot, but her spatial conceptual ability does not show in the Performance score, which was lowered by her poor coding.

It is informative to rearrange WISC-R scores according to the student's own mean score, figuring any deviation of plus or minus three (± 3) as significant. Making the individual's own set of clusters highlights strengths and weaknesses. Miranda's show the following patterns:

MARKEDLY LOW	IN THE MIDDLE	MARKEDLY HIGH
Coding 5	Arithmetic: 11	Information: 14
	Picture arrangement: 12	Vocabulary: 15
	Digit span: 12	Comprehension: 15
	Object assembly: 12	Block design: 15
	Picture completion: 13	Similarities: 18

What do we learn? There are many more significant strengths than weaknesses, and the strengths are all in conceptual and acquired knowledge tasks, auguring well for learning new information and enjoying intellectual work.

Much early schoolwork requires memory and speed, and Miranda's rote memory work is only slightly above the national norm (see Arithmetic and Digit span). Her high conceptual levels, however, will help her develop her own compensatory strategies. The analysis of clusters points an imperative finger at the need to shore up the weakness in Coding, a debilitating problem, dangerous to both self-concept and output if neglected. A numerical grouping such as the one here paints a clear picture. Thank you, Miranda.

"Memory-Myra," whose full-scale score puts her in the Superior category, scores high in the mechanical and memory subtests of Coding, Digit span, and Arithmetic. Her middle scores are in acquired information subtests, and her low scores are in conceptual areas. She was a strong student in the early years of school: she learned sight words, memorized number facts, and recited the capitals of all the states. But when the curriculum shifted to abstract thinking, she began to sink through no fault of her own. Her parents, and some teachers, assumed her full-scale IQ certified giftedness and needed to be let down gently.

Edward's conceptual scores are high, but his scores for acquired information are low. This was the tip-off to an auditory processing problem and hitherto undetected hearing loss.

Full-scale, verbal, and performance are the traditional ways to categorize WISC-R scores. Bannatyne[3] suggests an additional way to interpret them by allocating subtests to the following three categories:

SPATIAL	SEQUENTIAL	CONCEPTUAL
Object assembly	Digit span	Comprehension
Block design	Coding	Similarities
Picture completion	Picture arrangement	Vocabulary

Bannatyne shows that the subtest scores of many smart kids with school problems cluster together within these categories. Here are some examples.

Mickey does well in math and science and is a good athlete, but his language weakness shows in reading comprehension and trouble with figures of speech. He scores high on spatial tasks, and low on sequential ones.

Conversely, Adam, the potential English major who does poorly in math, scores high in sequential/conceptual work and low in spatial tasks.

By adding two more categories, Acquired information and

Memory, to Bannatyne's trio we could contrast acquired information with conceptual manipulation, and conceptual manipulation with rote memory.

Dr. Jane Holmes, a neuropsychologist at Children's Hospital in Boston and adjunct faculty member at the Harvard Medical School, points out another cluster. She calls it the "green beans phenomenon."

Numerous children with difficulty in concentration, selective attention, and rote memory show clustering scores in Arithmetic, Coding, and Digit span. She and her colleagues became tired of saying the whole phrase "low in Arithmetic, Coding, and Digit span"; abbreviated it to Ari., Co., D.S.; and then realized that the French word for green beans is *haricots* (pronounced "arico"). Because children with this pattern jump around a lot, she connected green and jumping beans and nicknamed them "Green Beans." Thank you, Dr. Holmes, for one more pattern. Meet Big Boy Smith.

VERBAL	PERFORMANCE
Information: 16	Picture completion: 15
Similarities: 19	Picture arrangement: 13
Arithmetic: 10	Block design: 13
Vocabulary: 19	Objection assembly: 13
Comprehension: 19	Coding: 7
Digit span: 4	

Here are two conundrum kids' WISC-R scores for the reader to interpret and recategorize.

ICHABOD Q. STUDENT
Full-Scale: 139

VERBAL: 135	PERFORMANCE: 135
Information: 15	Picture completion: 19
Similarities: 18	Picture arrangement: 16
Arithmetic: 17	Block design: 19
Vocabulary: 13	Objection assembly: 16
Comprehension: 14	Coding: 5
Digit span: 13	

Where is Ichabod strong, where is he weak, what does he need, what academic situations will present problems, and where will he shine?

JOE X
Full-Scale: 113

VERBAL: *125*	PERFORMANCE: *96*
Information: 13	Picture completion: 10
Similarities: 15	Picture arrangement: 8
Arithmetic: 12	Block design: 10
Vocabulary: 12	Objection assembly: 12
Comprehension: 19	Coding: 8
Digit span: 8	Mazes: 15

See what happens when we recategorize Joe's scores as Bannatyne suggests:

SPATIAL	CONCEPTUAL
Object assembly: 12	Comprehension: 19
Block design: 10	Similarities: 15
Picture completion: 10	Mazes: 15
	Vocabulary: 12

SEQUENTIAL
Digit span: 8
Picture arrangement: 8
Coding: 8

It is easy to see where Joe X is strong, where he is weak, and why he thought he was stupid in the early years of school.

Familiarity with these patterns is useful for educational planning as well as understanding of current function. We might flip the coin, using the scores and categories prescriptively as well as descriptively to hypothesize that a student whose scores are high in one area will be good at particular types of studies.

For example, if a class is going to be studying the exploration of the American West, a student with a high score in Block design and a low score in Vocabulary might make a significant contribution by creating and interpreting relief maps, increasing his vocabulary along the way as he uses words to describe what he is trying to depict. He can use his spatial conceptual strength to shore up his linguistic weakness.

A well-administered WISC-R, interpreted in several different ways, is a solid foundation first for understanding and then for helping a smart kid with school problems. As this student moves through school, it is wise to get another. The first one sets the stage; subsequent ones show consistency in pattern and evidence of growth. An eleventh grader with two or three in his file has solid ground on which to base curriculum choices and college decisions.

FRAMES OF MIND: THE THEORY OF MULTIPLE INTELLIGENCES

If no standardized test accompanies Gardner's book and there is no curriculum syllabus, why does it deserve our space and time?

First, the interested reader deserves access to the neuroanatomical reasons for learning styles. These patterns, and the intelligences Gardner describes, are precisely those that we have explored in the students whose stories are in this book.

Second, he explains from a medical and scientific standpoint that unusual talents can be hidden and damaged by single-dimensional educational values.

Third, this is one of those rare works that draws together literature, high-level scientific research, and human understanding.

Fourth, the parent or educator who develops the student's master file, plans his curriculum, and attends to both talents and weaknesses needs to describe the student in light of Gardner's intelligences. This view adds an important dimension.

Throughout *Frames of Mind*, the author's language is so precise that I have frequently quoted it, because it is hard to paraphrase without blunting his points.

Impatient with the limiting quality of existing methods of measuring intelligence, and moving well beyond current Western ideas of what intelligence is, Gardner expands to seven the number of separate "intelligences" that should be explored in evaluating individual potential and achievement.

> I argue that there is persuasive evidence for the existence of several relatively autonomous human intellectual competences, abbreviated hereafter as "human intelligences.". . . In ordinary life these intelligences typically work in harmony, and so their autonomy may be invisible. But when the appropriate observational lenses are donned, the peculiar nature of each intelligence emerges with sufficient (and often surprising) clarity. . . . I have reviewed evidence from a large and hitherto unrelated group of sources: studies of prodigies, gifted individuals, brain-damaged patients, idiots savants, normal children, normal adults, experts in different kinds of work, and individuals from diverse cultures.[4]

Gardner describes each of the seven intelligences scientifically, historically, and anecdotally. They are linguistic intelligence, musical intelligence, logical-mathematical intelligence, spatial intelligence, bodily-kinesthetic intelligence, and interpersonal and intrapersonal intelligences.

LINGUISTIC INTELLIGENCE

Readers of Chapter 6 will feel at home in this section. A Gilbert Islander, Lillian Hellman, T. S. Eliot, Robert Graves, and Stephen Spender are the voices that summon us into this chapter. Through them we are privy to the arduous process of searching and sorting that results in the perfect metaphor or the pleasing phrase.

Gardner explores four major uses of language: the rhetorical aspect whose purpose is persuasion, the mnemonic potential whose purpose is memory for items and methods, the role of language in explaining ideas and phenomena, and the uniquely human ability to use language to explain and reflect on its own activities.

These four functions of language depend on the linguistic foundations we explored in Chapter 6: gesture, labels, two words, articles and affixes, word order, and semantics. Gardner adds *pragmatics*, the uses to which language may be put.

He gives examples of high linguistic intelligence through the words and experiences of both budding and mature authors and demonstrates the influence of neurology on language through descriptions of the linguistic consequences of disturbance in various parts of the brain.

The relationship between human language and the auditory-oral tract receives considerable attention, both for itself alone and for its role in separating language from spatial forms of intelligence.

> My belief in the centrality of the auditory and oral elements in language has motivated my focus upon the poet as the user of language par excellence and my citation of the evidence from aphasia as a strong argument in favor of the autonomy of language. . . . Reading is invariably disturbed by injury to the language system, while, amazingly, this linguistic decoding capacity proves robust despite massive injury to the visual-spatial centers of the brain (p. 98).

MUSICAL INTELLIGENCE

Throughout this book, we have met many smart kids who have both school problems and musical talent. Gardner believes that musical intelligence, in a performer, a composer, or an active listener, is a separate entity, neither part of language nor part of mathematics.

The core components of music, as Gardner explains them, are pitch, rhythm, and timbre. He points out that rhythm can exist independently of auditory competence. For example, deaf people can begin to comprehend music through feeling or watching rhythm. (As an aside, anyone interested in "visual music" should read Douglas Hofstadter's article in the July 1983 issue of *Scientific American*.) Through these, together and separately, music holds powerful sway over affect. Music can serve as a way of capturing feelings: "Of all the gifts with which individuals may be endowed, none emerges earlier than musical talent." "Except among children with unusual musical talent or exceptional opportunities, there is little further musical development after the school years begin." Although these observations have been made before, people concerned with conundrum kids cannot read them too frequently.

Gardner says,

> Investigators working with both normal and brain-damaged humans have demonstrated beyond a reasonable doubt that the processes and mechanisms subserving human music and language are distinctive from one another. . . . Whereas linguistic abilities are lateralized almost exclusively to the left hemisphere in normal right-handed individuals, the majority of musical capacities, including the central capacity of sensitivity to pitch, are localized in most normal individuals in the right hemisphere. . . . As the names promise *amusia* is a disorder distinct from *aphasia.* . . . What is really crucial is whether other abilities predictably occur together with music such that when musical ability is destroyed, so are the others. So far as I am aware, none of the claims with respect to musical breakdown suggest any systematic connection with other faculties such as linguistic, numerical or spatial processing: music seems, in this regard, *sui generis* (p. 118).

LOGICAL-MATHEMATICAL INTELLIGENCE

As is the case with musical intelligence, logical-mathematical intelligence appears early, and "the major work of most mathematicians is over by the age of twenty-five or thirty." The hallmark of this intelligence is a love of dealing with abstraction, asking questions, identifying problems, and finding ways of solving them. Throughout this book we have seen instance after instance of gifted mathematicians who were struggling in school. To jeopardize their gifts is criminal.

SPATIAL INTELLIGENCE

Many smart kids with school problems have unusual spatial function, either in talent or in difficulty.

Spatial intelligence, unlike language, music, and the abstractions of mathematics, is tied to the objects in the real world. People use spatial intelligence to identify objects whose positions have been changed or rotated, to orient themselves, and to navigate their way. Spatial intelligence is fundamental to sculpture, architecture, painting, navigation, and some kinds of scientific thinking. Reflecting Gardner's interest in abnormal functioning is his documentation of what happens when parts of the brain controlling spatial intelligence are damaged. Here as in other instances he makes his case for the existence of a discrete intelligence by describing its absence as well as its presence.

Then Gardner takes us on one of his philosophical vaults. "In my view the metaphoric ability to discern similarities across diverse domains derives in many instances from a manifestation of spatial intelligence. For example, when gifted essayist Lewis Thomas draws analogies between micro-organisms and an organized society, depicts the sky as a membrane, or describes mankind as a heap of earth, he is capturing in words a kind of resemblance that may have occurred to him initially in spatial form." This reminds me of the irony of the physically clumsy fairy-tale writer in Chapter 4.

Gardner concludes this section with cheerful news indeed:

> My own view is that each form of intelligence has a natural life course: while logical-mathematical thought proves fragile later in life and bodily-kinesthetic intelligence is also at risk, at least certain aspects of visual and spatial knowledge prove robust, especially in individuals who have practiced them regularly throughout their lives. There is a sense of the whole, a gestalt sensitivity, which is central in spatial intelligence and which seems to be a reward for aging. . . . Perhaps wisdom draws on this sensitivity to patterns, forms and whole (p. 204).

BODILY-KINESTHETIC INTELLIGENCE

Marcel Marceau, the noted mime, is the guide Gardner selects to usher us into an exploration of bodily-kinesthetic intelligence. "I treat these two capacities—control of one's bodily motions and the capacity to handle objects skillfully—as the cores of bodily intelligence." His exemplars, then, go beyond the predictable athletes, dancers, and hunters to include artisans, instrumentalists, inventors, and actors. Fine-motor skills rank alongside gross-motor in this discussion. Readers of Chapters 3 and 4 in particular will resonate to Gardner's words.

And just as the reader feels a subversive inclination to say, "Wait a minute, maybe this isn't a separate intelligence at all," Gardner says,

> Buttressing my claim for a separate bodily intelligence, it turns out that injuries to those zones of the left hemisphere that are dominant for motor activity can produce selective impairment. Neurologists speak of the *apraxias*, a set of related disorders, in which an individual physically capable of carrying out a set of motor sequences, and cognitively capable of understanding a request to do so, is nonetheless unable to carry them out . . . limb-kinetic *apraxia*, ideamotor *apraxia* or ideational *apraxia* (p. 212).

Tucked in the middle of the text is this simple statement with profound implications for educators: "The fact that some individuals prove skilled at this kind of learning, but that it is accorded a low priority, may help explain why many promising young performers and dancers in our culture become alienated from school at an early age." This is a group the educational system can ill afford to lose. The reader may remember this when meeting Peter Boal, the dancer whose story appears in Chapter 10.

INTERPERSONAL AND INTRAPERSONAL INTELLIGENCES

Gardner explores personal intelligences from the points of view of both interpersonal and intrapersonal life, saying, "The core capacity here is access to one's feeling life."

"I feel that these forms of knowledge are of tremendous importance in many, if not all societies in the world—forms that have, however, tended to be ignored or minimized by nearly all students of cognition." (He footnotes a bouquet to Wechsler.)

He describes the development of the personal intelligences in the infant, the child aged two to five, the school-age child, and the periods of middle childhood, adolescence, and maturity. The section on the school-age child is particularly clear and poignant as he describes the growing sense of self that is rooted in "I am what I can do." His points here are in close agreement with Erikson's and tie in closely with many of the case histories at the conclusion of each of the chapters in this book.

Gardner is the originator of a term that should be used in education and in the study of intelligence. He talks of people as being "at promise" for certain kinds of tasks.

> What recent research has shown, virtually incontrovertibly, is that whatever differences may initially appear, early intervention and consistent training can play a decisive role in determining the individual's ultimate level of performance. Conversely, and perhaps more obviously, even the most innately talented individual will founder without some positive supporting environment. Discovery of an individual's inherent intellectual profile, which I believe may be possible, need not serve, then, as a means of pigeonholing the individual or of consigning him to an intellectual junk-heap; rather, such discovery should provide a means for assuring that every individual has available to him as many options as possible as well as the potential to achieve competence in whatever fields he and his society deem important (p. 116).

Although Gardner's view of intelligences has not yet become a part of formal evaluation procedures, it adds a critically important way of understanding human beings. Intuitively, clinically, and intellectually Gardner's assessment rings true. To the mind's ear, it is like the sound of a ting on fine crystal.

PRINCIPLES OF GOOD PRACTICE

When a smart kid has school problems, educators and parents should review the master file, bearing in mind the intelligences Gardner cites and making additions to the file accordingly. They should review test scores, arrange for an individual evaluation, and study the results carefully, using some of the methods suggested in this chapter. If the test results do not ring true, it is important to probe further. A tester sees the student a few times; educators and parents see the student over a long period.

Familiarity with testing terminology, types of testing, and test interpretation frees educators and parents to ask better questions, understand the answers, and be full partners in planning what comes next.

Test numbers should work *for* the educators and parents. After all, considerable time, effort, and money (even if it's the taxpayer's) has gone into accumulating them. They should do more than sit on a piece of paper or rest in a file drawer.

Insofar as possible, concerned adults, with the help of the educational overseer, should try to arrange for instruction that harmonizes with the student's preferred method of learning.

The student deserves to know his own patterns of strengths and weaknesses and benefits from learning test results in an age-appropriate way. Starting with strengths and their implications, the adult can move to weaknesses, always mentioning the available strategies for overcoming them. Self-knowledge and self-acceptance lead to healthy self-concept.

A CASE HISTORY: JODY

Jody is a bright eighth grader with a poor academic record. From early childhood he has been physically agile and daring, impatient with "scaredy-cats," eager to learn, and reluctant to be put on the spot. His strongly developed social sense (*personal intelligence* in Gardner's words) and knack for telling jokes have kept Jody in the "in-group" all along despite academic failure.

In kindergarten, Jody missed many school days because of recurrent ear infections, flu, and his grandparents' offer to take the whole family on a three-week trip to Spain in April. "After all, it's only kindergarten," his parents said, so off they went.

Jody finally learned individual letter sounds in first grade, but he had trouble trying to blend them into words; by the time he got to the end he had forgotten the beginning, would try to start over, and became badly discouraged. One day he threw his book on the floor, saying, "This dumb book doesn't work." Sometimes he would try to make the other children laugh to distract attention from his own failures.

Although he had a fine innate sense of numbers and was accurate with money in his extracurricular life, numerals were almost as hard for him to manage as letters. He wrote them backward or out of sequence, writing 96 for 69 as often as he wrote *was* for *saw*. His teacher believed in compartmentalized language-arts instruction, teaching reading during one period, spelling in another, math in another, and handwriting twice a week. Once a week the children were asked to copy a poem from the board and illustrate it. Jody responded enthusiastically to hearing the poem, as well as to memorizing and reciting it, but, although his illustrations were lovely, his copying was awkward and inaccurate.

In second grade his seeming improvement in reading proved to be an illusion; Jody was memorizing the morning's selections by having another child read them to him on the bus ride to school. His behavior grew increasingly disruptive, and although the other children laughed at his jokes, his teacher was not amused. Jody began to apply his powerful social skills to intellectual tight spots.

In the middle of the year an assistant teacher arrived, a young woman finishing her graduate degree in learning disabilities who needed one more semester of student teaching to complete her requirements. She chose Jody for her case study. She reviewed his records, screened him for learning disabilities, and identified some specific weaknesses. From watching him in class she knew he was smart and decided he would profit from multisensory training. She began working with him individually, in the classroom, during the time the other children were doing their seat work. She arranged with the head teacher to excuse Jody from some of his regular seatwork requirements, because, of course, it would be ridiculous to penalize him for being given extra help. He bloomed.

Everything improved. Jody was a highly intelligent little boy whose brightness helped him learn the strategies she taught him, and, because they made sense and he could apply them right away, he absorbed them all and reached for more. By the end of the school year, he was reading on grade level, his numbers were well formed, he had memorized all his math facts, and he was considered "cured."

When he started third grade, everyone assumed that "the trouble" was like chicken pox: having had it once, he would be immune for life.

Jody's native intelligence, social skills, naturally competitive streak, and new but unsolidified academic skills supported him through the first part of third grade, but as January closed in, the curriculum shifted, and life did too. Jody tried to make his pen keep pace with his ideas, and his jokes. It wouldn't. He began to flounder. Because he had a new friend, one his teachers and parents disapproved of, his slide was attributed to the "evil companion" and his parents tried to break off the friendship.

By the middle of fourth grade Jody's family was told that he was sinking to the bottom of the class. They were worried, he was frightened (though he tried to conceal it), and his teacher thought he wasn't trying. They dropped him down to the lowest reading group and put him into a remedial spelling class twice a week during the time the others went to art.

His standardized testing showed a wide discrepancy: verbal aptitude in the ninety-fifth percentile, verbal achievement in the fifty-sixth; quantitative aptitude in the ninety-eighth percentile, achievement in the sixtieth.

Well-meaning people tried persuasion, threats, bribery, and withdrawal of privileges without success. In retrospect, his best time had been his half year with the graduate student, but real life isn't a one-on-one teaching/learning setup.

His parents agreed with the school's suggestion to get an individual evaluation. In addition to some psychological testing that showed a wobbly self-concept, he was given a WISC-R. The results of the WISC-R were remarkably similar to Miranda's. In other words, he was very high conceptually (a cluster of 19s) and very low mechanically (a 5, 6, 7, and 8). His rote memory was weak, and his visual-motor integration both slow and imprecise. He impressed the examiner as being humorous and self-protective: "He will do beautifully in life but suffer through school."

The educational overseer, in this instance the learning specialist, scheduled two meetings: one with Jody and his parents, one with his current teacher, his next year's teachers, and his academic adviser. Together they discussed which subjects were likely to be difficult and laid out their teaching plans, incorporating many of the ideas that have appeared throughout this book.

Jody has access to a word processor for his written work, he uses manipulatives as well as paper and pencil for math, he is getting spelling help from a tutor twice a week at home in the afternoons, and he is working alongside his classmates.

Although the meetings took some time, they required a lot less than would otherwise have been spent discussing the whys and whats of a failure. By involving Jody himself in the program planning, they ensured his cooperation and gave him a feeling of being an agent of his own destiny rather than an object of fate.

Jody feels smart. He will never outgrow his learning style, but he has made friends with it.

9

MATURATION AND HIGHER EDUCATION

GETTING IT ALL TOGETHER

Last week a friend invited me into her darkroom to watch her develop a roll of film. I had been with her when she took the pictures, but because I hadn't been looking through the camera, I didn't know what shots she had or what angles she had used. We had been at a beach picnic, so I assumed we would see sand, water, blankets, and people. I could anticipate the general ideas but not the specifics. The outside of the roll of film certainly gave no clue.

As she did her alchemy with solutions and pans, images began to appear, general patterns of light and dark first, then human shapes, then human features. The negative, showing black where there would be white and space where there would be shape, was ready to print. Looking at the positive print, I could identify the same face under a hat, in the sun, in the shade, scowling, smiling, close-up or farther away. Yet, even though those images had been on the film the whole time, I couldn't tell what they were until the developing process was complete. The same is often true of the student between sixteen and twenty-one.

Intellectually and emotionally these are years of maturation and negative or positive consolidation. Erik Erikson calls the internal struggle of this age "identity versus role confusion." In the adolescent, the outcome of the "crisis" of identity versus role confusion is weighted by the outcomes of the previous crises. The child with a positive resolution of basic trust versus mistrust is well positioned for the pull between autonomy versus shame and doubt. A positive ratio for autonomy predisposes a healthy outcome in the push me-pull you of initiative versus guilt and industry versus inferiority. The influence of these cumulative ratios touches the entire course of the individual's adult life, sometimes treacherously. In the smart kid's journey through school, he may have accumulated shame and doubt, inferiority, guilt, and role confusion. In the most solemn sense of the phrase, this is a matter of life and death.

Adolescent suicide is increasing at an alarming rate. Reports submitted to the Senate Judiciary Juvenile Justice Subcommittee in October 1984 say that "suicide is the third-leading cause of death among 15–24 year olds, whose suicide rate rose dramatically from 1960 to 1980. In 1980 one of five suicides was a 15–24 year old male. . . . The experts said teen-agers with family troubles, low grades and overly high expectations were more prone to suicide, as are drug and alcohol abusers, those who lost a friend, and those trying to adjust to a new town or country."[1]

We know from the traits explored in Chapter 1 that smart kids set extremely high standards for themselves, have heightened perceptions, and are keenly aware of patterns. Smart kids with school problems feel tremendous pain from the gap between their expectations, their own ideals, and the work they actually produce or the grades they receive. The pressure from this pain is sometimes unbearable.

Although the pressure sometimes comes from adults, often it is self-generated. The pressures vary: to be accepted by the group, to do well enough to avoid being noticed, to give birth to an artistic or intellectual dream, to escape the ridicule of an unsympathetic teacher, to please a beloved teacher. Whatever the reason, self-generated pressure to close the gap between external demands and internal capacities is a force powerful enough to kill.

When the combination of high intelligence and school problems brings despair, we see throwaway kids who shrivel. When it generates violence we see throwaway kids who boomerang.

Studies such as those by Hogenson, and Hernnstein and Wilson, show the correlation between learning disabilities and delinquency, both urban and rural. It makes sense that the smart kid who cannot get what others are getting from society (and a student's society is his school) will either be angry at himself or at the successful others and the institutions that confer that success. Studies of inmates in penal institutions point over and over again to the high rate of illiteracy and the correlation between illiteracy and crime, also pointing to the high level of abstract intelligence in master criminals. In adolescents the combination of high intelligence with school failure is a loaded gun.

In less dramatic situations that bring neither physical death nor incarceration, other kinds of death occur: the death of concentration and the death of hope.

What kills concentration in the adolescent? The same processes we explored at length in Chapter 7. Hope? The future can seem bleak to the smart adolescent with school problems he doesn't understand. He needs explanations of why schoolwork is hard, reassurances of help, an internalized locus of control, and some power of choice. But there are happy fulfilled adults who used to be smart kids with school problems.

A marketing manager in New York has risen quickly to very responsible positions because in her boss's words, "She'll sell the world to the world." She says of her school career, "I hated doing all that bookwork. I was a slow reader and I wanted to get on with things, not sit inside chained to a desk reading about them. I loved athletics (figuring out strategies as well as physical movement), being out-of-doors, and being with people." Asked how she survived as well as she did, she said,

My family never bugged me about grades. I had lots of opportunity to do the things I liked after school, and the summers were wonderful.
When I was sixteen I went on a five-week National Outdoor

Leadership School trip in Montana. I learned I was a good decision maker. I also knew I enjoyed being with people and discovered I could get along with many different kinds. On a trip like that you learn to trust yourself as well as others. I even went on to college, although I had sworn I'd never crack a book after I graduated from high school. I loved college. It was for ideas instead of for memorizing. People I respected thought my ideas were good. When I got my first real job, I started to believe what my parents had said all along: "You're one smart kid!"

Higher education can open new worlds or be a tunnel. College-bound students, even those with impeccable academic credentials, face bewildering decisions. They must ask themselves

What courses should I select to get or maintain a good grade-point average?

Should I risk lowering my GPA by taking a course I may not be good at?

How many times should I take the SAT?

If I take it several times will my scores go up or down?

Should I take an SAT coaching course?

If I do, will it really raise my score?

If I take one, should I admit it to my school and prospective colleges?

How do I know whether I'm college material?

How many colleges should I apply to?

How do I select a long shot, a likely shot, and a sure shot?

How should I present myself?

Should I choose extracurricular activities with an eye to what looks good on an application?

Supposing I get into college, will I survive academically, emotionally, socially?

If these issues are perplexing to students with strong academic records, how doubly perplexing they are for smart kids with school problems. To help them make good decisions about higher education, we need to explore issues and plans.

ISSUES

As we did with testing, let's begin by clarifying some terms.

Grade-point average. A grade-point average (GPA) is just what it says, an average. It may raise up low scores and flatten high ones. Conundrum kids have profiles more like a cross section of the Alps than a side view of gentle hills. A poor or failing grade in one subject pulls down the grade-point average, leaving no place to show an outstandingly high grade. Our students frequently do poorly on tests and exams while doing beautifully in three-dimensional, hands-on work. But as noted throughout the book, art, music, sports, leadership, photography, school club activities, these "extras," are seldom factored into the GPA. Because of this, it is virtually impossible for a smart kid with school problems to have a high GPA, a score that is included on a college application and is supposed to be evidence of a student's ability to handle academic work.

SAT and achievement tests. The Scholastic Aptitude Test (SAT) is a multiple-choice, group-administered, timed, pencil-and-paper test that purports to measure scholastic aptitude. Critics, whose numbers are increasing to include college admissions officers, see it as one indicator of a student's ability to manage course work in the first year or two of college but not as an accurate measure of aptitude. The difference between GPA and SAT is the difference between evidence and prediction.

Students with many of the intelligences Gardner cites may do poorly on the SAT. The student who reads slowly may not finish; one who reads inaccurately may misperceive key words. The ruminative student may think about individual questions and forget to race through. A brilliant student may think beyond the test designers and be unable to find a palatable answer in the proffered multiple choices. In addition, the setting and the format of the SAT are anxiety-provoking to many students. Throughout this book we have seen those who think clearly in class, contribute to class discussions, and enjoy learning who score poorly on timed, standardized pencil-and-paper tasks. Although, as we will see in a later section of this chapter, the SAT hammerlock is gradually being broken, for now, many college applicants feel they must submit this test score. We shall explore SAT coaching courses shortly.

Achievement tests, although presenting some of the same problems as the SAT, are fairer. They do not pretend to measure aptitude; they give a student a chance to show what he has learned in the courses he has taken. The residual dyslexic, the slow or inaccurate reader may still have trouble managing a large amount of material in a small amount of time, but the smart kid with school problems generally finds it easier to do well here than on the SAT.

If SAT scores don't do the job, what are more reliable predictors of success in higher education and beyond?

Douglas Heath, sociologist, psychologist, and professor at Haverford College in Pennsylvania, has studied this question extensively. His findings, garnered from teaching his own students, from wide reading and research, and from a longitudinal study in which he interviewed his subjects at three different times, are particularly encouraging for smart kids with school problems.

Heath's longitudinal studies show little correlation between high scores on standardized tests early in life and feelings of fulfillment and success in later life. He finds that high scorers on timed, pencil-paper tests are more likely to experience dissatisfaction, frustration, intellectual atrophy, and a high instance of mental health problems. This is no wish list from a flower child: these are the research findings of one who revels in intellect.

Using his longitudinal study as a backdrop, Heath goes on to project which qualities will bring satisfaction to adult lives in the year 2000 and beyond. He says that as the nature of work changes, and as traditional sex roles lose the rigidity of their former boundaries, interpersonal skills, managerial skills, and skills in juggling and sorting information will assume increasing importance, as will the ability to be a self-educating person and to sustain intellectual curiosity.

According to Heath, the qualities found in, and valued by, people who were functioning at a high level of success, who felt fulfilled, and whose emotional health was very sound were sense of humor, self-confidence, enthusiasm and energy, honesty, self-discipline, intuition, empathy, ability to be a good listener, self-aware-ness, persistence, and willingness to take risks.

What about conundrum kids? We know from our own expe-rience and from the preceding chapters in this book that, in addition to areas of vulnerability, our students frequently have extraordinary interpersonal sensitivity, open-mindedness, persistence, and ability to get an idea across and are divergent thinkers who welcome ques-tions as well as answers. They are alert to patterns and take delight in testing out new ones. Having been bruised themselves, they are often tolerant. Having had to struggle, they have self-awareness. Having survived, they probably have humor. In short, if not dis-couraged by failure, they have in abundance the qualities Douglas Heath's studies show to be the ones that really count in college and later in life.

Other voices join with Heath's. Former Yale president A. B. Giamatti wrote a letter to the incoming freshman class in 1981. He said,

> I believe a liberal education is an education in the root meaning of "liberal"—"liber"—"free"—the liberty of the mind free to explore itself, to draw itself out, to connect with other minds and spirits in the quest for truth. Its goal is to train the whole person to be at once intellectually discerning and humanly flexible, tough-minded and openhearted; to be responsive to the new and responsible for the values that make us civilized. It is to teach us to meet what is new and different with reasoned judgment and humanity. A liberal education is an education for freedom, the freedom to assert the liberty of the mind to make itself new for the others it cherishes.[2]

Theodore Sizer, former dean of the Harvard School of Edu-cation and author of *Horace's Compromise: The Dilemma of the American High School*, regrets what he considers the national "col-lection of schools in pastel colors" and decries their vernacular of donation: "we give courses," "we deliver services," "we offer." "High schools must respect adolescents more and patronize them less. The best respect is high expectations for them, and a level of account-ability more adult in its demand than childlike. We should expect them to learn more while being taught less. Their personal engagement with their own learning is crucial; adults cannot 'give' them an education."

The common threads linking Heath, Giamatti, and Sizer with Gardner, Erikson, Seligman, and many other voices in this book are the importance of active involvement, willingness to take risks, self-knowledge, and self-respect.

Three particular personal qualities in some high-scoring students augur poorly for success in higher education and fulfillment in life thereafter: passivity, dependence on high scores for self-esteem, and premature or pseudo-sophistication.

Real learning is aggressive exploration. Passive absorption of predigested ideas may permit tidy performance on a test or term paper, but it will generate few original discoveries.

In exploring dependence on high scores, Heath discusses the student accustomed to As and high scores on standardized tests. Often these students, according to Heath, enter college with their goals established. They have already determined what they will study, their class rank, where they will go to graduate school, what salary will buy them the life-style they have selected, how to go about earning that sum of money, and how to stay on the top of the pile.

At each step up, success is harder to capture because the pyramid narrows. But the student whose identity is bound up in grade-point average can't abandon the chase for high grades without risking annihilation. The pressure intensifies, placing iron bands around the student's intellect at just the time it should be expanding.

Premature or pseudo-sophistication is as restrictive as dependence on high scores. It is a mask that controls the wearer.

Between the ages of sixteen and twenty, a blessed phenomenon may occur. Some troublesome aspects of the student's learning style may simply dissolve through maturation. The young child's developmental readiness for school is well charted: metaphorically and actually he loses his baby teeth and steps up to a new level. A less-documented developmental shift often occurs in late adolescence. Educators, parents, and students who are aware of this possibility can avoid premature rejection of higher education.

Betsy had been plagued by poor spelling throughout her early years of school. She never checked her words against a dictionary because, she said, "How do I know which ones to check? They all look right to me, and if I think about it too long, none of them look right." During her sophomore year of college, she suddenly knew which words to check, and many of her habitual errors fell away. Never again did she write that she was "re-nude." She was renewed!

Andrew who had avoided reading anything but assignments and the sports page discovered spy stories and tales of horror. When his mother took his jacket to the cleaner recently, she was amazed to find a John Le Carré paperback in one pocket and a volume of Edgar Allan Poe in the other. When she returned them to him, he said, "Thanks. I've been looking all over for those books. I've got to find out what happens next."

All of a sudden, Sam could identify a main idea in a story and do word problems in math. Terms such as *area, ratio, volume,* and *mass* became friendly words in addition to being concepts he had understood intuitively since his childhood block-building days.

Amelia, a college freshman, has discovered child psychology. Finally free of the foreign language and algebra courses that had been torture to her, she carries her textbooks as badges of honor and reads them eagerly. Her smiles are ready and her contribution to the professional field may very well be outstanding.

Jackson can concentrate. That simple three-word sentence is a miracle. He thumped, zapped, rocked, wiggled, bumped, and irritated his way through grades one through ten and gradually calmed down in the middle of eleventh grade. In the days when many young men, particularly boys with school problems, served a post–high school stint in the military, people would notice their new maturity, saying, "Soldiering brought that boy around." And although uniforms, structure, and responsibility undoubtedly played a part in the maturational process, there were other internal battles being fought and victories being won.

Even though the issues are complicated, the conundrum kid may do as well as or better than problem-free students if he has acquired self-knowledge, reinforced self-respect, received good compensatory training, and nourished his gifts and talents.

What an irony it is that the person who ultimately stands to make great good use of higher-level education may be the one who initially has great trouble gaining access to it.

PLANS

Getting from here to there requires good use of test scores, maturity in three areas, and appropriate choices.

TEST SCORES

How much weight do standardized test scores actually carry, what factors outweigh or counteract them, what about coaching courses, and are there some shifting patterns?

How much weight does an SAT score carry? In October 1984 William C. Hiss, dean of admissions at Bates College, wrote,

> Three recent efforts can help us address these questions. First, our staff has just completed a three year study of the relation between statistical predictors and personal qualities under a grant from The National Association of College Admissions Counselors. . . . Second we sent a questionnaire on SAT coaching to 100 colleges . . . 74 were returned: 41 private colleges, 21 private universities, 6 state universities and the rest anonymous or unsure what to call themselves. . . . Finally we can draw upon our own discussions and talk with guidance counselors.

The findings point to a diminished reliance on SAT scores and an increased reliance on the combined achievement test scores, written work, and a transcript reflecting a demanding course load. "Many deans sensed some swingback in high school transcripts toward tougher courses. I recall seeing three courses on one transcript with the bewildering titles 'Rocks and Ropes,' 'Things Russian,' and 'Things British.' This, all agreed, is often the kiss of death in the admissions office."

Personal qualities matter very much.

We found that a number of self-rated personal qualities added significantly to our formula for prediction of grade-point average. "Energy and initiative," for example, is often as strong as any single statistical measure in predicting variation in grade point average. Many other personal evaluations . . . creativity, independence, widening of perspectives, insight and humor . . . added to the prediction formula. . . . To allow anxiety over SATs, and sustained, intense coaching to set the tone of the junior and senior years is to misdirect seriously one's energies. These personal qualities, and not simply the standardized testing, are an integral part of being a good student and therefore a good candidate for top colleges. . . . Many felt that the SATs, if they do not control school curricula, very often distract a student's attention . . , and thus real growth as a student . . . from those factors that do control admission decisions: tough courses, good grades, hard thinking, good writing and significant other achievements.[3]

Where does this leave a conundrum kid? It diminishes the influence of the SAT, on which many of our students do poorly for the reasons cited earlier. It gives more power to the achievement tests on which our students may do well, particularly if they take advantage, where necessary, of the options for nonroutine administration of those tests. It gives our student a chance to demonstrate his intellectual power through written work and verbal expression, at which he may excel if he has received the kind of training and help suggested in this book. It puts the question of GPA in good perspective; a transcript that shows high performance in physics, algebra, and precalculus with lower performance in language is an accurate picture of a learning profile, showing areas of a student's interest and willingness to tackle tough subject matter. It indicates active involvement in learning.

Someone may argue, that's all very well to say, but does it really happen that way, and if an SAT score is going to be part of the record, why not take a coaching course? If they seem to work, why not get the benefit of the doubt? If they don't help, what harm has been done? If the school doesn't recommend it, why not just do it on the side without telling anyone?

Dorothy Dillon, assistant head of Kent Place School, Summit, New Jersey, wrote an article citing the research on actual gains from coaching courses and the time/numerical gain ratio involved.

For example, eight hours of mathematics coaching is needed for a 10 point gain, nineteen hours for 20 points, the equivalent of two additional problems on the SAT. In the verbal area, twelve hours of coaching will yield a 10 point gain, 57 hours a 20 point gain or the difference of three correct answers. . . . Carrying these figures farther, we find that 300 hours would be necessary for a 31 point verbal gain and another 300 hours for a 53 point gain on the mathematics section.[4]

If the ability to use time well is one important predictor of success and fulfillment, what does this use of time suggest?

Is it a worthwhile trade-off to take this much time for possible numerical gain on one single instrument? What gets pinched or cancelled in such a regimen? Very often it is the music, the art, the photography, the athletics—in short, the talent—that must be sacrificed. Ridiculous! In later life, once college admissions decisions are history, no one will know, much less care, what an individual got on the SAT. Dillon continues, "As far as college admissions officers are concerned, the solid commitment in time to a hobby or job or homework has far more influence than any small gain in SAT points obtained by hours away from constructive pursuits."

There are some practical guidelines to giving a student the best possible shot at his best potential score. Dillon lays them out clearly:

We need to let our students know what the SAT is all about, give them sample tests, let them practice analogies and antonyms, go over their PSAT [Preliminary Scholastic Aptitude Test] performance, and share with them the College Board booklet "Taking the SAT." . . . We must take the initiative in informing our parents and students about the results of research on the impact of coaching for the SAT, as follows.

They can expect without any review an average SAT score gain of about 18 points on the verbal and 15–20 points on the mathematics section between junior and senior year.

The expected gain varies with the initial score. For a

score of 700, a decrease of 7 points is expected; for an initial score of 500, an increase of 7 points; for a 400 score, plus 18 points; and for an initial score of 300 an increase of about 36 points.

In schools where students take advanced mathematics courses, the effect of coaching is negligible, even though the mathematics section of the SAT has been shown to be more responsive to coaching than the verbal.

The analogies portion of the SAT is the most responsive to short-term instruction. Even brief practice and instruction in this area can help "highly able students."

"Familiarity with the test . . . should assist them in attaining scores better representative of their abilities."

Although the mathematics required to answer SAT-M items is intentionally limited to ninth and tenth grade content, mathematics beyond that level serves not only as review but also to facilitate answering SAT-M items.

The general level of developed ability largely determines a student's SAT mathematics or verbal score.

What does all this have to do with conundrum kids? We can consider what Dillon says about analogies and antonyms in the light of Chapter 6. We can listen to what she and Hiss, as well as other college admissions officers, say about the use of time and reflect on the gifted thinker's need to keep his talent alive. We can interpret Dillon's comments about natural gain in the light of what we know about spontaneous growth. We can consider the frequent discrepancy between doing well on standardized tests and possessing one or many of Gardner's intelligences. We can remember Heath's fulfilled and unfulfilled adults.

Words from these experienced professionals can free our students from hours of needless, pointless drudgery. The following shifting patterns will benefit our students, particularly as these procedures become standard practice.

At a growing number of competitive colleges a student may submit an extra achievement score in place of the SAT. Almost all colleges will accept the results of specially administered achievement tests. It may be untimed, a reader may read the questions aloud to the student, an amanuensis may write out the student's answers for him. College admissions officers say that the need for a special administration does not jeopardize the chance for acceptance. However, some college advisers suggest that the student take a regular form of the test the first time and request an untimed or special administration a second time. This demonstrates the student's willingness to tackle regular work and also allows for a comparison of the two scores.

In August 1984 the Harvard Business School announced that applicants would be asked to submit essays in place of standardized multiple-choice test answers. This is one more example of growing disaffection with standardized tests as predictors of ability and increasing reliance on *how* the student thinks, his ability to put his thoughts into words and organize words into clear exposition.

MATURITY IN THREE AREAS

How can we help smart kids with school problems develop social/emotional maturity, intellectual maturity, and linguistic maturity?

Social/emotional maturity. In reaching for social/emotional maturity, young people between the ages of sixteen and twenty struggle with internal and external ambiguities. They want desperately to conform; at the same time they long to glory in their own individuality. They must try to develop self-control at the same time they have no control over the ways their bodies change daily. Developing aesthetic and athletic tastes whet lifelong appetites, yet scholastic requirements may absorb most of the available time and energy. Students this age are subject to the societal pressures of drugs, alcohol, and sexual experimentation. Their decisions may have irreversible consequences, yet they receive conflicting advice from all sides: "Stick with your friends, be loyal, don't tattle." "Be responsible for the well-being of other people; caring for your friends means helping them stay out of trouble." "Real learning depends on the willingness to take risks." "Don't take chances." "Listen to the voice of experience." "Be your own person."

External forces set requirements: courses a student must take, hours of driver education to be completed, minimum balances for a checking account. These externals are superimposed at the same time the young adult needs the locus of control.

If these forces pull the trouble-free student in opposite directions, how do they affect a smart kid with school problems? He may be ahead of the game. If he has been raised with understanding and has received appropriate training, he may have already accepted himself as different and feel free to join others without disguise.

Social/emotional maturity comes from self-respect, self-knowledge, and an attribute that can be described in a four-letter word.

Self-respect grows from competence. A student who is competent in a particular field, academic or nonacademic, has something to dream about and hang on to. We need to remember Gardner's intelligences here. The very existence of an area of competence contributes stability to the adolescent's internal gyroscope.

Self-knowledge is what this book is all about. The student whose parents and teachers revere his strengths and understand his weaknesses experiences the acceptance that allows him to know himself without fear.

The four-letter word comes from the British neurologist Macdonald Critchley, who writes, "Lastly, and perhaps most important of all, a personality trait on the part of the patient: sheer dogged determination to succeed. . . . This is what American psychiatrists call ego-strength; in Great Britain we prefer the simpler term 'guts.' "[5]

Intellectual maturity. Intellectual maturity comes from exposure to ideas and from practice with comparison, abstraction, and patterns. These are magnets to original thinkers. Yet frequently the kids who are the subject of this book are pulled in the opposite direction by educational requirements for factual recitation and rote memory.

Conundrum kids need remedial training, but not at the expense of intellectual stimulation. As we have seen, they need opportunities to join music with words, words with art, art with music, art and music with dance, or dance with language, using their strengths to support weaknesses.

Linguistic maturity. Linguistic maturity grows with social/emotional and intellectual maturity as we saw in Chapter 6. The absorption and exercise of all the levels of language development foster linguistic maturity. Language is the verbal medium for explanation, request, permission, compromise, planning, anticipation, mediation, and congratulation. Our kid may need to dicker, tinker, barter, and tailor. He needs to be able to express his self-awareness and determination through language.

APPROPRIATE CHOICES

This section is written as a checklist for the student. Those who don't want to read it probably don't think they want to go to college. That's one choice. But it is unwise to rule out higher education because of fear of rejection. Choosing a college and being chosen are more than a petal-plucking game of "loves me, loves me not." Here are some steps to take to reduce the complications and increase your chances of being admitted and succeeding once you begin your college career.

Know your own interests and strengths. Pick a school that emphasizes those areas and disciplines. Don't pick a place for its prestigious name or because someone you know went there. This choice is for you.

Know your area of difficulty and what courses and requirements you will need to meet in order to graduate. Don't pick a college with a four-year language requirement if you can't do Latin.

Find out as much specific information about the college as possible. Learn its size, faculty/student ratio, and whether freshman and sophomore courses are taught by full-time professors, part-time visiting firemen, or graduate students. Although this is a generalization, smaller institutions are likely to be more responsive to individual needs. Graduate students are likely to be the most inflexible grade givers, and full-time professors have a deeper investment in the institution than visitors or graduate students. In addition to reading the catalogue, talk to students who have been there. If at all possible have a personal interview.

Lay your cards on the table. Be forthright about your strengths and open about your weaknesses. Don't try to slide in and patch things up afterward. You are shopping for an education just as much as colleges are increasingly shopping for students. The only way to expect a good fit is to be honest with one another from the very beginning. Show that you have self-knowledge and strength and that you have done your research thoroughly. This will mean much more to an admissions officer than a 10- or 20-point difference on an SAT.

Find out what extra help the college offers or would be willing to offer.   Susan Vogel, Ph.D., writes in her article "On Developing LD College Programs," "Depending on the stringency of the admissions requirements of the institution, there are some gifted LD students who are presently enrolled or who have completed degree programs in undergraduate, graduate and professional schools. There are far more however who are average or above in ability, and who, after a year in college, are in serious academic difficulty, have dropped out, or who have been asked to leave."[6] Ask whether the college offers study skills classes, tutors (and at what price), flexibility in core requirements, the possibility of waiving or trading a requirement, computers or word processors and training in how to use them, alternative formats for taking exams, curriculum specifically designed for dyslexics or different learners. There are some colleges designed specifically for the learning disabled; Curry College in Milton, Massachusetts, and Landmark College in Putney, Vermont, are two of many. (The Bibliography for Chapter 9 and the Resources list offers sources for finding others.) In addition, many art and engineering schools are now adding remedial and developmental reading and writing programs to their offerings because many of their most spatially gifted students are deficient in this area. Don't be embarrassed to inquire.

Get your study habits well organized ahead of time.   They won't develop spontaneously. It's hard to catch up once you get behind. The principles will stand you in good stead all your life. See the section on Principles of Good Practice for specifics, and the Resources list for references.

Choose with an eye to recreation time too.   Don't put yourself into a situation in which bare survival will consume all your time and in which success is a question mark even when you are working your hardest. Save time for nurturing your strengths, for friends, for fun, and even for a little frivolity.

Although this type of educational planning is complicated, it represents the ability to identify and work out an intricate pattern.   In and of itself, this is an extremely valuable life skill and one at which conundrum kids, with their alertness to pattern, may excel.

PRINCIPLES OF GOOD PRACTICE

Consult the master file and add to it. Consult with your overseer. Keep the file up to date with evidence of talent as well as admissions of weakness. If it is an accumulation of many years it will be a real help to you. If you have a summer job or an after-school job or have done some volunteer work, be sure to get a letter from your boss or supervisor when the job ends. Put it in your record.

Plan your courses with an eye to balancing your strong and weak areas. If you are a slow reader or a residual dyslexic, do not take a reading course in Tolstoy and Dostoevsky in the same semester as philosophy and world history. Spread them out.

Be flexible in your planning and be willing to bargain. Take tough courses one at a time in a January term or over the summer.

Follow the study skills suggestions outlined by Milton Academy in conjunction with Harvard University, those outlined by the Forman School, those in the paperback book *Study Smarts,* and those outlined in the articles in *The Journal of Learning Disabilities.* Although the sources are as different as can be, the principles remain constant. (See Resources list). Some specifics follow.

Organize your belongings, your materials, your time, and your obligations. Keep a calendar with dates assignments are due. Hang it above your desk.

Transcribe your lecture notes daily. This will help you keep a tidy notebook and will also serve as a double review.

Develop a note-taking shorthand for high-frequency phrases.

Have a separate notebook for each course. Keep all notebooks in one backpack or briefcase.

Discuss your needs with your professors the first day of the semester. Do not wait until you are floundering.

Sit in the front row away from your friends. Keep eye contact; write notes as accurately as you can. Raise your hand if things go too fast.

Make a course outline. This will serve as the organizational grid on which to slot incoming information.

Learn the vocabulary for each subject. Don't skip new words even when you are tempted to do so.

Arrive before class starts, get your materials organized, and preview the topic. Do not leave class if there is anything you have not understood.

Line up your support systems before the semester starts. It's always easy to discard them, but don't put yourself in the position of having to scramble around trying to find a tutor after you're already in trouble.

Get to know the librarian. She could be your best friend.

Set up outlines, grids, previews in as many ways as you can, for the reasons we have discussed throughout this book.

Get enough sleep.

Keep your gifts alive and well. Exercise them and enjoy them.

Trust in yourself.

Returning to the metaphor of the photographer's darkroom, how clouded the images are of those in transition between childhood and adulthood. And how obvious the patterns seem once the salient features emerge. The next chapter offers three such portraits.

10

THREE SUCCESS STORIES

In spite of obstacles, in spite of the lifelong nature of learning styles, success is possible, even inevitable, if greater emphasis is placed on children's strengths than on their weaknesses. Let these three stories speak for themselves.

PETER

Peter's story is one of a brilliant student whose high school transcript would appear to be work of a mediocre (at best) student, one who would in no way meet federal or local numerical criteria for inclusion in programs for the gifted. Yet Peter Boal (his real name) is a member of the New York City Ballet, founded by George Balanchine and now under the direction of Peter Martins and Jerome Robbins. At nineteen he is the youngest male ever to have been given many of the roles he has danced. In the fiercely competitive world of the ballet, Peter's rise to the top has the same certainty and precision as his physical leaps and jumps.

As a young child, Peter was a sensitive, highly intelligent child, skillful with words; a rapid, precise learner; a lithe athlete; and a young boy with an extraordinary sense of justice. Others' suffering gave him pain in a way far beyond his years.

All schoolwork came readily: reading, writing, spelling, math, science, art, social studies, and athletics. He was popular albeit reserved. He listened generously to others but kept his own counsel.

In third grade he enrolled as a student in the School of American Ballet, commuting daily for dance classes from his home in the country, an hour outside New York City. Because he was a boy in a predominantly jock community, he concealed this activity, saying he "took gymnastics."

His cover was blown when, in sixth grade, he starred as the prince in the well-known annual production of *The Nutcracker*. He danced the Prince for three years, all the while managing to stay afloat academically. His innate sense of order kept him on the track for his homework assignments, which he completed on the train, and his contributions to classroom discussions added depth to any and all topics.

But as his interest in ballet grew, and as his emotional attention was drawn more and more in that direction, the world of words lost its previous fascination for him. Already at eleven and twelve he was trying to live two lives, each demanding. His high personal standards would not let him be comfortable with slipshod performance in anything he undertook, yet satisfying the demands of both an academically demanding school and an art form such as ballet seemed nearly impossible to the adults in Peter's life.

At thirteen he had to make a choice. He could turn away from dance, relegating it to "something he did in his childhood" and something he would always enjoy watching. That would free him to pursue his studies in the best of schools and universities. He had the intellectual muscle to move in any abstract direction he chose.

Or he could turn to ballet as a serious pursuit, recognizing that it would be all-encompassing. He was told that his was the kind of talent that comes perhaps once in a century, but that, no matter how great his dedication, adolescence was going to change his body, perhaps allowing him to grow into an even finer dancer, but perhaps turning his talent to mediocrity. There was no way to predict, no exercises to do, no guarantees that single-minded study would finish his preparations and allow him to continue his high performance level.

His parents left the decision to Peter. As he climbed into the sleigh for his last performance as the Prince no one knew whether his journey was away from dance, to what some would call "the real world," or into dance for the realization of a dream.

Peter chose dance, knowing that it would be extraordinarily difficult to keep on with academic study at any kind of acceptable level, yet realizing that his mind as well as his body needed continuing training.

It is interesting to note his standardized test scores at the end of seventh and eighth grades, the years just preceding his decision. On the Secondary School Aptitude Test (SSAT) his quantitative scores were medium to high, reflecting his mathematical ability and, doubtless, his spatial awareness. But his verbal score was much lower than one would have anticipated from his early schoolwork and his capacity to think. Peter likes to work slowly when precision is important, and all his standardized test scores were lowered by his reluctance to rush.

His scores on standardized achievement tests were respectable, but not remarkable, reflecting the same patterns as his standardized aptitude tests. Nowhere in these numbers was there any indication of his extraordinary talent and reasoning ability and high personal dedication and standards. Anyone looking solely at his numerical transcript would have had no hint of the person behind the scores.

Peter moved into an apartment in New York, managed his own marketing and daily living (he had just turned fifteen), and enrolled in a school that strove to meet the needs of students who were also performing artists. But while "ought" was attached to academics, his heart was in his dancing. He found little time to study, and when he did crack the schoolbooks, either fatigue or his love of dance pulled his attention away.

His mother was insistent that Peter at least pass a high school equivalency test. Not having a high school diploma is reckless in today's world.

As Peter struggled to complete the requirements he was not interested in, he also struggled to discipline his growing artistic competence and to resist temptation to capitalize on it prematurely. He was offered a contract for a piece of work that would have brought him a large amount of money and public exposure. It was the kind of offer many performing artists dream about, and yet Peter turned it down. He made the decision himself, telling his family after the event. He knew, somewhere in his artistic soul, that he needed more training, that using his talent before solidifying it would jeopardize the long run for short-term glory.

As the competition grew more intense, and others were eliminated or moved sideways, Peter kept moving up. His body was powerful now as well as graceful, sinewy as well as slender, his artistry was maturing with depth and breadth. But the studies, the hateful requirements wouldn't go away. For all his ability to land precisely at the end of a predetermined arc, he didn't have the book learning to do formal geometry. For all his ability to see and move himself in relation to others, ratio and area were obstacles on paper. In spite of his capacity to communicate in English words and the additional language of space and movement, he couldn't pass French. For all his ability to be friends with many different types of people in the ballet world, he had no grade in civics or deportment to codify his leadership and personal integrity. There is no space in the professional dance world for the adolescent rebellion to which others his age feel entitled. Perhaps in academics he snitched a bit of the teenage irresponsibility denied him elsewhere.

At this same time that he was wrestling with the high school equivalency requirements, he voluntarily signed up for a college level literature course. A paper he wrote discussing a point in *Six Characters in Search of an Author* was praised by his professor as one of the most insightful pieces of criticism he had ever read. But how to pass social studies?

Peter's story has no tidy ending, thank goodness. He has finally passed his high school equivalency and is free to think, to learn, and to dance. Unshackled from academic requirements, he can soar in intellectual leaps, delighting his watchers and satisfying his soul.

In the summer of 1985 he performed in the amphitheater in Taormina, Italy. He described the moon rising behind the dancers, the powerful presence of Mount Etna, the look and feel of the stones, the sense of history of those who had seen and given performances here, century after century. He was not just one dancer in one time, but part of the magic alchemy between audience and artist, part of a tradition of movement and expression, part of a whole and greater power—from the past and of the future.

RICHARD

Richard Strauss told his story at the Twenty-eighth Annual Conference of The Orton Dyslexia Society in 1977 in Dallas, Texas. The son of a locally and nationally prominent family, Rick is now a husband and father himself, as well as being president of the Realty Development Corporation in Dallas. His story comes from a time when understanding of learning styles was limited and help unavailable.

When I was asked to give a speech at the annual conference of the Orton Society, I said that if I had to prepare one to read, it would take me an hour and a half to get through what would take a normal person only ten minutes. Rather than do that, I decided to tell a little bit about my life, about some of my educational experiences, and about some of the good and bad in it.

I started in public school in the first grade like most people. But by the fourth grade, my teachers called in my parents to inform them that I was totally unable to read or write and for that reason, they suggested, I should not progress into the fifth grade. At that time, my parents enrolled me at St. Mark's, a very fine private school with small classes. I was still unable to compete with the other students. I can remember that in the fourth grade there, the teacher had to write my last name on the bulletin board for me because I could not spell it.

I went to St. Mark's from the fourth grade through the eighth grade and continued to have great difficulty in competing with the rest of the students. In fact, the more difficulty I had, the more I cut up in class. I was probably the leading juvenile delinquent in St. Mark's history, and I was asked not to return for ninth grade for disciplinary reasons. I had spent more time skipping classes than in attending classes. I would have gotten away with that except when I skipped classes, I would go into the different classrooms and steal pens and pencils out of the desks and sell them to other kids on the campus to make a few dollars. One day on the way home on the bus, I sold back to a guy his own pen that I had stolen that day. That was the end!

In the ninth grade, then, I went back to public school for another try. At the same time, I was being tutored just about every afternoon. Off and on, I was taking speed reading courses, and I was spending most of my life in summer school. Finally we found a doctor who "realized" what my problem was. He suggested that I buy bifocal glasses and that would cure it all.

So, wearing my bifocals, being tutored, and taking my speed reading course, I was making great progress! In fact my parents thought that I was making exceptional progress until one day my Latin teacher (I had started Latin in the ninth grade) called them about midway through the semester and said, "Mr. and Mrs. Strauss, I'll make a deal with you. I'll pass Rick in this semester if you will promise—in writing—that he will never take another foreign language until he gets out of high school. This is the dumbest kid I've ever seen in my life." He said, "I've had him for nine weeks and he doesn't know one word of Latin and I'm not sure that he knows many more in English." This sounded pretty good to me at the time because it looked as though it might be the only course I was going to pass that year.

As time went on there were still problems with my conduct, or at least my parents seemed to think so. I seemed to think I was having a lot of fun. I was out of school more than I was in. I was caught riding go-carts through the halls of the school. I did all the usual things!

Every morning, announcements would come over the loudspeaker mounted high on the wall of the classroom. In my classroom there was a bolt missing from the bottom of the mounting which would always shake a little. One day when it snowed in Dallas, I put a snowball on top of the speaker. The teacher sat down beneath it, and as soon as the morning announcements began, down came the snowball . . . and out went Rick!

I finally wrapped up my high school career with my second attempt at my senior year when I took woodshop, speech, and—for the third time—freshman English. I took those three courses and finally got out.

It was early during that senior year that my father contacted a person in New York who was supposed to be one of the leading people on learning problems in children. He suggested that I go to the Scottish Rite Hospital in Dallas to be tested for dyslexia. I did get tested and for the first time was made aware of exactly what my problems were. I was then tutored by Mrs. Bywaters in the Orton-Gillingham method all through my last year in high school.

Then it was time for me to try college, so I sent my applications off to ten schools thinking that I would get four or five acceptances and then pick the one I wanted to go to. When all ten rejected me we found an organization that, for $250, would enroll a student in any [*sic*] college or university in the United States. We paid the $250 and I received three acceptances, one of them from a college that received a lot of publicity about 12 years ago. It was Parsons College but when *Life* magazine did a cover story on it, *Life* called it "Flunkout USA." As long as your father was willing to pay the high tuition, you could go there no matter what your grades were . . . and nobody had ever failed out. Well, I proved them wrong in twelve easy months!

From Parsons I went to another school, Henderson County Junior College in Texas. There I managed to do in six months what had taken me a whole year at Parsons. After about six months there my father took me into the sunroom one day and said, "Son, you know some kids are born students and some aren't, and you definitely fall in with the latter. Maybe we ought to try something else." So I got into the Air Force Reserves and, after a short time of active duty, was stationed near Dallas. I went back to Mrs. Bywaters and was tutored some more.

After my period of service, I went to work for a real estate brokerage firm in Dallas. At the age of 22, I opened my own real estate firm. That was ten years ago. Since that time I have built over 5000 apartment units in four states and have managed over 10,000 units. We have done the corporate restructuring for a major American Stock [Exchange] company after it went through bankruptcy. The company had 900 stores and 250 million dollars in assets and liabilities. We represented another American Stock Exchange company in the acquisition of a third American Stock Exchange company which was doing 80 million dollars a year in business and making a little over $8 million a year in profits. I am Chairman of the Board of a bank in Dallas and also chairman of the loan committee.

All of the successes I've had were possible to me for a few simple reasons. I learned that every person has strengths. For some it is in finance, being able to study financial information; for others it is being able to read well; for others it is writing well; and for others it is common sense. Every person has certain strengths. What is most important for students with dyslexia—or adults with dyslexia—is to locate those strengths and learn how to capitalize on them, and learn how to do the things that come naturally to them, and not to spend their whole lives concerned about the things that are the most difficult.

Another important reason for my successes is that I was very fortunate in having understanding parents. They understood that I was trying. They understood that I could spend two hours studying for a test on which others would need to spend only fifteen minutes. The others would get an A on the test and I would get an F. My parents did not concern themselves as long as I was applying myself and trying. The more trouble I got into, the more understanding they were. The worse I did in school the more understanding they were. They understand that some people are born to be students and others are not born to be students. When I was having my most difficult time in high school, when I was on my third round with freshman English, and when I couldn't pass any of the courses, I would go home at night and sit down with my father and compute the depreciation schedules on his radio station with him and do the budget for the next month. Yet, at the same time, I could not compete in my class with kids who were fifteen and sixteen years old.

Another thing is important for people with dyslexia. At an early age they must have explained to them what their problem is and that they are not mentally retarded, and that there isn't anything that makes them much different from other kids. They have got to know what their problem is, and it's got to be explained to them in a way that they can understand. There is nothing worse than not understanding—and I know because I went through it.

In my opinion the disciplinary problems come from not being able to compete in class with others or to get the attention of other students or feel equal to them. You've got to do something else whether it is cutting up in class or becoming the fastest runner on the track team or the best passer on the football team. If you are five feet seven and a half, as I am, with short legs, you aren't going to be a great football player or track star, so I thought cutting up was best. Had I known myself, had I not had the problem of wondering why I couldn't compete with the kids next to me, why I couldn't answer the questions they could answer, couldn't make the grades they could make, and couldn't achieve scholastically like them—had I understood all this, then I believe I would not have had so many disciplinary problems. The problem must be recognized and must be explained to children.

There is something else I think we need and that is important. I came from a very fortunate situation in that my parents did not believe there was something mentally wrong with me. They could afford to spend the time and the money and the effort—a lot of years and a lot of work—trying to find out what my problem was and why I could not read or write. Not many children in our school systems today have that opportunity. Therefore we must give that opportunity to them. We must teach teachers in the public schools to be able, first, to recognize children with dyslexia while they are in class and second, to teach them to read and write in that class along with the other students. If you do that in the schools where the children are—the children who do not have the opportunities I had or the parents who understand the problem and can afford the special help—then, in my opinion, this will help the children with dyslexia more than anything else I that know of. Dyslexia is real, and it can be dealt with, and the most important thing a person with dyslexia can have is the understanding of the people around him.[1]

EVA

Eva's story is also in her own words, a forty-five-page manuscript. For this book, with Eva's permission, I have included only those parts that bear on school problems. One day, when she reveals her identity, perhaps her whole story will be published. For now, Eva (a pseudonym) is a nationally respected authority on child development. She titles her story

MEMORIES OF A BRIGHT CHILD WHO COULD NOT— WOULD NOT—LEARN: THE DOUBLE MASK

This is the story of a double mask.

The disabilities, at first particularly the speech defect, served to hide from other people my ability to think so well. At times it even made ME doubt that I was so bright, although at other times, the enforced unintelligibility increased my sense of arrogance. Later on, the wretched handwriting and spelling and other difficulties with the mechanical part of learning masked my ability to think and acquire material. That was the first mask.

The other mask was one I could don. Increasingly, after I learned to speak clearly, I would use my fine intelligence and wide range of knowledge to bemuse people to camouflage my various disabilities. With these two masks coming on and off I often felt like a sham and would speculate who the Real Me was.

The double mask bewilders the child herself and is also hard on adults. As a child I had no margin of sympathy for grown-ups: my own woes were too big. In retrospect, I sympathize with my parents and even my nefarious teachers Ms. Clyde and Ms. Shaw.

This is not a full autobiography, but the focused story of a selective portion of my life, dealing with academic and physical skills. My early learning was a complex interaction between a mind, a family, and a cultural background that were operating on one level and a neurophysiological structure with lags and deficits.

Everybody talked in my family, and talked very well. My father was a minister and my mother a professional lecturer and writer. The sound of their voices was beautiful even when they were saying very ordinary things. And they both used words that had all kinds of colors and tones about them that I enjoyed hearing even when I didn't know what the words meant. My parents talked to me and my brothers (one older, one younger) the way they talked to other grown-ups, which made it even better to listen.

It was different talking to other children, or other grown-ups, than it was at home. Father and Mother tried never to be angry or to make me hurry when they couldn't understand me, but would wait patiently and ask me to try the word again or say it with other words. When I finally got the word out correctly, if I could, they would suggest I practice it so next time it would come out better. But the next time I might be so excited about what I wanted to say that I would stumble again.

I was in a hurry when grown-ups talked in an exasperatingly overdetailed manner; long before they had finished a sentence I would anticipate the ending and, in my arrogant way, try to finish the sentence for them. When my words came out jumbled I would be accused of interrupting with silly sounds. I learned to finish the sentences inside my head, simultaneously exulting in being so much smarter than they were, and fuming at not being able to talk right.

In the early 1920s, the time of which I am writing, schools did not expect children to read before first grade and most parents thought that children should wait until school to be taught. My parents, intellectual, constant readers, gave us beautiful picture books and read aloud to us, but did not expect us to master our letters until "the time was right."

I had trouble with coordination as well as speech, but since my parents were not athletic they did not notice my difficulty learning to ride a tricycle, jump rope, or play jackstraws. Jump rope started around the first grade, and paralleled the exclusion my garbled speech produced in kindergarten. It seemed so easy when I watched the others, but when I tried to jump over the rope, I would trip and fall. Instead of knowing how to arouse compassion in my peers, I would go into a rage, denouncing them for turning the rope the wrong way, and become excluded again. Even when I took a turn at rope turning, I could not synchronize with the other rope turner, the jumper would get mad, and there would be another fight.

Playing jacks, or jackstraws, overlapped with jumping rope, but lasted well into third grade. I alternated between making a fool of myself trying to learn from other girls in a group and trying to practice alone. My cat was fascinated by the little rolling ball and the tiny jacks he could field and hide so that at least was a little fun. But jackstraws never worked for me. The girls I tried to play with were as impatient as the jump ropers. Once a kid screamed at me, "What's the matter! Are you a cripple or something?" As usual, when I was upset or lost my temper, my retort came in garbled speech. So they added jeers that I couldn't even talk right. Unfortunately, I had to face these same girls in class every day. I always thought of them as "The Other Children."

When I was around five, an optometrist who had come to our house as a visitor watched me trying to pass a plate of cookies to our guests. When he saw how often I bumped into the furniture, he said to my parents, "Bring that child to my office in the morning."

The glasses he prescribed meant a whole new view of life. I had heard people talking about the way leaves looked, but up to then they had been a mass of green. Now, suddenly, leaves took on different shapes as if they were flowers. I could even see the way they were attached by twigs to branches. The American flag, which we had to salute in school daily, was now a clear set of red and white stripes and definite five-pointed stars on a blue background. The 1920s was a period of unabashed patriotism and I had heard the song "The Stars and Stripes Forever" many times, but for the first time I saw what they were.

The acquisition of glasses also led to some of my first metaphysical speculations. I would look at something with my glasses on, seeing a clear and sharp image, and then take my glasses off, seeing a vague and fuzzy image but sometimes one whose colors seemed more vivid in the absence of contour. I would wonder which image was real and what other people saw.

It would be good to report that the improvement with vision solved everything. It helped me avoid some accidents and embarrassment at breaking things, but I remained awkwardly unable to do, even with GREAT effort, what other children could do easily. Late in second grade, I still couldn't tie my shoes, a disgrace in class when everyone else got up from "rest," put on and tied his own shoes. I had to ask the teacher to do mine, and she would invariably respond that someone as smart as I could do it if I tried.

First grade taught me that there was no place for a left-handed child. Until then I had not been bothered by my handedness or even paid it much attention. The very first day of first grade, the teacher whose name I still remember as one of the ugliest words in the language, Miss Clyde, leaned over me when I was trying to copy a letter from the board, yanked the pencil from my left hand, and thrust it into my right hand, making a little speech about why I should always use the right.

We had wide-lined paper for practicing our letters. Mine went off the line and were too high or too low, too big or too small. I soon learned that certain letters and numerals were as troublesome as certain sounds, *b*, *d*, *p*, *q*, and *s*, and my *3* always went in the wrong direction. Fortunately there were 40 or 45 "Other Children" in the classroom, so Miss Clyde was too busy to pay much attention to me, but suddenly she would descend to insist that I change back to my right hand if I was sneaking in a little left-handed work or criticize what I was doggedly accomplishing with my right hand.

In hindsight, I wonder why I never told my parents about this, but it never occurred to me that what went on at school and at home had anything to do with each other.

Then came the reading. Or, rather, it did not come. In this particular school in the 1920s each child was furnished with a box of letters printed on small cardboard forms, much like Anagrams or Scrabble, except that they were cardboard. Miss Clyde would write a word, or a "family" of words, on the blackboard (*at, cat, bat, sat,* etc.) and we were to copy them on paper or make them with our cardboard letters. Miss Clyde would say the word "B-at" and the class would chant back "B-at." The whole morning seemed to go by while we were doing one "family."

Often, even with my glasses, I couldn't see her words on the blackboard. My mind would wander, and since I had always liked to nibble on things, I might chew on one of the letters. Without realizing it, I might chew up a dozen or more during one interminable recitation. Then, when I looked for a particular letter, I would realize it had gone down my gullet.

School got worse and worse that whole first grade. Besides prowling around to change my pencil from my left to right hand, Miss Clyde caught on to my habit of "Eating School Property" and chastised me publicly. She wrote to my family and they had to pay for a new box of letters. I was so ashamed that they knew, but I still went on eating letters because that was all I could do with the terrible boredom and not knowing what was going on with the reading.

Although I was not reading yet in school, at home I was learning poetry at a great rate simply by listening to my parents recite it. My mother could not carry a tune well, and so, when she sat by our beds at night, she would put us to sleep by reciting poems. Many we would request again and again, and before long I found that I really had them for my own. I still loved to hear her say them because of the sound of her voice, but I could say them with her under my breath.

In school, the children were now called on to "recite." Miss Clyde would fire a question at me in a way that made it impossible for me to answer coherently. While The Other Children were answering I knew in advance what they ought to say and corrected them in my own mind if they made mistakes, but when I was called on, garbled speech was all that came out.

One very cold morning I refused to eat my oatmeal and went out fortified only with milk, juice, and a piece of toast. I remember with complete vividness that my habitual path through the empty lot was bumpy and the white frost was over all of the weeds and the frozen earth. My knees burned with the cold, I had lost my mittens so my hands hurt too, but most of all I remember the pain of my face. My metal-rimmed glasses cut like fire into my cheeks. Tears kept coming. I could envision being in the classroom with Miss Clyde scolding me for saying things wrong or eating some of my letters. Suddenly I knew I could NOT make it to school. I turned and stumbled home.

My father grasped that the problem was more than physical cold, but he did not let on. He rewarmed the oatmeal, and I ate it slowly. Probably he added an extra portion of brown sugar and raisins. By then it was obvious that I was terrified of going back to school. Father carried me on his shoulder, took me up to the classroom, and explained my lateness to Miss Clyde in a way that kept her from scolding me more than usual that day.

But this one moment of rebellion and flight did not dispel the anguish of first grade. I vented my frustration by going into tantrums at home. My parents had been quite lenient when we had cried or screamed as little children, isolating us in our rooms until we had cooled off. But six was too old for tantrums, particularly when the triggering events were so trivial. I would flail around on the floor, "kicking and screaming like a four-year-old" as one adult put it. Another would say, "Calm down and tell us what's wrong; don't howl like an animal." But I went on howling and flailing.

Even in those far-off days of the 1920s there were some psychologists in this country. My parents did not have much money but felt a consultation would be a wise investment. They took me to Dr. Jessie Taft, one of the first practitioners of child psychology in this country. I remember meeting a very kind, white-haired lady who knew how to listen to children. The way she listened helped me talk clearly enough for her to understand.

Dr. Taft saw that the current school situation was getting cumulatively worse. Since one could not alter a school, she said the best thing would be to take me out for "medical reasons" until the end of the term and give me a new start in the fall.

She not only suggested I leave school, but that there be some time with me and mother alone. Mother started the rental on our summer beach cottage in early April and took me there alone, except of course for my cat. Father came down midweeks to see us, but otherwise I did not see other members of my family until after the Fourth of July. By then, in those three months, much of the cure had been accomplished.

For my mother, as a working writer, this time in the cottage with only one small child was a godsend. She wrote, and wrote, and wrote; the sound of the typewriter was as constant in my ears as the sound of the waves on the beach. We both loved the ocean, the beach, and the dunes and explored them freely. Mother had time for me when I needed it.

Since there were only the two of us, we took turns cooking and I learned on a kerosene stove, and a pump instead of running water, to do practical cooking effectively. I was responsible for many of the supplies by picking blackberries and walking the half mile to the nearest farm to bring back fresh milk and fresh-churned butter. Visiting the farm people an hour or two each day was a joy. I saw how much wonderful work got done with so little talk. I learned the songs of the butter churn as the old woman sang them. Here, too, I talked much more clearly.

An awareness began to dawn. During those long, miserable days in school, with the dreary repetition of letters on the board and the cardboard messes, in spite of myself I had learned to associate sound and shape of letters, and even ideas of sound blends, word families, and patterns. But I had kept this skill in the back of my mind because I was so scared and furious. Also, with a number of beautiful fairy tale books at home, I had often sat looking at the books, the pictures and the words together, and may have learned to recognize many words by sight without realizing it. So I had all of these sound and sight recognition techniques buried somewhere within me, if only they had a chance to come out right. And in one afternoon they did.

The previous week my mother had read "The Ancient Mariner" aloud to me, all the way through. Some educators would have questioned the suitability of this for a six-year-old, even a bright one, but that didn't bother my mother. She loved the poem for the rich imagery, the moral, and she also felt that living within sight of the ocean was good reason to read things connected with the sea. I was enthralled and wanted to go over it again and again, hoping I could memorize it and make it all mine. The sheer length seemed no obstacle because it was all so wonderful.

When I decided I needed another exposure, Mother was typing, and I knew she was only to be interrupted for a severe emergency. So I found the book myself and started looking at it. It happened not to be an illustrated edition but a very small little paperback copy. With this little book, I began reading, filling in from my memory, deciphering, decoding, and probably using what we would now call context clues. I was keenly attuned to the rhymes, and if a final word needed one, I could supply it. I have seldom in my entire life had the same heady, exhilarating experience, and it mounted and mounted as the poem went on. When the sound of the typewriter stopped and Mother came in to see what I was doing, I had completed the poem all by myself.

I exultantly told her and asked if I could read it to her. She was as happy as I and listened all the way through, and only on the rarest occasion did she tactfully interject a correction when I had grossly altered or mispronounced a word. I compare this moment of having finished "The Ancient Mariner" with the same kind of incredulous excitement I had two years earlier, discovering a whole new world by wearing glasses. But now it was my own mind that had the sharp vision. There was nothing artificial I had to put on.

The rest of the summer I read and read. Most of the books were for children, of them we had a great store, but I was allowed to read anything I saw, and there was no end to things.

All of this made me happy, but the greatest happiness was in the written page itself and where it would take me. I would often stop in the middle of reading and "see" what I was reading ("and it grew wondrous cold, and ice, mast-high, came floating by as green as emerald"). And I would look out at the ocean, now so bright blue in the June sunlight and see those mast-high deep green icebergs. I never stopped reading "The Ancient Mariner" the rest of the summer, but each day added one or two other things. Before tackling a new poem, I would often reread one or two from the previous days so each day I built up the number with which I was thoroughly comfortable.

At the same time I was reading poetry, I started writing. I started by writing postcards or letters to Father or my brothers. Mother was endlessly patient about spelling the words for me. She offered to have me dictate letters to her on the typewriter, but somehow, once I could read I felt ready to write also. My letters must have been a terrific job of deciphering for my father. With my poor coordination and using my right hand, bad as it felt to use it, the letters were enormous and scrawly, and when I made a mistake, I tried to mark over it, not erase. Miss Clyde had not approved of erasing. Still, it felt wonderful to see a letter being folded up in an envelope, knowing it would take my words to Father before I saw him again.

It would be nice to end here and say that when I entered second grade I had my tools well enough in hand and that whatever early difficulties I had been suffering were all over, but it wasn't so. Elementary school and all the rest of the way was a hard pull.

In second and third grades, when we studied reading, each child would get up in turn and read one paragraph with the teacher correcting any errors. This took a great deal of time, so I would go ahead on my own and read the rest of the book. When I was called on, I might be on page 18 while the paragraph I was meant to read was on page 3. I tried to use a finger to mark the paragraph I had figured out would be mine, but that method never seemed to work. If the story was really good, I would be so involved with how to get the hero out of danger on page 19 that I would stumble in my reading aloud, exposing my speech difficulty to the whole class.

Writing and spelling have continued to be painful problems into adulthood. My spelling is a joke among my colleagues; I do as much as I can of dictating rather than writing. Many things contributed to my difficulty learning to spell. They were all there together making each other worse. One was my terrible handwriting. I really didn't know what a word looked like after I put it down. Like many bright children who are poor spellers, I would foul up my handwriting deliberately so people might give me the benefit of the doubt in judging the correctness of a word.

Spelling and handwriting became a power struggle between me and whatever teacher I had. I would be furious because I knew that my poems, stories, or compositions were the best in the class, yet the teacher would return them with comments such as "Disgraceful handwriting for a fourth grader" or "Copy this over with NO spelling mistakes." I was seldom given credit for fine content or rich ideas because teachers harped on technical trivia. Growing up in a family of writers, I knew that content and style are what matter.

I decided to teach myself to type. We had a little portable my father had used in World War I which we children were allowed to use. I was thrilled with my first half-page double-spaced composition and confident the teacher would eat her previous cruel words, finally praising me for my true worth. My parents suggested I "proofread" my page. I used a pen to correct what errors I thought I saw but must have chosen one with a bad nib and managed to make great blots. When I handed the paper to Miss Shaw (not quite as ugly a name as Clyde, but it comes close), she held it up to the whole class as an example of unacceptable work.

Although I used the typewriter at home for my personal writing, it wasn't until high school, when I had a very different relationship with the faculty, that I dared hand in another typed paper.

As a result of several years of speech therapy and spontaneous growth, my speech improved so much that by sixth grade few people were even aware of the problem, but in adulthood I still must be careful, especially when tired or upset. At certain points of fatigue, I am vulnerable to malapropisms, spoonerisms, and other mistakes. But because I am adult I can oass them off as intentional jokes.

Around sixth grade I got involved with children's theater, and found to my delight that when I was acting a character, reciting memorized lines, my speech would be flawless. This is a common phenomenon among people with speech defects, and I put it to use when I had to meet new people socially or speak out in a difficult class situation. I would cue myself by pretending to be someone else and the speech would come out clearly.

The physical awkwardness was a much harder and longer thing. While other kids learned to whistle, I could never make more than a tiny gasp. My brothers and I climbed trees, went on long hikes searching for fossils, bird's nests, or arrowheads. We were active but not in the way of other kids our age.

When, at my request, I received a bicycle for my fifteenth birthday, I was too proud to ask to be taught how to ride it and did not know about the coaster brake. I managed by some kind of image of having seen other people ride to get going, riding straight along until I came to a hill. Going down, I didn't know how to avoid an approaching vehicle, rode myself into a parked car, and broke my leg. So it went, one accident after another, but I didn't give up.

The after story is predictable. I seemed doomed by family background and my own values to enter some field of intellectual endeavor. I have loved it, done well, and, in the words of educators, "adequately compensated" for many of these early disabilities. But the adequate compensations are sometimes only partially successful.

In the pursuit of my Ph.D., I was required to take a French exam and reverted to the agonies of first grade. I was enraged that the university required me to pass a French exam that had nothing to do with successfully completing the doctoral program and writing a first-rate thesis. I failed the French qualifying exam three times and finally passed it with an average mark, one of the few "averages" I have received in my entire academic career. On the matriculation examinations for my doctoral program, I failed the multiple-choice questions more miserably, I was told later, than had any graduate student in the history of the program. I had trouble keeping my place on the separate answer sheet and felt insulted by the stupidity of the questions. At the same time, I made one of the very top ratings on the essay questions.

Part of my success on the essays was knowing the extent of my own disabilities. I knew that if I had to write for four hours with a pen, the sheer fatigue and preoccupation with ideas would make my handwriting increasingly illegible and invite all kinds of misspellings, omissions, or even reversals. Therefore I petitioned the department to let me write my essays on a portable typewriter. If I had had to write all that material in one stretch by hand, I might have scored as low on my essay questions as I did on multiple choice, although for different reasons.

My current professional life requires a considerable amount of telephoning, which I try to do in the morning when I am refreshed. If I must do it later in the day, I hold the number right in front of me and dial slowly. Otherwise, out of seven digits, I am likely to get at least five of them scrambled.

Somewhere in adolescence, I tried to settle on a few aids to orientation so I would not be caught going the wrong way. I wear my wristwatch on my right arm and a bracelet on my left. When I remember to look at either one before saying anything or turning one direction, I am usually all right. I say "usually" because there still seems to be some sort of gap between the word and the actual physical direction. I can be driving home in a taxi in the neighborhood where I have lived for twenty-five years and tell the cab driver, "Turn right at the next block" when I mean he should turn left.

Along with this I have better than average orientation in the physical world. Having once been to a place, I can revisualize it and have a good mental map. If I must drive a car in unfamiliar territory, I memorize the map ahead of time.

I do not want to conclude this narrative on a note of bewilderment about right-left orientation; it is such a small portion of the life that intellectually, professionally, and personally has become increasingly productive and joyful.

I began with the image of the double mask. The masks remain. It is no accident that even now I do not wish to use my name for this account. However, along with the concealment that has become such a way of living, when I look back over my sixty-seven years I see continuity and conviction. My early love of language, and the images language can create, has persisted. I have never lost the ultravivid eidetic imagery of childhood. A single phrase, in the words of John Donne, "Makes a little room an everywhere."

The experience of living with a double mask extends the boundaries of empathy. Feeling cut off from human communication, such a frequent part of my early childhood, has helped me communicate with the learning disabled, the intellectually limited, and the psychotic. Even the agony of having such teachers as Miss Clyde has helped me learn what teaching should not be and to recognize that whenever a student fails I must look beyond her errors to her intentions.

Whichever mask is on, the other one is still available. Yet I am slowly growing to where I can have an open face.

Peter, Richard, and Eva are child, man, and woman, representing the configuration of the human family. They are from the worlds of commerce, academia, and the arts and cut across many socioeconomic layers. Together their triumphs and their tribulations represent the universality of conundrum kids.

As their personal stories speak more powerfully than any description from a distance could, so the voices of two young poets tell what education can be to an atypical learner.

This first poem was written by a high school senior in Alton, Illinois, two weeks before he took his own life.

ON EDUCATION

He always wanted to explain things
But no one cared

So he drew.
Sometimes he would draw,
And it wasn't anything.
He wanted to carve it in stone
Or write it in the sky,
And it would be only him and the sky and
The things inside him that needed saying.
It was after that he drew the picture.
It was a beautiful picture.
He kept it under his pillow
And would let no one see it.
He would look at it every night
And think about it.
When it was dark and his eyes were closed,
He could still see it.
When he started school,
He brought it with him,
Not to show to anyone,
Just to have along like a friend.
It was funny about school.
He sat at a square brown desk,
Like all the other square brown desks.
He thought it should be red.
And his room was a square, brown room,
Like all the other rooms.
It was tight and close and stiff.
He hated to hold the pencil and the chalk,
His arms stiff, his feet flat on the floor,
Stiff,
The teacher watching and watching.
The teacher came and spoke to him.
She told him to wear a tie like all the other boys.
He said he didn't like them.
She said it didn't matter!
After that, they drew.
He drew all yellow.
It was the way he felt about morning,
And it was beautiful.

The teacher came and smiled at him.
"What's this?" she said, "Why don't you
Draw something like Ken's drawing?
Isn't that beautiful?"
After that, his mother bought him a tie,
And he always drew airplanes and rocketships
Like everyone else.
And he threw the old picture away.
And when he lay alone looking at the sky,
It was big and blue and all of everything,
But he wasn't any more.
He was square inside and brown,
And his hands were stiff.

He was like everyone else.
The things inside that needed saying
Didn't need it any more.
It had stopped pushing.
It was crushed.
Stiff.
Like everything else.[2]

The second poem, "The Wall," was written as a tribute to Henry Collis, for many years Director of The Association For Gifted Children in London. The author was an eleven-year-old boy who prefers to remain anonymous.

THE WALL

They laughed at me.
They laughed at me and called me names,
They wouldn't let me join their games.
I couldn't understand.
I spent most playtimes on my own,
Everywhere I was alone,
I couldn't understand.

Teachers told me I was rude,
Bumptious, overbearing, shrewd,

Some of the things they said were crude.
I couldn't understand.
And so I built myself a wall.
Strong and solid, ten foot tall,
With bricks you couldn't see at all,
So I could understand.

And then came Sir,
A jovial, beaming, kindly man,
Saw through my wall and took my hand,
And the wall came tumbling down,
For he could understand.

And now I laugh with them,
Not in any unkind way,
For they have yet to face their day
And the lessons I have learned.
For eagles soar above all birds,
And scavengers need to hunt in herds,
But the lion walks alone,
And now I understand.

Concerned adults, working together, have the power to choose what
education will be for
Smart Kids with School Problems.

NOTES

1. RECOGNIZING, UNDERSTANDING, AND HELPING CONUNDRUM KIDS

1. Norman Geschwind, "The Brain of a Learning Disabled Individual," *Annals of Dyslexia* 34 (1984).
2. G. H. Parkyn, Remarks presented at the World Conference on Gifted Children, London, England, 1975.
3. Shel Silverstein, *Where the Sidewalk Ends* (New York: Harper & Row, 1974).

2. THE YOUNG CHILD: DEVELOPMENTAL LEVELS AND ACADEMIC REQUIREMENTS

1. Jerome Rosner, Test of Auditory Analysis Skills, taken from *Helping Children Overcome Learning Difficulties*, rev. ed. (New York: Walker, 1979).

3. VISUAL LEARNING

1. LLoyd J. Thompson, M.D., *Language Disability in Men of Eminence*. Orton Monograph 27 (1969).

2. The Report of the Commission on Reading, *Becoming a Nation of Readers*, prepared by R. C. Anderson, E. H. Heibert, J. A. Scott, I. A. G. Wilkinson for The National Academy of Education, The National Institute of Education, The Center for the Study of Reading, 1985.

4. MOTOR FUNCTION AND SCHOOL ACHIEVEMENT

1. Melvin D. Levine, F. Oberklaid, and L. Meltzer, "Developmental Output Failure: A Study of Low Productivity in School-Age Children," *Pediatrics* 67, no. 18 (1981).

2. Nina Traub, Francis Bloom, et al., *Recipe for Reading*, rev. ed. (Cambridge, Mass.: Educator's Publishing Service, 1975).

5. AUDITORY LEARNING:
LEARNING TO LISTEN, LISTENING TO LEARN

1. Julie Reichman, M.S., and William C. Healey, Ph.D., "Conductive Hearing Loss Involving Otitis Media," *The Journal of Learning Disabilities* 16, no. 5 (May 1983): 272–78. "The most common cause of hearing loss in children in developed countries is Otitis Media with Effusion, OME, an unresolved middle ear inflammation . . . [which] may arise insidiously and painlessly, may produce only low-grade discomfort . . . a number of studies have been reported that show relationships between OME and impairment in intelligence, reading, speech and language; additionally increased behavior problems have been found in children with OME. It was concluded that the relationship between middle ear pathology and learning disabilities deserves intense and critical study because of a possible causal link."

2. P. A. Silva, C. Kirkland, A. Simpson, I. A. Stewart, and S. M. Williams, "Some Developmental and Behavioral Problems Associated with Bilateral Otitis Media with Effusion," *The Journal of Learning Disabilities* 15, no. 7 (August/September 1982): 417–21.

6. LANGUAGE AND LEARNING:
INTELLECT, LANGUAGE, EMOTION

1. Leon Eisenberg, M.D., "Psychiatric Aspects of Language Disability," *Reading, Perception and Language, Papers from the World Congress on Dyslexia* (Baltimore: The Orton Dyslexia Society, 1975).

2. Richard H. Masland, M.D., *The Advantages of Being Dyslexic*, Orton Monograph 72 (1976).

8. TESTING DEMYSTIFIED:
SCORES, INTERPRETATION, PLANNING

1. National Association of Independent Schools, *Glossary of Selected Terms for Testing*, compiled by Alice Jackson (Boston, 1982).

2. Priscilla L. Vail, Book review, *Independent School* (February 1984): 46–51. Many of my remarks on Gardner's work are taken from my review of his book, which appeared in *Independent School*, and are reprinted here with their kind permission.

3. A. Bannatyne, H. B. Vance, and M. G. Singer, "Recategorization of WISC-R Scaled Subtest Scores for Learning Disabled Children," *The Journal of Learning Disabilities* 12, no. 8 (August 1979): 63–66.

4. Howard Gardner, *Frames of Mind: The Theory of Multiple Intelligences* (New York: Basic Books, 1983).

9. MATURATION AND HIGHER EDUCATION:
GETTING IT ALL TOGETHER

1. *The New York Times*, October 9, 1984, sec. C, p. 11.

2. *The New York Times*, September 6, 1981, sec. C, p. 25.

3. William C. Hiss, "Coaching for the SATs: What the Colleges Think," *Independent School* (October 1984): 51–53. (Boston: National Association of Independent Schools)

4. Dorothy H. Dillon, "SAT Preparation and Independent Schools," *Independent School* (October 1984): 45–49. (Boston: National Association of Independent Schools)

5. Macdonald Critchley, M.D., *Dyslexia Research and Its Application to Education* (London: Wiley & Sons, 1981)

6. Susan A. Vogel, Ph.D., "On Developing LD College Programs," *The Journal of Learning Disabilities* 15, no. 9 (November 1982): 518–28.

10. THREE SUCCESS STORIES

1. Richard Strauss, "Richard's Story," *Bulletin of The Orton Dyslexia Society* 28 (1978): 181–85. (Baltimore: The Orton Dyslexia Society). "Richard's Story," in its entirety, is reprinted here with his kind permission.

2. *Scholastic Magazine* (October 10, 1970).

ANNOTATED
BIBLIOGRAPHY
AND RESOURCES

ANNOTATED BIBLIOGRAPHY

The following books and articles are pertinent to the contents of the entire book as well as to the specifics of Chapter 1, "Recognizing, Understanding, and Helping Conundrum Kids." Orton monographs are available by mail from The Orton Dyslexia Society, 724 York Road, Baltimore, Maryland, 21204.

Clarke, Louise. *Can't Read, Can't Write, Can't Talk Too Good Either*. New York: Penguin Books, 1973. This is the clearly written personal story of a parent who kept faith in her son, who struggled with severe school problems and who has gone on to have a rich professional career.

Erikson, Erik H. *Childhood and Society*. New York: W.W. Norton, 1950. Particularly Chapter 7, "The Eight Ages of Man," which describes the psychosocial stages of human growth, showing the influence of the child's experiences on his developing self-concept and view of the world.

Featherstone, Helen. *A Difference in the Family*. New York: Basic

Books, 1980. This book describes the ways in which one child's disability affects the rest of the family. It is simultaneously a personal and universal story.

Galaburda, Albert M., M.D. "Developmental Dyslexia: A Review of Biological Interactions." *Annals of Dyslexia* 35 (1985): 21–33.

Gardner, Howard. *Frames of Mind: The Theory of Multiple Intelligences.* New York: Basic Books, 1983. This scientific work is difficult reading for those unaccustomed to scientific terminology. But Gardner weaves in literature, anthropology, human understanding, and humor with his neurological research and offers tactful shortcuts to keep the lay reader from getting too bogged down. It offers an exciting and optimistic view of human intelligence.

Hampshire, Susan. *Susan's Story.* New York: St. Martin's Press, 1982. This gifted actress tells the story of her early attempts at learning to read; how her mother kept her artistic talents blooming; and how, in spite of poor reading, she learned to survive tryouts and new scripts and has enjoyed a career as an internationally known actress at peace with herself and at home in the world.

Healy, Jane M. *Your Child's Growing Mind: A Parent's Guide to Learning.* New York: Doubleday, 1987. This commonsense book by a neuropsychologist, who is also a teacher, learning specialist, and parent, is a gold mine of good advice and child-centered suggestions.

de Hirsch, Katrina. *Interactions Between Educational Therapist and Child.* Orton Monograph 53 (1977). (Baltimore: The Orton Dyslexia Society).

Masland, Richard L., M.D. *The Advantages of Being Dyslexic.* Orton Monograph 72 (1976).

Sapir, Selma G., and Wilson, Bernice. "The Selection of Special Educators and Learning Disability Specialists." *The Journal of Learning Disabilities* 15, no. 3 (March 1982).

Simpson, Eileen. *Reversals: A Personal Account of Victory over Dyslexia.* Boston: Houghton Mifflin, 1979. This is the first-person account of the author's disastrous, misunderstood school problems; her marriage to the poet John Berryman, who first diagnosed her difficulty; her triumph in earning a graduate degree in psychology, and her becoming a therapist.

Sizer, Theodore R. *Horace's Compromise: The Dilemma of the American High School.* Boston: Houghton Mifflin, 1984. This study of high schools, written by the man who was dean of the Graduate School of Education at Harvard University and head-master of Phillips Academy, Andover, Massachusetts, is a call for reform in which practical suggestions interweave with educational philosophy, human understanding, and clear writing.

Smith, Sally L. *No Easy Answers: The Learning Disabled Child at Home and at School.* New York: Bantam Books, 1979. This readable, clear introduction to learning disabilities is a reliable handbook for parents or professionals working in the field.

Vail, Priscilla L. "Pardon Parents and Pardon, Parents." *The Orton Dyslexia Society Newsletter* (February 1983).

———. *The World of the Gifted Child.* New York: Walker, 1979. This book was written for professionals and parents. A combination of theory, practical suggestions, and case studies, it explores Who They Are, How They Live, What Else They Need, and What They Say.

2. THE YOUNG CHILD: DEVELOPMENTAL LEVELS AND ACADEMIC REQUIREMENTS

Ames, Louise B. *Is Your Child in the Wrong Grade?* Available from Gesell Institute of Human Development, 310 Prospect Street, New Haven, Connecticut 06511. The title of this book is self-explanatory. They also publish *A Gift of Time,* a brief, jargon-free pamphlet summarizing the reasons for basing school-entry decisions on developmental criteria, which is very helpful in reassuring perplexed parents and educators.

Elkind, David. *The Hurried Child.* Reading, Mass.: Addison-Wesley, 1981. This important book has clear messages for both parents and educators.

Jansky, Jeannette J. *The Marginally Ready Child.* Orton monograph 68 (1975). The title is self-explanatory. Jansky is a careful researcher and experienced, intuitive clinician. This is for all audiences.

Rosner, Jerome. *Helping Children Overcome Learning Difficulties*. rev. ed. New York: Walker, 1979. This practical guide to identifying specific levels of difficulty in visual and auditory analysis is written for parents as well as educators and contains carefully sequenced exercises to help children overcome problems in these two areas.

Vail, Priscilla L. *Gifted, Precocious or Just Plain Smart?* New York: Programs for Education, 1987. (1200 Broadway, New York, N.Y. 10001.)

————. *The World of the Gifted Child*. New York: Walker, 1979. Chapter 1 describes the perils of acceleration (overplacement) through a case history.

3. VISUAL LEARNING

Cox, Aylett R. *Structures and Techniques: Remedial Language Training; Multi-Sensory Teaching for Alphabetic Phonics*. Cambridge, Mass.: Educator's Publishing Service, 1967, 1969, 1974. This highly detailed, technical manual of the structure of our language is an invaluable help to the teacher who wants to learn more about the rules that govern the decoding and encoding of English and wants to learn multisensory techniques.

Hogenson, Dennis. *Reading Failure and Juvenile Delinquency*, Orton monograph 63 (1974).

Keogh, Barbara K., and Pelland, Michele. "Vision Training Revisited." *The Journal of Learning Disabilities* 18, no. 4 (April 1985): 228–36.

Lieberman, S. "Visual Perception vs. Visual Function." *The Journal of Learning Disabilities* 17, no. 3 (March 1984): 180–81.

Orton, Samuel T., M.D. *Reading, Writing and Speech Problems in Children*. New York: W.W. Norton, 1937. Available from the Orton Dyslexia Society. 724 York Road, Baltimore, Maryland 21204. Dr. Orton's book is technical, but the general reader can also enjoy and learn from it.

The Report of the Commission on Reading. *Becoming a Nation of Readers*. Prepared by R. C. Anderson, E. H. Heibert, J. A.

Scott, I. A. G. Wilkinson for The National Academy of Education, The National Institute of Education, The Center for the Study of Reading. 1985.

Rosner, Jerome. *Helping Children Overcome Learning Difficulties*. rev. ed. New York: Walker, 1979. This clearly written, practical book is for parents and educators. Rosner's exercises work and students enjoy them.

Traub, Nina, and Bloom, Frances, et al. *Recipe For Reading*. rev. ed. Cambridge, Mass.: Educator's Publishing Service. 1975. This practical manual offers step-by-step lessons combining decoding, encoding, and handwriting. It is less complicated than Cox's *Structures and Techniques* (cited previously) and dwells more on practical exercises than on the research.

Welty, Eudora. *One Writer's Beginnings*. Cambridge, Mass.: Harvard University Press, 1983. This is the beautifully and simply told story of a romance with reading, writing, and language.

4. MOTOR FUNCTION AND SCHOOL ACHIEVEMENT

Duffy, Joan. *Type It*. Cambridge, Mass.: Educator's Publishing Service, 1974. This is a manual for teaching typing to students in grades one through twelve.

Levine, Melvin D., Oberklaid, F., and Meltzer, L. "Developmental Output Failure—A Study of Low Productivity in School-Age Children." *Pediatrics* 67, no. 18 (1981).

Plunkett, Mildred. *A Writing Manual for Teaching the Left-Handed*. rev. ed. Cambridge, Mass.: Educator's Publishing Service, 1967.

5. AUDITORY LEARNING:
LEARNING TO LISTEN, LISTENING TO LEARN

Lash, Joseph P. *Master and Teacher, the Biography of Helen Keller*. New York: Delacorte Press, 1980. Helen Keller's story belongs in any discussion of listening, learning, and alternative routes to language.

Oliphant, Genevieve. "The Lens of Language." *Bulletin of The Orton Dyslexia Society* 26 (1976): 49–62.

Rosner, Jerome. *Helping Children Overcome Learning Difficulties*. rev. ed. New York: Walker, 1979. This book for teachers and parents contains the test and exercises referred to in this chapter.

Vail, Priscilla L. *Clear and Lively Writing: Language Games and Activities for Everyone*. New York: Walker, 1981. Particularly the section on listening. This book for teachers and parents offers games and activities for developing listening, speaking, reading, and writing skills in students from kindergarten through twelfth grade.

Welty, Eudora. *One Writer's Beginnings*. Cambridge, Mass.: Harvard University Press, 1984. Particularly the section on listening. This 104-page volume is Harvard's first best-seller. It is a must for anyone who cares about words, children, learning, language, and listening.

6. LANGUAGE AND LEARNING: INTELLECT, LANGUAGE, EMOTION

Blachman, Benita A. "Are We Assessing the Linguistic Factors Critical in Early Reading?" *Annals of Dyslexia* 33 (1983).

Denckla, M. B., and Rudel, R. G. "Rapid 'Automatized' Naming (R.A.N.): Dyslexia Differentiated from Other Learning Disabilities." *Neuropsychologia* 14 (1976): 471–79.

————. "Rapid 'Automatized' Naming of Pictured Objects, Colors, Letters and Numbers by Normal Children." *Cortex* 10 (1974): 186–202.

Eisenberg, Leon, M.D. "Psychiatric Aspects of Language Disability." *Reading, Perception and Language*. Baltimore: York Press, 1975, 215–29.

Fraiberg, Selma H. *The Magic Years*. New York: Charles Scribner's Sons, 1959. This book, written for parents, is filled with warmth, wisdom, humor, and insight into the nature of the young child.

Geschwind, Norman, M.D. "Why Orton Was Right." *Annals of Dyslexia* 32 (1982): 13–30.

de Hirsch, Katrina. *Language and the Developing Child*. Baltimore, Md.: The Orton Dyslexia Society, 1984. This collection of de Hirsch's articles and papers is written for professionals, but anyone interested in the topic will find it readable in spite of its technical language, and helpful because of its profound understanding of language and the child.

Kastein, S., and Trace, B. *The Birth of Language*. Springfield, Ill.: Charles C. Thomas Publishers, 1966. This is the true story of an anguished mother who, guided by the renowned, warm language therapist Dr. Shulamith Kastein, helped her child, originally diagnosed as retarded, to acquire language. In addition to being a moving story, it is a step-by-step model of how to teach language to a language-disordered child.

Rawson, Margaret B. *Adult Accomplishments of Dyslexic Boys*. Cambridge, Mass.: Educator's Publishing Service, 1968, 1978. This is the true story of Rawson's dyslexic students at the heterogeneously grouped school in Rose Valley, Pennsylvania, and what they have done with their lives.

———. *Self Concept and the Cycle of Growth*. Orton Monograph 62 (1974).

The Report of the Commission on Reading. *Becoming a Nation of Readers*. Prepared by R. C. Anderson, E. H. Heibert, J. A. Scott, I. A. G. Wilkinson for The National Academy of Education, The National Institute of Education, The Center for the Study of Reading. 1985.

Selfe, Lorna. *Nadia*. New York: Harcourt Brace Jovanovich (by arrangement with Academic Press, Inc., London), 1979. This is the story of a nonverbal child with extraordinary ability to draw, particularly horses. This shows examples of her work and tells what happened to her art when she developed language.

Vail, Priscilla L. *Clear and Lively Writing; Language Games and Activities for Everyone*. New York: Walker, 1981. The title explains the contents, which are specific, detailed, and classroom- and family dinner table–tested.

———. *Limerence, Learning, Language and Literature: an Essay*. Orton Monograph 77 (1978).

Vygotsky, Lev. *Thought and Language*. Cambridge, Mass.: The MIT Press, 1962. This is the brief but powerful work of the Russian learning theorist and linguist. It is dense reading but important.

7. PSYCHOLOGICAL AVAILABILITY FOR SCHOOLWORK:
AROUSAL, ATTENTION, ACTION

Bowlby, John. *Loss, Sadness, and Depression.* New York: Basic Books, 1980. This excellent resource gives professionals and concerned adults a solid foundation of information and research.

Erikson, Erik H. *Identity: Youth and Crisis.* New York: W.W. Norton, 1968. Although this is not light fare, the interested reader will find wisdom and illustrative cases.

Francke, Linda Bird. *Growing Up Divorced.* New York: Simon & Schuster, 1983. This well-researched book is written primarily for the popular market.

LeShan, Eda. *Learning to Say Good-bye: When a Parent Dies.* New York: The Macmillan Company, 1976. This short, highly readable book written for the popular market is a wise, warm, practical exploration of a painful subject.

St. Exupéry, Antoine. *The Little Prince.* New York: Reynal & Hitchcock, 1943. Because this beautiful story can be read or heard on many levels, it is appropriate for students roughly from second grade on through old age. It should be read aloud *to* most children below fifth or sixth grade, giving them the chance to soak up the language and imagery.

Seligman, Martin E. P. *Helplessness: On Depression, Development and Death.* San Francisco: W.H. Freeman, 1975. This book is written for both the professional and popular markets, and although the subject matter is gloomy, the presentation is concise and interesting.

8. TESTING DEMYSTIFIED:
SCORES, INTERPRETATION, PLANNING

Bannatyne, A., Vance, H. B., and Singer, M. G. "Recategorization of WISC-R Subtest Scaled Scores for Learning Disabled Children." *The Journal of Learning Disabilities* 12, no. 8 (August 1979).

Gardner, Howard. *Frames of Mind: The Theory of Multiple Intelligences.* New York: Basic Books, 1983.

International Reading Association. *How to Use WISC-R Scores in Reading Diagnosis.* Newark, Del., 1986.

National Association of Independent Schools. *Glossary of Selected Terms for Testing, Commonly Seen Tests. Appendix: Test Publishers.* Prepared for NAIS by Alice Jackson. Boston, 1982.

Wechsler Intelligence Scale for Children, Revised, and its companions the *Wechsler Preschool and Primary Scale of Intelligence,* normed for children age three years, ten months, fifteen days, and the *Wechsler Adult Intelligence Scale,* normed for persons aged sixteen and above, are published by The Psychological Corporation.

9. MATURATION AND HIGHER EDUCATION: GETTING IT ALL TOGETHER

Ansara, Alice. *Language Therapy to Salvage the College Potential of Dyslexic Adolescents.* Orton Monograph 78 (1972).

Bright, George. *The Adolescent with Scholastic Failure.* Orton Monograph 33 (1970).

Brown University. *Dyslexics at Brown: A Student Perspective.* One of a Series of Occasional Publications of the Office of the Dean of the College, Providence, June 1985.

Cordoni, Barbara. "A Directory of College LD Services." *The Journal of Learning Disabilities* 15, no. 9 (November 1982): 529–34.

Cowin, Pauline, and Graff, Virginia. *Comprehensive Treatment of the Older Disabled Reader.* Orton Monograph 28 (1977).

Dillon, Dorothy. "SAT Preparation and Independent Schools." *Independent School* (October 1984). (Boston: National Association of Independent Schools)

Gillespie, Jacquelyn. "The Pushouts: Academic Skills and Learning Disabilities in Continuation High School Students." *The Journal of Learning Disabilities* 15, no. 9 (November 1982): 539–40.

Heath, Douglas. "Academic Predictors of Adult Maturity and Competence." *Journal of Higher Education* 48 (1977): 613–32.

———. "Adolescent and Adult Predictors of Vocational Adaptation." *Journal of Vocational Behavior* 9 (1976): 1–19.

———. "Some Possible Effects of Occupation on the Maturing of

Professional Men." *Journal of Vocational Behavior* 11 (1977): 263–81.

———. "Teaching for Adult Effectiveness." *Journal of Experiential Education* 1 (1978): 6–11.

Hernnstein, Richard J., and Wilson, James Q. *Crime and Human Nature*. New York: Simon & Schuster, 1985. This complicated, somewhat controversial book is intended for the professional.

Hinds, Katherine. "Dyslexia." *Brown Alumni Monthly*. Providence: Brown University, December 1984/January 1985.

Hiss, William. "Coaching for the SATs: What the Colleges Think." *Independent School* (October 1984).

Howe, Bill. "A Language Skills Program for Secondary LD Students." *The Journal of Learning Disabilities* 15, no. 9 (November 1982): 541–44.

Kesselman-Turkel, J., and Peterson, F. *Study Smarts*. Chicago: Contemporary Books, 1981. This eighty-five-page paperback is a concise and funny gold mine guide to study skills. The kids who need it will read it.

Liscio, Mary Ann, ed. *A Guide to Colleges for Learning Disabled Students*. Orlando, Fla.: Academic Press, with Grune & Stratton, 1985. The title is self-explanatory.

National Association of Secondary School Principals. *College Study Skills Program*. Reston, Va. Developed by Milton Academy and Harvard University, this is available in student texts and instructor's guides, and offers high-class practical advice from top-quality schools. It says in more solemn and thorough terms what *Study Smarts* says briefly and humorously.

Ostertag, B., Baker, R. E., Howard, R. F., and Best, L. "Learning Disabled Programs in California Community Colleges." *The Journal of Learning Disabilities* 15, no. 9 (November 1982).

Rawson, Margaret. *Dyslexics as Adults: The Possibilities and the Challenge*. Orton Monograph 22 (1977).

Vogel, Susan A. "On Developing College LD Programs." *The Journal of Learning Disabilities* 15, no. 9 (November 1982).

RESOURCES

The following organizations, through their publications, conferences, and research, are valuable resources for the concerned educator or parent.

The Alexander Graham Bell Association for the Deaf, 3417 Volta Place N.W., Washington, D.C. 20013, offers many materials that are suitable for students with marginal to moderately severe problems with auditory learning, as well as those whose hearing is severely impaired. Their catalogue is available free of charge.

The American Association for Gifted Children, 140 East Monument Avenue, Dayton, Ohio 45401.

Association for Children with Learning Disabilit.es, 155 Washington Avenue, Albany, New York 12210.

The Association for the Gifted (TAG), c/o Council for Exceptional Children, 1920 Association Drive, Reston, Virginia 22091.

Books on Tape (catalogue), P.O. Box 7090, Newport Beach, California 92660. Through Books on Tape, weak readers can hear books they can understand and enjoy but cannot yet read.

Educator's Publishing Service, 75 Moulton Street, Cambridge, Massachusetts 02238.

The Foundation for Children with Learning Disabilities, 99 Park Avenue, New York, New York 10016.

Literacy Volunteers of America, whose tutors are trained to work with adults, has branches all over the country. For information, contact their main headquarters: 404 Oak Street, Syracuse, New York 13203.

The National Association of Independent Schools, 18 Tremont Street, Boston, Massachusetts 02108.

The Orton Dyslexia Society, 724 York Road, Baltimore, Maryland 21204.

World Council for Gifted and Talented Children. Papers from their annual conference are published yearly by The Trillium Press, Box 921, New York, New York 10159.

PERIODICALS

Gifted Children Monthly. 213 Hollydell Drive, Sewell, New Jersey 08080. Articles and activities for roughly preschool through fifth or sixth grades.

The Gifted Child Today (formerly *G/C/T*), A Magazine for Parents and Teachers of Gifted, Creative and Talented Children. P.O. Box 6448, Mobile, Alabama 36660-0448.

School Success Network. Rosemont, New Jersey 08556. This newsletter, published three times a year, is written for parents and teachers of young children. Its title explains its emphasis.

INDEX

Abstraction
  affinity for, 179
  difficulty with, 127, 132–33
  verbal, 86–87
Acceleration, academic, 38
Adolescents, 187–205
Advocate, educational. *See* Overseer,
  educational.
Aesthetic values and nourishment, 13–
  14
Age (chronological) and developmental
  level, 30–31
Alcohol and drug abuse, 152, 200
Allergies
  and auditory learning, 93–94, 101
  and psychological availability, 138
Alphabet Phonics. *See* Multisensory
  training.
Alternative styles and methods
  for handwriting problems, 82
  for learning, 8
  for reading, 56
  for test-taking, 81, 199–200
American Speech, Language and Hearing Association, 128
Ames, Louise Bates, 34

Analogy
  in language development, 114
  See also Metaphoric language.
Anger
  from academic frustration, 27; audi-
    tory problems, 106; and delin-
    quency, 189; handwriting failure,
    68–69; language disorder, 135;
    reading failure, 55
  in case studies, 27, 68–69, 107, 135
  depression as, 149, 151
Anticipation, motor memory and, 64,
  65
Anxiety
  and reading problems, 55
  and speech problems, 90, 225
  and writing and test-taking, 124
  See also Pressure, academic
Aphasia, 123
Arousal, 136, 137–39, 153
Articulation problems. *See* Speech
  problems.
Assessment, educational. *See* Evaluation, educational; Screening, academic; Testing, academic; Tests,
  academic.